artsy
toddler
storytimes

Neal-Schuman purchases fund advocacy, awareness, and accreditation programs for library professionals worldwide.

artsy toddler storytimes

A Year's Worth of Ready-To-Go Programming

CAROL GARNETT HOPKINS

Neal-Schuman

An imprint of the American Library Association

Chicago 2013

WEB

Don't miss this book's companion webpage!

To download and share ten "Artsy Helper Sheets," complete with phrases, tips, and tricks that inform parents and caregivers about the benefits of doing art activities with toddlers, go to **alaeditions.org/webextras**

Printed in the United States of America
17 16 15 14 13   5 4 3 2 1

Extensive effort has gone into ensuring the reliability of the information in this book; however, the publisher makes no warranty, express or implied, with respect to the material contained herein.

ISBNs: 978-1-55570-792-7 (paper); 978-1-55570-891-7 (PDF)

Library of Congress Cataloging-in-Publication Data

Hopkins, Carol Garnett.
    Artsy toddler storytimes : a year's worth of ready-to-go programming /
Carol Garnett Hopkins.
        pages   cm
    Includes bibliographical references and index.
    ISBN 978-1-55570-792-7 (alk. paper)
    1. Children's libraries—Activity programs—United States. 2. Libraries and toddlers—United States. 3. Creative activities and seat work. I. Title.
    Z718.3.H66 2013
    027.62'5—dc23   2012018140

Cover design by Rosemary Holderby/Cole Design and Production.
Text design in Mercury and Vista by Kimberly Thornton.

♾ This paper meets the requirements of ANSI/NISO Z39.48-1992 (Permanence of Paper).

To Robert and Patrick,
thank you for the time to get this done.

contents

Preface   xi

Part I: Toddler Art Fundamentals   1

Using Different Mediums to Exercise a Toddler's Ability in Art   2

Art Supplies to Have on Hand   3

Using Food as a Medium and Other Considerations   9

A Few Words about Safety   9

A Look at Coloring Sheets   10

Part II: Making the Most of Your Artsy Storytime Program   11

Storytime Themes Are for Organizational Purposes Only   14

Some Tips for Working with Toddlers at Storytime   14

Part III: A Year's Worth of Storytimes   17

THEME 1   Apple Munching   18

THEME 2   Autumn   24

THEME 3   Aviation   28

THEME 4   Bath Time Bubbles   32

THEME 5   Bears   36

THEME 6   Berry Delicious   40

THEME 7   Birds of a Feather   44

THEME 8   Boats in the Water   48

THEME 9 Bugs and Other Creepy Crawlies 52

THEME 10 Cats and Kittens 57

THEME 11 Chickens 61

THEME 12 Clothing and Hats 65

THEME 13 Colors and Patterns 68

THEME 14 Community Workers 72

THEME 15 Construction Site 76

THEME 16 Cool Pool of Water 80

THEME 17 Counting 84

THEME 18 Dinosaurs 87

THEME 19 Dogs and Puppies 91

THEME 20 Farm Animals 94

THEME 21 Fire Trucks and Firefighters 99

THEME 22 Flowers and Gardens 104

THEME 23 Food, Yummy Food 107

THEME 24 Frogs and Toads 113

THEME 25 Garbage and Recycling 118

THEME 26 Gingerbread and Other Cookies 123

THEME 27 Green for St. Patrick's Day 128

THEME 28 Halloween 132

THEME 29 Lunar New Year 137

THEME 30 Monsters 141

THEME 31 Music and Movement 146

THEME 32 My Body and Me 150

THEME 33 Nighttime 154

THEME 34 Nocturnal Animals 159

THEME 35   Opposites   163

THEME 36   Pet Parade   166

THEME 37   Pirate Treasure   172

THEME 38   Rabbits and Bunnies   176

THEME 39   Royalty   181

THEME 40   Silly Fun   185

THEME 41   Spiders   188

THEME 42   Springtime   191

THEME 43   Summer in the Sun   194

THEME 44   Thanksgiving Turkeys   199

THEME 45   Toys   204

THEME 46   Trains on the Track   208

THEME 47   Under the Sea   212

THEME 48   Valentine Hugs and Kisses   217

THEME 49   Weather   222

THEME 50   Wheels on the Road   226

THEME 51   Wild Animals   230

THEME 52   Winter Snow   236

About the Author   *241*

Index   *243*

 Don't miss this book's companion webpage!
To download and share ten "Artsy Helper Sheets," complete with phrases, tips, and tricks that inform parents and caregivers about the benefits of doing art activities with toddlers, go to **alaeditions.org/webextras**

preface

**TORYTIME FOR TODDLERS IS A MAGICAL TIME. IT IS A TIME** to explore language, sound, movement, and printed books. For toddlers, every storytime can be a new adventure. The room may be new; the storytime leader may be unfamiliar; the child must learn to sit quietly; there are new books to hear, a whole roomful of other children to greet, songs to sing, rhymes to act out, and even new ways of moving the body. The children at storytime, ranging in age from one to three years old, are learning from all these new opportunities. They are learning how to interact with other children and adults, how to sit with a large group of peers, how to listen, and how to communicate. Now, challenge the children further. Add an art or craft activity after the stories. The tots can explore impulse control, fine motor control of the fingers and hands, eye–hand coordination, following directions, and imaginative play. Put together, these storytime experiences, these learning opportunities, help children develop school-readiness and preliteracy skills

Art and craft activities appropriate for toddler skill sets are hard to find. Small toddler fingers are still learning how to move, how to act on command. The challenge lies in finding an activity that requires little or no adult assistance. Yet, it is rewarding to watch these young children take pride in their art creations. These children are happy to successfully glue shapes onto a mask or paper plate, to add spots to a cow. They are rightfully proud of these small accomplishments.

Art-filled storytimes are an opportunity to expose children to more than just stories, songs, and rhymes. With this book in hand, the search for developmentally appropriate art activities to use at storytime becomes much easier. The goal of *Artsy Toddler Storytimes* is to help busy teachers, librarians, and storytellers easily match age-appropriate books with art activities suitable for use with toddlers. The little tykes benefit by practicing skills that form the foundation of later school success.

How to Use This Book

In the pages to come, you will find 52 thematic storytime plans, one for each week of the year. Each theme includes books, fingerplays or action rhymes, plus two or more art encounters on a variety of topics appealing to this age group. In Part I of the book you will also find information on the fundamentals of conducting art activities with toddlers. These pages discuss the differences between art and craft activities, the use of different art mediums when working with young children, and supplies to have on hand. Part II describes the routine of a great artsy storytime for young children and offers tips on working with toddlers. Part III contains the storytime themes themselves.

The included art activities found in the thematic storytime plans are more than crafty projects; they are open-ended art experiences. Great care was taken to find activities in which there is no "one" way to complete the project at hand. The children are free to explore the process and tools used to make the art. A particular end product that looks the same as everyone else's is not needed with the chosen projects, although some projects do include figures to help you visualize the final creations.

Each storytime plan is meant to be fingertip ready. This means the storytimes are ready to go with a little preparation. Book titles, rhymes, songs, and fingerplays are listed and/or written out in full. If the art activity requires a drawing, then the drawing is provided as a pattern on another page sized appropriately for 8.5-by-11-inch paper (it is best to provide little hands with limited movement control larger drawings when possible). I provide these patterns because I find it very frustrating to discover a great art idea but then be left on my own to figure out how to implement it. Sometimes I find art ideas that need a drawing, but the drawing is the size of a silver dollar. Once again, I am left on my own to enlarge the drawing at the copy machine. But here such frustration is set aside. One example is the Farm Animal theme. Pick two books, two movement activities to get the wiggles out, and then pick one of the two art experiences to create an age-appropriate artsy storytime within minutes. If you choose the spotted cow art experience, the included pattern of a cow is ready for decorating with thumbprints. Photocopy a supply of cows for your storytime kids and you are ready to go.

Why Do Arts and Crafts with Toddlers?

Sometime between age one and the time they start kindergarten, children are expected to learn how to control a pencil, cut accurately with scissors, and glue small pieces of paper onto precise locations. All of this takes small (or fine) motor control (also called muscle control) of the hands and fingers. While most toddlers may never master this small motor control before the age of four, they can get a start at learning to maneuver these small muscles. To develop the dexterity, control, and strength to cut a straight line with scissors, many hours must be spent exercising the muscles needed to perform this movement. Fingerplays along with art and craft activities at storytimes provide great exercise opportunities for these tiny hand muscles.

Art and craft experiences are also a time of experimentation. Children this age should be allowed to experiment on their own about how to hold a crayon or paintbrush. Holding a color pen or paintbrush in different grips provides different outcomes: the lines on the paper may look different, the thicknesses of paint on the page may vary, and even the muscles in the fingers may feel unusual. Experimenting with glue can produce similar results: the amount of glue flowing out of a glue bottle can change; glue may or may not come off a glue stick.

Then there is impulse control. Art and craft activities help children learn to control small muscle impulses. A certain squeeze of the glue bottle could mean the difference between a puddle and a small drop. Using a color pen over and over on the same spot of paper may result in a small hole. Stickers may not come off in whole when peeled too quickly. While doing art and craft activities children learn why impulse control is important. They see firsthand the large and small consequences of not being in control.

Learning to place an object in the exact location the brain wants to put it is the skill of eye and hand coordination. The eye sees where the paint should go. The eye tells the brain and in turn the brain tells the hand where it should move to make this happen. For toddlers, the precision to make this happen right on target is still under development. While bouncing a ball develops the large muscle coordination between the eye and hand, art activities develop the small muscle controls between the eye and hand.

Following simple one-, two-, or three-step directions is another skill children learn about during art activities. Listening to and then following directions is a learned skill. For some children, this skill is not learned easily or quickly. An art experience after stories is a fantastic chance to teach children why one must listen to instructions. What do you do with the art supplies on the table if you did not listen to the given directions? Even the simple task of "paint the leaf on the paper" needs to be followed or the paint may end up on the table, chair, or wall. Because of the capabilities of the toddlers, art instructions with this age group are short. There is no need for lengthy explanations. "Glue the feathers onto the baby bird" is the only direction needed to get most children going. Children should experiment with the placement of the feathers, so the teacher, librarian, or storyteller does not need to say anything more.

While the storybooks and rhymes used in storytimes help children build their preliteracy skills, art activities help children develop imagination and manual dexterity in the hands. Yes, all of this is important in getting children ready to start school, but let us not forget the fun and almost game-like atmosphere children feel as they experiment within the art experience. The little tykes explore the look, the sounds, the smells, sometimes the taste, and even the feel of a variety of art mediums. Textures can be soft or smooth, rough or sticky. A child can discover so much in a format that is fun and entertaining. An art and craft activity also allows you, the storytime leader, to interact with the children on a whole new level. Now you can learn their favorite colors, their preference for stuff on the hands, how much they experiment with glue, and so much more. With the storybooks you can see the children enjoy a story told by someone else. With an art experience you can see children enjoy something they made on their own. It is not just the end product that is fun for the child; it is also the process of making it.

Despite the numerous skill sets that art activities bring to a child's developing body, I acknowledge that finding age-appropriate art and craft experiences is difficult. Children of toddler age have short attention spans, they are still learning how to hold a pencil/crayon/pen, their ability to cut accurately with scissors is abysmal, and they haven't quite figured out how much glue is enough. For more than eight years I struggled to find art activities that fit with a variety of storytime themes. When I first started out, I relied too heavily on coloring sheets because I could not find good sources of information on what to do with toddlers and art. Then I started to experiment and truly understand toddler capabilities. As time went on, my belief in the value of art experiences within a storytime setting grew. Watching a child start off with puddles of glue and then improve to total control of the glue bottle is wonderful. My repertoire of art experiences grew as well, and now here I am writing this book.

As an added bonus, *Artsy Toddler Storytimes* also includes a free companion webpage available at **alaeditions.org/webextras**. There you can find ten tip sheets about the benefits of doing art activities with toddlers ready for you to share with parents and other caregivers. These "Artsy Helper Sheets" contain phrases, tips, and tricks to let caregivers know how certain art behaviors help children in developmentally appropriate ways to learn the skills and muscle control they will need in the future. Print out and distribute these and invite families to take them home. Feel free to add information about your next scheduled storytime or use them to remind parents they are doing great things with their young children by participating in your storytimes and art activities.

Week after week, my storytime kids and their families returned to the library for more stories and more art. For some young children, the art experience is the highlight of storytime. I present to you short, easy to do, inexpensive art experiences appropriate for use with toddlers. I share these with you because I enjoy sharing them with my storytime kids. May you find joy using the ideas in *Artsy Toddler Storytimes* with the children in your life.

PART I

Toddler Art Fundamentals

THINK OF A TIME WHEN YOU SAW A BULLETIN BOARD display of student artwork. Did all of the artwork look the same? Did all of the students follow the same directions? When you look at the display of artwork can you point out the "correct" ones and the ones that look "wrong"? For example, when there is a display of Halloween pumpkins all looking the same, that is a craft. But when one pumpkin in the bottom corner is different from all the other pumpkins, that is art.

Truly, the distinction between a craft and art is a little fuzzy. Oftentimes the process of making a craft and a piece of art can be the same but the outcome may be different. While working with toddlers, the following definitions are useful:

Craft: Creating something with step-by-step directions so that each effort looks exactly the same.

Art: Creating something in which each outcome looks different; there is no right or wrong way of doing something.

In showing the difference between the two concepts, think of the example of making a flower with a yellow circle as the center and paper strips as the petals. For a craft activity the children will be expected to neatly place the ten paper petals equally around the yellow circle center. In an art experience the children will be told to make a flower with the materials provided. One child may choose to place a single petal next to the yellow circle and then stack the other nine paper petals at the bottom of the paper. So the artwork in this example does not technically look like a flower, but there is nothing wrong with this! The child was experimenting. The child was playing around with the materials on hand. The child was using his or her fine muscles in the hands and fingers to put the glue on the materials and move the materials around in some fashion. When it comes to art experiences for children it is the process that matters, not the end product.

The art activities provided in this book are intended to be "art experiences." They are meant to be open ended with no right way of doing them. When working with toddlers, it is interesting to watch how they use the materials placed in front of them. Give toddlers a context with a minimal set of directions and the materials. The rest is up to them. During a storytime in which the art activity is a kite, the librarian might say, "Today we will be making kites to fly in the wind, like the story we read today. The streamers are meant to be the tail of the kite. Let's see how your kite will look."

Using Different Mediums to Exercise a Toddler's Ability in Art

During the time in life called the toddler months, children are learning how to move their bodies. They are still learning how to control the large and small muscles in these bodies. The ability to do small intricate art activities is limited at this age. These tykes just do not have the muscle control for many things. Instead they are developing, practicing, and experimenting with this newly developing body control. Art experiences are a great introduction to skills children will need in school. Holding a pencil, coloring inside the lines, and even cutting with scissors are all learned skills. Children are not born with these abilities. Therefore, the art experiences used along with storytimes are designed to exercise the small muscles in the hands, as well as improve hand–eye coordination, impulse control, and the ability to follow directions.

Expecting a toddler-age child to cut something accurately inside a ten-minute art experience is absurd. Very rarely does a child between the ages of one and three years old have the control of scissors for a turtle to still look like a turtle after it is cut from a piece of paper. For this reason, precut anything that requires scissors. The children can concentrate on the creative aspect of the project at hand instead of the frustrating lack of control with scissors. If a child does want to cut some part of the art project, suggest that he or she do so at home after storytime. If you do want to use scissors during an art activity, make the act of cutting the project goal.

Most often, art experiences used with toddlers tend to fall into four main categories: coloring, painting, gluing, and stickers. Sometimes art experiences include the use of play clay, ink pads, and other art tools (food, glitter, stringing items, shaving cream, etc.). It is easy to stretch the four most common experiences categories into a 16-week storytime session by changing the medium used in the art activities. When using glue, the children might glue pieces of paper one week, feathers the next week, pieces of colored tissue paper another week, sewing notions yet another week, and buttons on a different week. These are all art activities that involve glue; the only difference is how the children arrange the different mediums. These different mediums also give the children different tactile and visual experiences. The glue comes through feathers and some lace trims but not regular paper. The colors in tissue paper may change or bleed when wet with glue. For some projects the children might use white glue, while for other projects they might use a glue stick. All of these projects use glue, yet no two experiences are exactly the same.

When it comes to coloring and painting, again, it is the use of different mediums that creates the different art experiences. Coloring can involve crayons, color marker pens, pencils, or even chalk. Painting can involve water colors or tempera paint. Painting can also vary if using cotton swabs, paintbrushes, or the bingo-style bottle paints. Each different medium provides different effects and different chances for creativity.

Stickers are always a favorite with children. Learning how to peel the paper off the back of a sticker is a great exercise for the small muscles in fingers. Do check out the stickers in advance of using them with toddlers. Some stickers are almost impossible for an adult to peel apart. If it is difficult for an adult, then a toddler will get too frustrated and need adult help. Try to provide art activities that need a minimal amount of adult interference.

Art Supplies to Have on Hand

Purchasing brand new art supplies for each art experience can get very expensive. The cost of everything needed to create different experiences using different methods can add up quickly. For this reason, do not forget to recycle, reuse, and request donations whenever possible. It is possible to offer a wide range of art experiences at little cost. Some libraries successfully keep to a small art supply budget. At one library, the library's Friends group buys the white glue and a few other miscellaneous supplies while the library itself picks up the tab for paper. Various materials may come from recycled materials found around the house. Several libraries and daycare centers make their dollars stretch by requesting community donations for art supplies.

Essential Art Materials to Have on Hand

- Buttons
- Chalk
- Color pens
- Construction paper
- Craft sticks or popsicle sticks
- Crayons
- Crepe paper
- Paint (tempera paint)
- Paintbrushes
- Paper (8.5-by-11-inch printer/copier paper)
- Paper plates (cheap white ones)
- Paper towel tubes
- Pie tins
- Plastic tablecloths
- Sewing notions
- Stickers (dots or circles)
- Stickers (miscellaneous)
- Tissue paper
- White glue or Elmer's glue
- Yarn

One method of keeping costs low while purchasing supplies is to buy the amount needed when it is needed. There is no reason to buy cotton balls now if there is no plan to use them anytime soon. What's more, there is no need to buy eight bottles of paint when one is plenty. If storage space is available, be sure to put away leftovers for the next time you need the materials.

One favorite cost-saving measure is to ask for donations. Many people are happy to clean out a drawer or cupboard of materials no longer in use. Need some cloth scraps? Ask your community. Chances are you will get more than enough. One teen librarian once asked for donations of baby food jars for a teen art program. This appeal appeared in the library's monthly newsletter as well as personally requested at toddler and preschool storytimes. The library received more than enough. People were happy to give up their baby food jars for a good cause. Do be careful what you ask for. You may or may not get what you really need. In the case of the baby food jars, the teen librarian needed jars with lids. She got more jars without lids than those with lids. Be sure to check your employer's policy about asking for donations. Some organizations, including some libraries, have strict rules about asking for any type of donation. Library Friends and volunteer groups are another great resource when inquiring about recycled donations.

Here is a list of art materials to look for and keep around for use during storytime art experiences:

Aluminum foil: Not an essential purchase, but it can come in handy when you want something shiny.

Baking cups: These paper cups used to make muffins or cupcakes are nice, but buy them only when needed.

Bingo bottle paints or dabber dot markers: These pens or bottles stamp great circles. They make a great alternative to dot stickers or Q-tips. Their price makes them a nonessential purchase.

Buttons: Look for buttons at thrift stores or ask for donations from your community. Buttons can get expensive when bought through a craft store. They are very useful so keep a large supply of them on hand. A shoebox half filled with buttons is a good start.

Cardstock or index paper stock: This is much thicker than regular printer/copier paper but easier to cut than cardboard. It can even go through most copy machines. Since it can be expensive, buy it only as you need it.

Chalk: Used on paper, chalk acts and feels different than crayons. This difference makes it a good alternative to crayons. The bright art chalks feel like silk sliding across the paper, but they can stain clothing. The sidewalk variety of chalk is great for children to experiment with. Fat or skinny, sidewalk chalk is easiest and cheapest to find in the summer months. When coloring with chalk, construction paper is recommended. The chalk tends to stick and rub off in fun ways on the rough texture of construction paper.

Cloth: There are many uses for scraps of cloth in art activities. Ask for donations or cut up a colorful bedsheet found at a thrift shop.

Coffee filters: Not an essential purchase, but they are useful in a number of ways.

Color pens: These are a must for any list of art supplies. At one library, they keep a supply of odd color pens in a bucket as well as a supply of color pen sets in their original boxes. When working with toddlers, one handful of pens placed in a pie tin or shallow tray is plenty. Place several tins at each table.

Construction paper: Construction paper feels different from regular printer/copier paper. It is usually more coarse and easier to tear. Be careful when using this paper in machines, as many copy machines will not use construction paper.

Cotton balls or cotton fiberfill: While not cheap, toddlers do not need a lot of cotton to experience the fun of using it. For most toddler art experiences, using five to ten cotton balls will do the trick. Cotton fiberfill is a nice alternative to using cotton balls.

Craft foam shapes (foam circles and other miscellaneous shapes): These are not an essential purchase but are fun to have around. Foam shapes can sometimes be found on sale, but otherwise they are somewhat expensive. Don't be afraid to use leftover craft foam from other art activities. During one library summer reading art program for older kids, the children made rings with craft foam and pipe cleaners. The larger scrap pieces were later cut up and used as foam shapes at a storytime. At this particular storytime, it did not matter that these pieces had no definable shapes.

Craft sticks or popsicle sticks: These make great handles for stick puppets or masks.

Crayons: These are another must for any list of art supplies. At the author's library, crayons are never purchased. Instead, the library receives a steady stream of crayon donations from patrons young and old. Do not bother keeping the crayons in their original boxes. That is too much of a headache. Keep them in a big bucket. When using crayons at storytime, place them in pie tins or other small trays, boxes, or bowls around the tables. Containing the loose crayons in small containers makes cleanup move a lot faster. Toddlers do not usually care if the paper is still on the crayon or not.

Crepe paper streamers: Shop around for good prices and buy it only as needed. There are several uses for crepe paper.

Feathers: While not an essential purchase, they are fun to use.

Felt: White felt is nice to keep on hand because it can be used with color pens. Unfortunately, felt is not always cheap. Buy felt as you feel the need to use it.

Glue sticks: While not essential, glue sticks do offer an alternative to using white glue in bottles. Glue sticks are best used with paper only. This glue does not tend to stick to other objects like craft foam, buttons, cloth, or yarn.

Googly eyes: These can be an expensive item, so beware. While these silly eyes can add a nice finishing touch to an art activity, they are not usually needed. If these eyes are outside your budget, feel free to substitute with buttons, dot stickers, or paper circles.

Ink stamp pads: Nontoxic stamp pads are not cheap. So do not worry if this is outside your budget. Stamp pads can also be made by putting a sponge or several layers of folded paper towels in a pie tin. To add ink to this makeshift stamp pad, just pour in some watered down paint.

Paint (tempera paint): Buy this one bottle at a time. When working with toddlers, you do not need a lot of paint. In fact, most painting activities with toddlers require only one color of paint. On a few rare occasions, two colors may be called for. Water down the paint a little to make it last longer. One children's librarian recommends mixing two big squirts of paint along with one small squirt of dish soap and some water. The dish soap helps make the paint easier to clean up. A small, clear dish soap bottle is a great storage vessel for paint. On the art table, place the paint in pie tins or other small bowls with enough paint to cover the bottom. Oftentimes, two to three children can share one bowl of paint.

Paintbrushes: Of course these go hand in hand with paints. Luckily, you do not need the expensive paintbrushes. Cheaper plastic paintbrushes are easy to find. For longer lasting paintbrushes, be sure to thoroughly clean them after each use. Store them standing vertical in a can or cup with the brush end up.

Paper (8.5-by-11-inch printer/copier paper): This is used for printing or copying pictures as well as the background for some art experiences. Sometimes this paper can be used in long strips or other shapes. Always keep white paper on hand. Purchase other colors as needed.

Paper lunch sacks: Whether they come in brown or other colors, these small paper bags can make fun art activities. Buy them only as needed.

Paper plates: Most art experiences that call for paper plates need the thin, cheap white plates. Occasionally a colored plate might be requested, but otherwise, get the cheapest plates you can find.

Paper towel tubes: Most people prefer to work with paper towel tubes rather than toilet paper tubes. You can never be sure of the cleanliness of the hands that touched the toilet paper. Generally, this germ issue is not considered so much of a problem with paper towels. Paper towel tubes can easily be cut down to any desired size. A good rule of thumb is to always keep two boxes full of paper towel tubes on hand at all times (paper ream boxes make great storage boxes). Ask coworkers, storytime parents, and other people in your community to help collect and recycle these hidden gems.

Pie tins: Ask coworkers to wash and keep all metal pie tins that come with holiday pies. These small metal bowls are very versatile. During art activities place these tins on the table to hold small objects such as crayons, pens, craft foam shapes, buttons, pom-poms, pasta, and so much more. Just wash and dry between uses. These tins can also be used to hold paint, glue, or even water.

Pill bottles: These small round bottles that usually hold medicine can come in handy for certain art experiences. Be sure they are well sanitized with the labels peeled off.

Plastic tablecloths: The cheap ones found with party supplies are all you need. Tablecloths can help speed up the cleaning process. Tablecloths are not necessary for every single art experience, but they come in handy when paint is around. Of course this goes without saying: reuse those tablecloths as much as possible.

Q-tips or cotton swabs: These make a nice alternative to paintbrushes.

Scotch tape or cellophane tape: This is essential to keep on hand because sometimes it is easier to use tape than it is to use glue. Most of the time, one or two tape holders are all you need for everyone to share.

Sewing notions: This is a catchall phrase for lace, ribbon, scraps of cloth, and sewing edging. Get in the habit of keeping every bit of ribbon that comes your way. Was that a ribbon around the neck of your chocolate Easter bunny? Add that to the stash. Most art experiences that call for the use of sewing notions need them to be in one- to two-inch chunks. It is always amazing how creative the children can get using these odds and ends.

Shaving cream: One cheap can of shaving cream will go a long way. This makes a great alternative to finger painting. Place a dollop of shaving cream in front of each child on a bare table and then let the children go to it. The children help to clean the table while "painting." Yes, this is not an activity where the children will take something home, but they will have great fun experimenting and exercising their fingers. To clean up, first wipe off the shaving cream with a dry cloth towel. Then go through and clean up anything remaining with a wet paper towel or cloth towel.

Stickers, dots or circles: The various colors and sizes of these circle-shaped stickers make them very flexible to use with toddlers. They can be spots or berries or just a colorful decoration. The packages are not very expensive and tend to hold a lot.

Stickers, miscellaneous: Any time you receive free stickers, stash them away. They might come in books, in magazines, or even in the mail. During most art activities, the toddlers will never notice that everyone holds different stickers. At this age, the children are more focused on peeling the stickers off the paper, not on what the sticker says. Got some stickers that celebrate a special date over eight years ago? Don't worry, the children will be happy to peel and stick them to something.

Tissue paper: Sheets of colorful tissue paper usually come in large quantities of 50 to 100 sheets per package. For this reason, they are not cheap. But on the positive side, one package of tissue paper will last a long time. Tissue paper can be used in strips or cut up into small squares.

White glue or Elmer's glue: When working with toddlers, this all-purpose glue is perfect for practically everything. Obtain a set of bottles that you refill from a gallon-sized bottle. Using white glue during art experiences offers the perfect experiment for impulse control.

Yarn: This material can be requested from your community. Knitters are happy to clean their cupboards and then donate a skein or two of yarn. For safety reasons, toddlers seldom use long lengths of yarn; be careful with lengths long enough to choke a child.

Using Food as a Medium and Other Considerations

It is rude to do any sort of art or craft activity involving food with a child who may be going hungry at home. The librarian or storytime leader may never realize that a child sitting in storytime went without breakfast that day because of parental finance problems. For this reason, if a craft includes a food component, ALWAYS offer extra food that can be eaten. Also make sure to tell parents at the beginning of art time that the children have permission to eat the food. Sometimes there is a child who does no art but will eat all the food. Sometimes a child will do the art project but will never consider eating it. There is nothing wrong with either child, and be quick to tell parents this is so. Every child is different, so expect different outcomes. How children react to food is different as well.

The only food item this author uses regularly that is not eaten is uncooked wheelie pasta (rotelle). Technically, this hard pasta can be eaten, but most children do not consider this yummy food. These beautiful, round fabrications are too much to resist. They make perfect wheels in a transportation theme.

Practically speaking, use food during storytime art experiences only two to four times a year. When food is used, children should consider it a genuine treat. Remind parents to police the dietary restrictions of their own children, so no child eats a food that he or she should not eat. If a parent informs you of an allergy problem, change plans or offer an alternative if possible.

A Few Words about Safety

At all times be aware that many toddler-age children are still at the oral developmental stage. This means that if something is in the hand of a one- or two-year-old child, then it is also in the child's mouth. Repeatedly remind parents to supervise their children as they use the art materials. Many of the best art supplies (craft foam, large buttons, cotton balls, etc.) can also be choking hazards. This warning should also be applied to life outside the storytime room. Except with adult observation, artwork that includes small pieces should be kept away from small hands. Caution parents again and again about the dangers of small objects. This includes during times the child is in the stroller and in the car. While driving around town, a child should not be able to pull a feather off a finished baby chick artwork and then pop this feather in his or her mouth.

This should go without saying, but check for nontoxic materials at all times. Unless your glue, paint, stamp pad, or whatever else you use during an art experience specifically states "nontoxic," then be especially careful about using it.

A Look at Coloring Sheets

Coloring sheets present two moral questions: Do coloring sheets stifle a child's ability to learn to draw? Do coloring sheets help a child develop the small motor skills in the hand that help him or her learn to write? Some people believe that coloring books and coloring sheets teach children that their developing drawing skills are inferior and stifle their desire to learn drawing skills. Others believe that coloring books and coloring sheets help young children develop fine motor control in their hands, which is a necessary step in learning to write with a pencil. This author falls in the middle. It appears as if muscle control develops more strongly in the children who are exposed to coloring sheets and coloring books. These children appear more advanced in their ability to control the tiny hand muscles and stay in the lines of the picture. At the same time, many children learn at an early age that their drawings are not as good as those an adult can draw and therefore stop learning to draw. For these reasons, if coloring sheets are used as part of an art experience, keep the drawing simple. Simple outlines work best. Do not use a detailed cow drawing that shows where the spots on the cow should be. Use a simple outline of a cow and invite the children to choose where and how many spots should be there. Coloring sheets should give just enough detail to indicate what the drawing is about but leave the other details to the imaginations of the children.

PART II

Making the Most of Your Artsy Storytime Program

HILDREN THRIVE ON ROUTINE. ROUTINES BRING comfort and understanding to the world of a toddler. A storytime with a definable routine tells a toddler what to expect and in which order it will happen. The storytime plans (sometimes referred to as lesson plans or outlines) included in this book provide an example of such a routine. These storytimes run from 15 to 25 minutes to account for the short attention span of the audience. The storytimes are then followed up with a small art experience. Of course, these plans can be adapted to suit the needs of any particular group. Add more books or fingerplays to simply extend the length of the storytime. The important thing to remember is to keep the routine consistent.

A great storytime designed for toddler children consists of an opening song, two books, two movement activities, a flannel board or other activity, and a closing song followed by an art experience. The storytime plans included here are presented in the style preferred by the author. However, these elements can be rearranged to fit any style or group.

OPENING

Start with a song or rhyme. One preference is to sing a sit-down action song. This tells everyone in the room to sit down and stop talking because storytime is about to start. This is a message that children and parents both need to understand. For toddlers, one such opening song is a recorded version of "Skinnamarink" (favorite source: *Car Songs: Songs to Sing Anywhere* by Dennis Buck) followed by the chant "Sticky, Sticky Bubblegum" (favorite source: *Songs of the Month Volume 2* by Nancy Stewart). By starting off with the same songs and rhymes, the children and adults in the room hear a cue to switch gears, recognize the start of storytime, and allow the late stragglers to come in the room before the books start.

Easy-to-Follow Toddler Storytime Routine

- Opening
- Book #1
- Stand-up activity
- Flannel board or math activity (optional)
- Book #2
- Another movement activity
- Closing
- Art experience

BOOK #1

Use any book you feel comfortable starting with. If there is one long book and one short book, place the longer book here. By their nature, great books for toddlers tend to be short. Few words fill the pages. When using a long, wordy book, check to see if sections can be skipped while leaving the essence of the story intact.

STAND-UP ACTIVITY

This is a chance for everyone to get up and move. The children have now been sitting for about six to ten minutes. It is time to move around. Use a song, rhyme, chant, or fingerplay in which you must stand up in order to act it out. If you want to use a fantastic sit-down fingerplay, then stand up to do it. Urge those kiddos to move, to get out the wiggles and increase their concentration for the next book.

FLANNEL BOARD

Insert your favorite flannel board or math activity here. This author has an affinity for counting flannel board rhymes and songs (forward and backward counting). If a suitable flannel board cannot be found, then use a math activity. Two favorite math activities include graphing and pattern recognition.

A professional quality flannel board can be expensive but there are many alternatives: cover a large rectangular piece of cardboard with felt or flannel cloth, tape the pieces to a wall, find a used white board at a thrift store, or use an old metal cookie sheet. A flat surface to place the pieces onto is essentially all a librarian or storytime leader needs.

Flannel board pieces are remarkably easy to make with the use of clip art. Need a cat for a particular flannel board activity? Look up a cat image in your favorite word processing software. Then print it and cut it out. Next, to stick the picture to the flannel side of your flannel board, glue felt or sandpaper to the back side. Some librarians even use self-stick Velcro. If your board is magnetic, glue or tape magnetic strips to the back side of the picture. A relatively inexpensive magnetic tape comes on a roll just like cellophane tape. When time is short, feel free to tape flannel board pieces to the board with cellophane tape. Or, if you are the patient type, create unique flannel board pieces using felt and other patterned cloth.

Puppets are a great alternative to flannel boards. Many flannel board stories or rhymes can be adapted for use with puppets. These puppets offer a great hands-on visual for toddlers.

BOOK #2

Another great book for toddlers goes here. Oftentimes this book is shorter than the first book. The toddlers in the audience have been engaged for more than 15 minutes now. Their attention will soon disappear.

ANOTHER MOVEMENT ACTIVITY

Another song, rhyme, chant, or fingerplay should go here. Feel free to stand or sit for this wiggle opportunity.

> **TIP** **Movement Activities Using Sign Language**
>
> Sign language is a fun way to bring meaningful actions to a fingerplay or rhyme. If a movement activity suggests the use of sign language, the storytime leader can make up an action or look up the word in an American Sign Language (ASL) dictionary. Some popular online ASL dictionaries include Signing Savvy (www.signingsavvy.com/) and Handspeak (www.handspeak.com/word/).

CLOSING

Use an action song or rhyme for your closing. This is a great opportunity to introduce children to some aspects of the performing arts. Let them explore musical instruments and dance or movement-inspiring objects. Bring out tambourines, egg shakers, scarves, rhythm sticks, or a parachute. But be careful not to overwhelm the tykes. Use the same closing song and object for the whole 8- to 12-week storytime session. Allow the children to get acquainted with and feel good about using one object or instrument at a time. Again, keep the routine consistent. Do feel free to switch out the closing song and try new ones at the start of each storytime session block. When the egg shakers (rhythm sticks, scarves, etc.) come out, the children will know that the story component of storytime is coming to an end.

> **TIP** **Some Favorite Storytime Closing Songs**
> - Egg shakers with the song "I Know a Chicken" from *The Best of the Laurie Berkner Band* by Laurie Berkner.
> - Parachute with "Five Little Monkeys" from *Car Songs: Songs to Sing Anywhere* by Dennis Buck.
> - Rhythm sticks with the song "Goin' on a Bear Hunt." Many versions of this song exist but one favorite source comes from *Kids in Action* by Greg & Steve.

- Scarves with the song "Flitter, Flutter" from *The Second Line* by Johnette Downing.
- Tambourines with the song "Did You Ever See a Lassie?" Many versions of this song exist but one favorite source comes from *Playtime: 49 Favorite Action and Sing-Along Songs* by CEMA Special Markets.

ART EXPERIENCE

The art experience should provide hands-on fun that encourages the use of fine and gross motor skills and continues the storytime theme.

Storytime Themes Are for Organizational Purposes Only

This should be a mantra of each and every person conducting storytimes for children of any age. Themes are a convenient method of organizing your materials. It is by no means the one and only way to conduct storytimes. For the purposes of this book, the picture books, songs, rhymes, and art experiences are organized around central themes only because it was convenient. Go ahead, mix and match as the whim takes you. For example, in one storytime about fathers, a decorative fish art experience went along with the book *Just Like Daddy* by Frank Asch. The book *Splash!* by Ann Jonas can be followed by the song "I'm Bringing Home a Baby Bumblebee" because there was a dragonfly, an insect, in the story. One time, this author presented a construction-themed storytime but used no songs or rhymes that had anything to do with construction or trucks. In this particular storytime, the wiggle activities consisted of a rhyme about washing and the song "The Noble Duke of York." And guess what? It turned into a fantastic storytime.

Some Tips for Working with Toddlers at Storytime

The variety of newly introduced stimuli at this age is mind-boggling. For this reason, storytimes can be a difficult time for a good number of children. Some children show this by constantly wandering around the room. Other children show this by becoming statuesque bumps on a parent's lap. Then there are the seemingly perfect participants. No matter how the children act, if they are in the room and listening, then they are taking it all in. The constant repetition of a storytime routine, including favorite songs and rhymes, and even the exercise of gross and fine motor skills—it all eventually sinks in. The toddler brain processes it, experiments with it, and acts on all the new stimuli over and over and over again. These young children learn the beginning steps to literacy. They learn the first skills needed to function in an elementary school classroom. They learn how to control their rapidly growing bodies.

At the author's storytime, we start off each book with our bottoms on the floor, our hands in our laps, our eyes on the book, our ears listening, and our mouths quiet. The author has no delusions that the whole room will still be in this state by the end of the book. With 15 to 30 toddlers at varying stages of development, this is a pipe dream. Be sure to tell parents that it is alright and expected for their children to move during a book reading. Tell this to them repeatedly! As long as the movers are not disrupting another child, then they are free to keep moving. The child constantly flopping around in his mother's lap is still listening and absorbing the rich language of storytime. The child looking out the window will probably recite parts of the story on the car ride home. Sitting attentively, listening to a teacher is a learned skill. Storytime is the perfect opportunity to learn and practice this skill. It does not happen immediately for some children. In fact, some children take several years to learn how to sit quietly in a classroom. But a moving toddler is still a learning toddler.

No matter how the child acts, keep encouraging the child. Keep providing the fun and exciting stimuli that storytimes so generously evoke. Try out new books and songs. Bring back favorite books and familiar rhymes. Toddlerdom is such a short span of time in the life of a child. This is a time for us teachers, librarians, and storytellers to have fun while bringing so many new experiences to the children in our lives.

Storytimes at a public library usually include parents or other caregivers, especially for toddler-age children. It is important to remember that parents also need encouragement. The frustrated parent whose child is touching another child's stroller or running to the window may be thinking that storytime is not ideal at this time in his or her child's life. A few words of encouragement—telling the parent there is nothing unusual in the behavior of his or her child, to keep coming—are sometimes just what a parent needs to hear. Some parents have preconceived ideas that their little darlings will be good students and instantly sit through a whole storytime. These parents just need a little gentle educating about the skill development of toddlers. These parents need reassurances that the repetition of attending storytime numerous times will help their children learn the skills they do not seem to have yet. Countless times, you should remind parents to keep coming. After a few months or a couple of years, their children will go from room roamers to storytime leaders, sitting in front through the whole book and acting out every rhyme.

PART III

A Year's Worth of Storytimes

THERE ARE PLENTY OF TOPICS PERFECT FOR THE IMAGI-nations of the toddler crowd. The following pages contain storytime themes that are crowd pleasing, age appropriate, and seasonal. Mix and match them, or take them straight as they come. There are plenty to choose from to fill up a whole year of storytimes.

Apple Munching

Opening Song and Rhyme

Book #1 *Apple Pie Tree* by Zoe Hall, illustrated by Shari Halpern

Stand-Up Activity
Sung to the tune of "Are You Sleeping?"

Great Big Apple Tree

Great big apple tree, great big apple tree, (*Use sign language for "apple."*)
Standing tall, standing tall. (*Raise hands up high.*)
Moving your branches, when the wind blows. (*Move hands in the air, swaying side to side.*)
Then the apples fall, down to the ground. (*Drop to ground.*)

Flannel Board
Pieces: Five apples (use Pattern 1.1)

Five Red Apples

Five red apples hanging on the tree.
Five red apples, big and round and shiny.
Along came a child with a hungry, grumbly tummy,
And picked one apple right out of the tree.

Four red apples hanging on the tree.
Four red apples, big and round and shiny.
Along came a child with a hungry, grumbly tummy,
And picked one apple right out of the tree.

(*Continue counting down to zero apples.*)

Book #2 *Apples! Apples!* by Salina Yoon (lift-flap)

Action Chant

Way Up High in the Apple Tree
(*Traditional*)

Way up high in the apple tree, (*Raise hands up high.*)
Two little apples I did see. (*Make two fists for apples.*)
I shook that tree as hard as I could, (*Pretend to shake tree.*)
And d-o-w-n came the apples. (*Let hands fall to ground.*)
Mmmm, were they good! (*Rub tummy.*)

Closing Song

Art Experience

Colorful apples:
1. Print out or precut apple shapes on red construction paper (use Pattern 1.1).
2. Invite children to decorate apples by coloring with color chalk.

Bonus Storytime Resources

More Books
Apple Farmer Annie by Monica Wellington
Little Apple Goat by Caroline Jayne Church
Orange Pear Apple Bear by Emily Gravett
Ten Red Apples by Pat Hutchins
Ten Red Apples: A Bartholomew Bear Counting Book by Virginia Miller

Extra Fingerplay
Sung to the tune of "This Old Man"

Apples in a Pie
Apples red, (*Use sign language for "apple" and "red."*)

Apples yellow, (*Use sign language for "apple" and "yellow."*)

Apples green, (*Use sign language for "apple" and "green."*)

In a great big barrel. (*Make large circle with arms in front of body.*)

Just wash them up, (*Pretend to wash something with hands.*)

Cut them up, (*Make chopping motion with one hand.*)

And bake them in a pie. (*Cup hands together in front of body.*)

Now there's some for you and I. (*Point away then at self.*)

Additional Art Experiences

Apple pie:
1. Print off or precut large circle shapes on brown paper (use Pattern 1.2).
2. Precut or purchase small red, yellow, and green paper apple shapes (use Pattern 1.3).
3. Invite children to glue these apple shapes onto the circle pie crust.

Apple tree:
1. Print off tree drawing (use Pattern 1.4).
2. Invite children to add red dot stickers to the drawing to make it an apple tree.

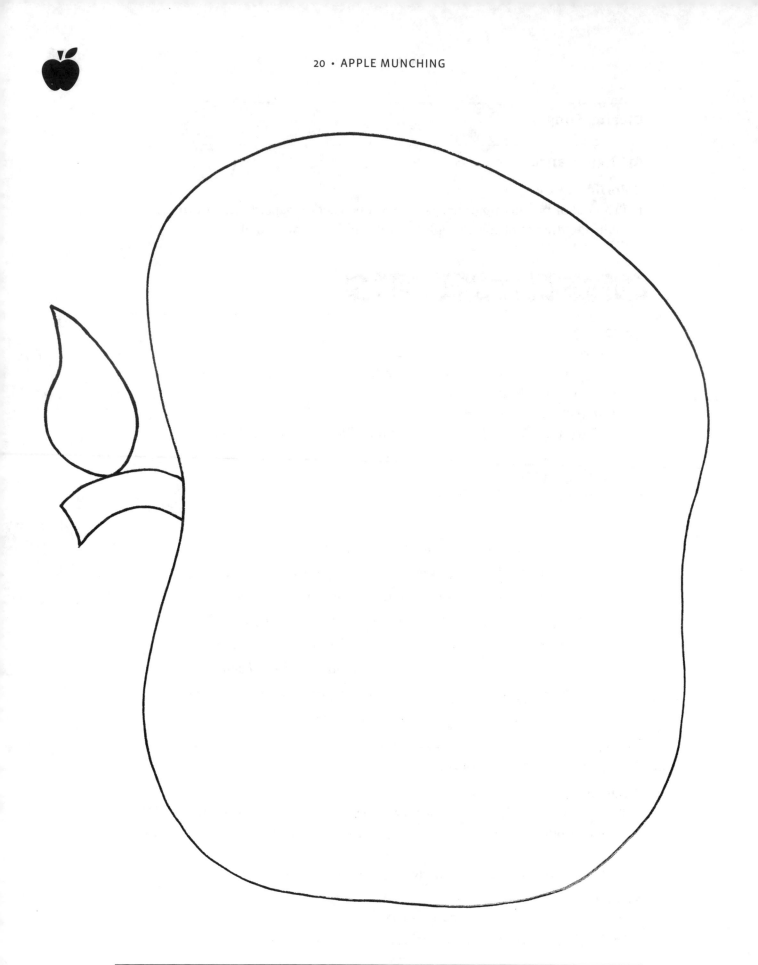

Pattern 1.1 **Apple**

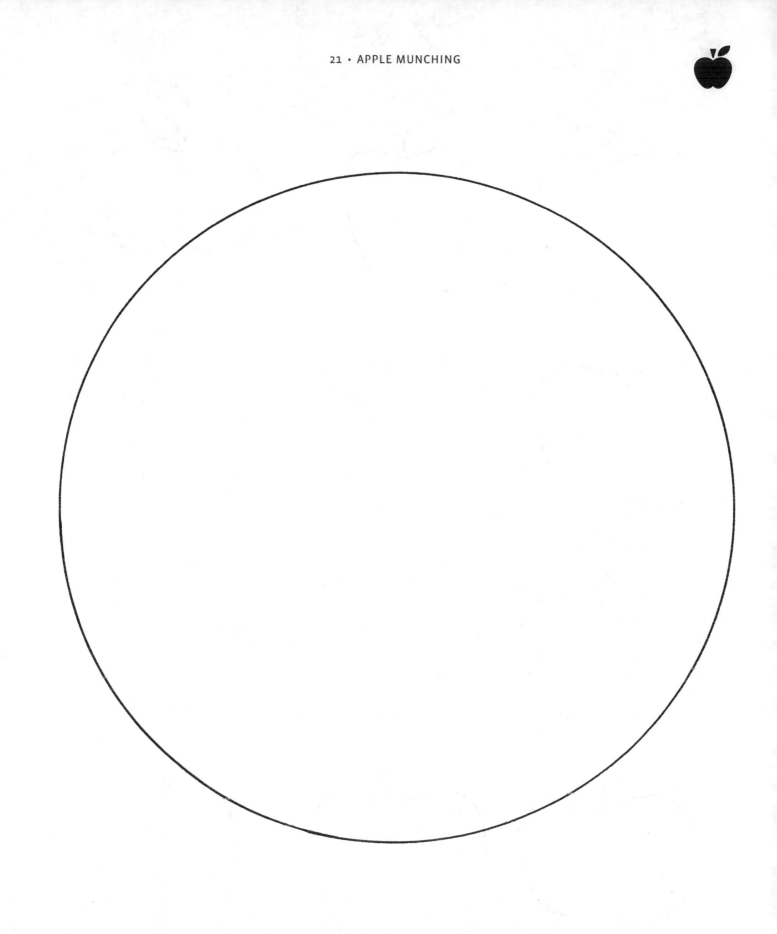

Pattern 1.2 **Apple pie crust**

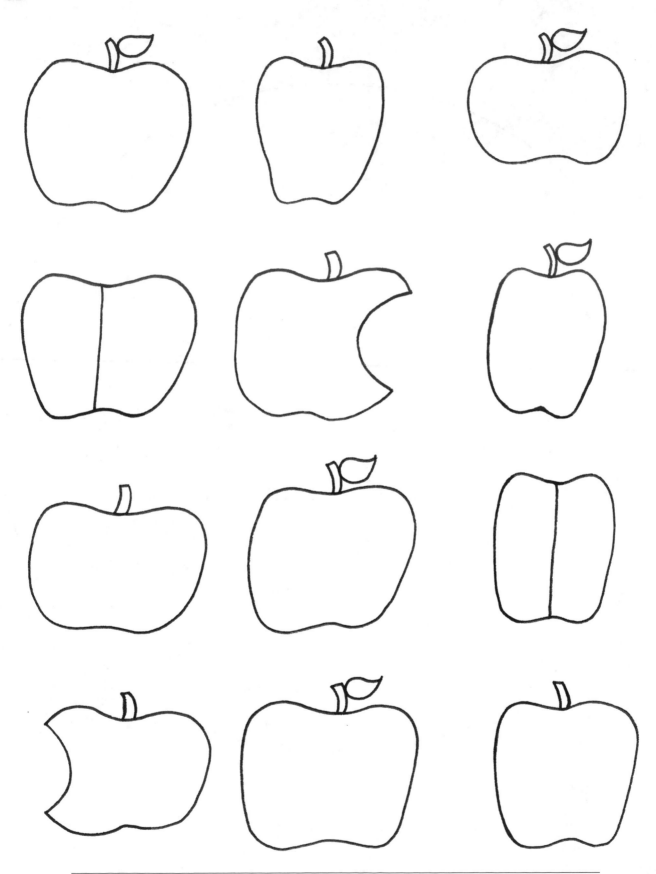

Pattern 1.3 **Small apples**

Pattern 1.4 **Apple tree**

Autumn

Opening Song and Rhyme

Book #1 *Ska-Tat!* by Kimberley Knutson

Stand-Up Activity
Sung to the tune of "London Bridge Is Falling Down"

The Wind Is Blowing All Around

The wind is blowing all around, all around, all around.
(Spin in a circle.)

The wind is blowing all around; the wind blows the leaves right off.
(Wiggle hands in front of body.)

The leaves are swirling through the town, through the town, through the town.
(Move hands from side to side.)

The leaves are swirling through the town; one landed on my head!
(Place hands on head.)

Flannel Board
Pieces: One large red leaf (use Pattern 2.1), one smaller yellow leaf with a smile, two small orange leaves, two small green leaves, and two small acorns
Sung to the tune of "Do You Know the Muffin Man?"

Do You Know the Leaf People?

Do you know the leaf people? The leaf people? The leaf people?

Do you know the leaf people, who come in the fall?

The leaf people have red bodies, red bodies, red bodies.

The leaf people have red bodies, who come in the fall.

The leaf people have yellow heads . . .

The leaf people have two orange hands . . .

The leaf people have two green feet . . .

The leaf people have acorn eyes . . .

The leaf people do not like the wind, do not like the wind, do not like the wind.

The leaf people do not like the wind, because when it blows . . .
(Make a blowing sound with mouth.)

They fall into pieces!
(Move pieces around on the board.)

Book #2 *Busy Little Squirrel* by Nancy Tafuri

Action Chant

Scamper Little Squirrel

Scamper, scamper little squirrel, (*Run in place.*)

Up the tree, (*Reach up high.*)

And down again. (*Touch the ground.*)

Grab an acorn. (*Pretend to grab something with one hand.*)

Grab that peanut. (*Pretend to grab something with other hand.*)

Stuff them in your puffy cheeks. (*Point to your cheeks as you puff them out.*)

Swish your tail. (*Wiggle your bottom.*)

Look around. (*Look around with one hand above eyes.*)

Coast is clear, scamper up that tree again. (*Run in place.*)

Closing Song

Art Experience

Colorful leaf:

1. Print out or precut leaf shapes (use Pattern 2.1).
2. Invite children to decorate the leaf by painting with one or two fall colors.

Bonus Storytime Resources

More Books

Acorns Everywhere by Kevin Sherry

Every Autumn Comes the Bear by Jim Arnosky

Leaf Man by Lois Ehlert

Mouse's First Fall by Lauren Thompson, illustrated by Buket Erdogan

Red Are the Apples by Marc Harshmann and Cheryl Ryan, illustrated
by Wade Zahares

Extra Action Song

Sung to the tune of "The Ants Go Marching"

The Leaves Are Falling Down Today

The leaves are falling down today, hurrah! Hurrah!
(Flutter hands downward.)

The leaves are falling down today, hurrah! Hurrah!

The leaves are falling to the ground,
(Touch the ground.)

Where I can jump and play around.
(Jump.)

Oh, the leaves are falling down, to the ground, where I can . . .

Stomp! Stomp! Stomp! Stomp! Stomp!
(Stomp.)

Additional Art Experience

Fall crown:

1. Precut two long strips of cardstock paper, two inches wide, for each child.
2. Purchase, find, or precut a supply of fall objects such as colorful leaves (real, paper, or silk), sunflower seeds, pumpkin seeds, small pinecones, acorns, small twigs, and dried grasses.
3. Invite children to glue these objects onto one of the paper strips (see Figure 2.1).
4. When done, tape the two ends of the paper together to make a crown. You may need to use the second strip of paper if the crown is not long enough to go around the child's head.

Figure 2.1 **Fall crown**

Pattern 2.1 **Leaf**

Aviation

Opening Song and Rhyme

Book #1 *I Wish I Were a Pilot* by Stella Blackstone, illustrated by Max Grover

Stand-Up Activity
Sung to the tune of "You Are My Sunshine"

I Am an Airplane

I am an airplane,
(Use sign language for "airplane.")

A flying airplane.
(Make airplane arms out to the sides.)

A propeller spins 'round, at my front end.
(Move one arm around in a circle.)

I fly really high up, all over towns.
(Make airplane arms out to the sides and spin around.)

Flying up, and up,
(Raise arms up.)

And flying down.
(Lower arms.)

Flannel Board

Pieces: Five hangar buildings of different colors; one airplane that will fit under a hangar

Directions: On the board put out the five hangars with the airplane under one hangar. Sing the song, then let the children guess which building the airplane is under.

Sung to the tune of "The Farmer in the Dell"

Hangar Home for My Airplane

My airplane is in its home.
The hangar is its home.
Hi, ho, the derry-o,
Which hangar is it in?

Book #2 *Flying* by Donald Crews

Action Song

Sung to the tune of "Row, Row, Row Your Boat"

As a Pilot Does

Drive, drive, drive your plane,
(Sway side to side with airplane arms.)

As a pilot does.

Merrily, merrily, merrily, merrily, flying is fun for me.

Up, up, up you fly,
(Jump with airplane arms.)

As a pilot does.

Merrily, merrily, merrily, merrily, flying is fun for me.

'Round, 'round, 'round you fly,
(Spin around in place with airplane arms.)

As a pilot does.

Merrily, merrily, merrily, merrily, flying is fun for me.

Land, land, land your plane,
(Slowly sit on the ground with airplane arms.)

As a pilot does.

Merrily, merrily, merrily, merrily, flying is fun for me.

Closing Song

Art Experience

Paper airplanes:

1. Prefold one paper airplane for each child. (For simple folding directions go to www.amazingpaperairplanes.com/Basic_Dart.html.)
2. Invite children to decorate their airplanes by coloring with crayons or color pens.

Bonus Storytime Resources

More Books

Air Show by Anastasia Suen, illustrated by Cecco Mariniello
Five Trucks by Brian Floca
I Love Planes! by Philemon Sturges, illustrated by Shari Halpern
Planes by Anne Rockwell
This Plane by Paul Collicutt

Extra Action Song #1

Sung to the tune of "The Noble Duke of York"

My Red Hot Air Balloon

My red hot air balloon,

It's big and round and red.
(Hold arms in large circle in front of body.)

It floats up into the sky,
(Raise hands high into the air.)

And then down to the ground.
(Lower hands to the ground.)

When you're up, you're up,
(Raise hands high into the air.)

And when you're down, you're down,
(Lower hands to the ground.)

When you're only halfway up,
(Place hands at hip level.)

You're neither up,
(Raise hands high into the air.)

Nor down.
(Lower hands to the ground.)

Extra Action Song #2

"Airplane" action song from *Whaddaya Think of That?* by Laurie Berkner

Additional Art Experience

Helicopter propellers:
1. Print out the helicopter drawing on colorful paper (use Pattern 3.1).
2. Precut small strips of colored paper, approximately four inches by ¼ inch.
3. Invite children to glue the propeller strips onto the helicopter picture.

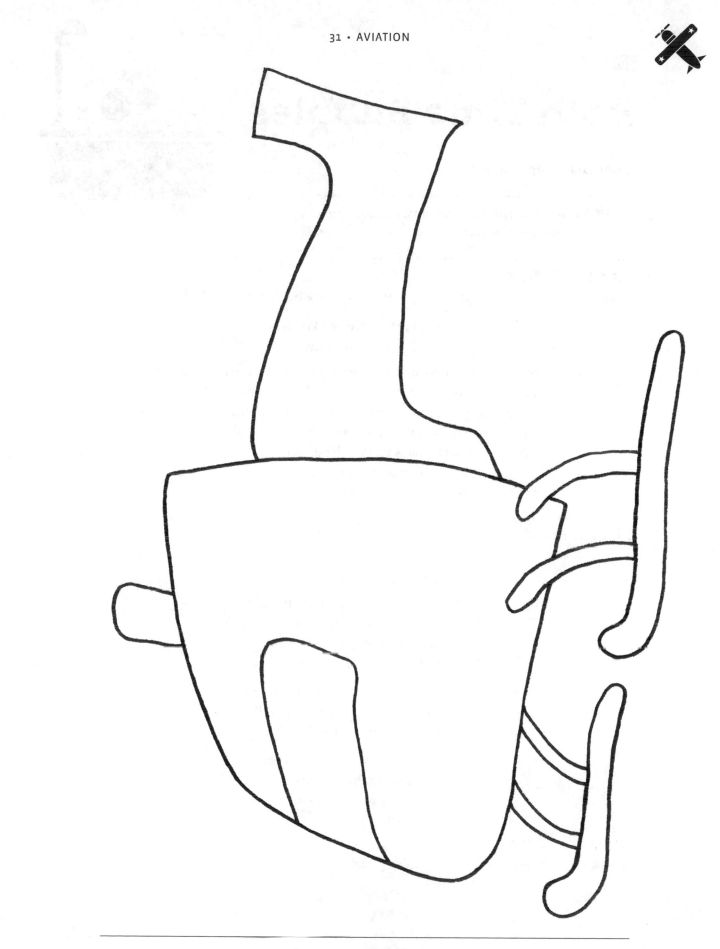

Pattern 3.1 **Helicopter**

Bath Time Bubbles

Opening Song and Rhyme

Book #1 *Big Red Tub* by Julie Jarman, illustrated by
Adrian Reynolds

Stand-Up Activity

Adapted traditional song sung to the tune of "Here We Go 'Round the Mulberry Bush"

This Is the Way We Wash
(Suit actions to words.)

This is the way we wash our hands, wash our hands, wash our hands,
This is the way we wash our hands, when we get all dirty.
This is the way we scrub our face, scrub our face, scrub our face,
This is the way we scrub our face, when we get all dirty.
This is the way we rub our ears . . .
This is the way we rinse our hair . . .
This is the way we sponge our tummies . . .

Flannel Board
Pieces: Five pigs

Five Piggies Taking a Bath

One little piggy was taking a bath.
The water was splashing and the bubbles were rising,
When another little piggy came to join the fun.
Two little piggies were taking a bath.

The water was splashing and the bubbles were rising,
When another little piggy came to join the fun.
(Continue counting up to five pigs.)

Five little piggies were taking a bath.
The bathtub was full.
The piggies were now clean.
And the slippery little piggies got out of the bath.

Book #2 *Maisy Takes a Bath* by Lucy Cousins

Action Chant

This activity is even more fun while someone is blowing bubbles.

Bubbles

(Suit actions to words.)

I like to pop, I like to pop, I like to pop, pop bubbles.
I like to pop, I like to pop, I like to pop, pop bubbles.
I like to pop, I like to pop, I like to pop, pop bubbles.
Bubbles, bubbles, bubbles, bubbles, bubbles!

I like to blow, I like to blow, I like to blow, blow bubbles.
I like to blow, I like to blow, I like to blow, blow bubbles.
I like to blow, I like to blow, I like to blow, blow bubbles.
Bubbles, bubbles, bubbles, bubbles, bubbles!

I like to clap, I like to clap, I like to clap, clap bubbles.
I like to clap, I like to clap, I like to clap, clap bubbles.
I like to clap, I like to clap, I like to clap, clap bubbles.
Bubbles, bubbles, bubbles, bubbles, bubbles!

I like to stomp, I like to stomp, I like to stomp, stomp bubbles.
I like to stomp, I like to stomp, I like to stomp, stomp bubbles.
I like to stomp, I like to stomp, I like to stomp, stomp bubbles.
Bubbles, bubbles, bubbles, bubbles, bubbles!

Closing Song

Art Experience

Shaving cream finger painting:

1. Place a large gob of shaving cream on the table in front of each child.
2. Invite children to finger paint using the shaving cream on the table. This is also a great way to clean tables! (When ready to clean off the table, first wipe off the shaving cream with a large, dry cloth towel. Then use a wet cloth to finish cleaning the table.)

Bonus Storytime Resources

More Books

Bath Time by Eileen Spinelli, illustrated by Janet Pedersen
Big Smelly Bear by Britta Teckentrup
Bubbles, Bubbles by Kathi Appelt, illustrated by Fumi Kosaka
Mrs. Wishy-Washy by Joy Cowley
Scrubbly-Bubbly Car Wash by Irene O'Graden, illustrated by Cynthia Jabar

Extra Action Song

Sung to the tune of "London Bridge Is Falling Down"

Bubbles Floating All Around

Blowing bubbles fat and round, fat and round, fat and round,
(Make large circle with arms in front of body.)

Blowing bubbles fat and round, watch them float all around.
(Spin around.)

Bubbles swirling through the air, through the air, through the air,
(Raise arms up high and sway side to side.)

Bubbles swirling through the air, watch them float all around.
(Spin around.)

Bubbles popping here and there, here and there, here and there,
(Pretend to pop bubbles.)

Bubbles popping here and there, watch them float all around.
(Spin around.)

Additional Art Experience

Bubbles around a bathtub:

1. Print out a bathtub drawing (use Pattern 4.1).
2. Gather a supply of small round objects that can stamp circles (pill bottles, yogurt containers, etc.).
3. Invite children to dip their round objects into a very thin layer of paint and then stamp the circles as bubbles around the bathtub drawing.

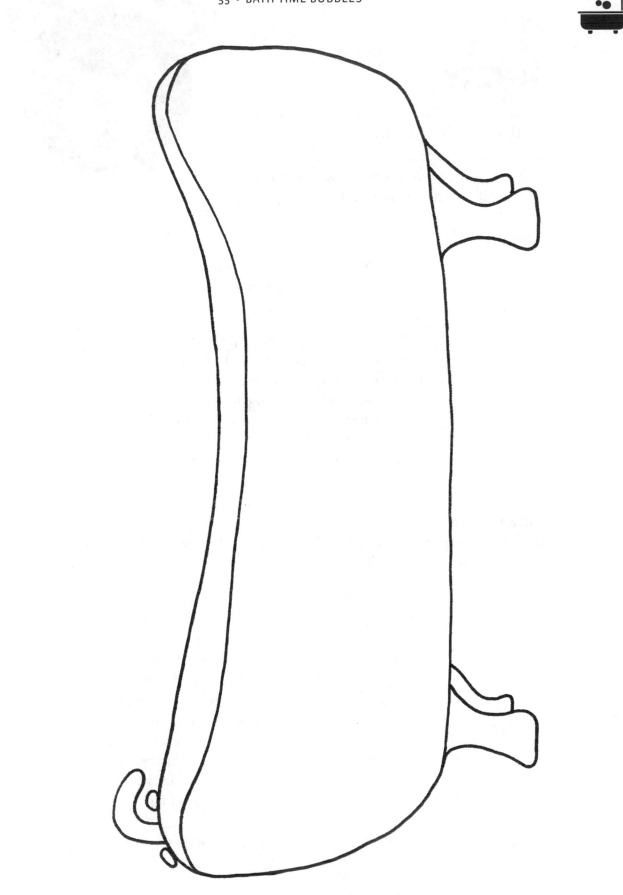

Pattern 4.1 **Bathtub**

Bears

Opening Song or Rhyme

Book #1 *My Bear and Me* by Barbara Maitland,
illustrated by Lisa Flather

Stand-Up Activity

Teddy Bear, Teddy Bear
(Traditional jump rope rhyme)

(Suit actions to words.)

Teddy bear, teddy bear, turn around.
Teddy bear, teddy bear, touch the ground.
Teddy bear, teddy bear, dance on your toes.
Teddy bear, teddy bear, touch your nose.
Teddy bear, teddy bear, reach up high.
Teddy bear, teddy bear, jump to the sky.
Teddy bear, teddy bear, touch your feet.
Teddy bear, teddy bear, find your seat.

Flannel Board

Pieces: Brown bear, polar bear, panda bear, koala, teddy bear
Sung to the tune of "Mary Had a Little Lamb"

All Types of Bears

Grizzly bears are big and brown, big and brown, big and brown.
Grizzly bears are big and brown, and live in the woods.
Polar bears are soft and white, soft and white, soft and white.
Polar bears are soft and white, and live where it's cold.
Panda bears are black and white, black and white, black and white.
Panda bears are black and white, and live with bamboo.
Koala bears have great big ears, great big ears, great big ears.
Koala bears have great big ears, and live high in a tree.
Teddy bears are just my size, just my size, just my size.
Teddy bears are just my size, to cuddle with at night.

Book #2 *Brown Bear, Brown Bear What Do You See?* by Bill Martin Jr. and
Eric Carle

Action Chant

The Great Big Bear

The great big bear, (*Use sign language for "bear."*)
Gives a warning with a soft little growl. (*Growl.*)
Waves its paws in the air. (*Move hands like claws.*)
Shakes its great big head. (*Shake head.*)
Rubs its furry little ears. (*Rub ears.*)
Gives a great big roar. (*Make a loud roar.*)
Then goes to sleep in its lair. (*Put hands together on the side of the face.*)

Closing Song

Art Experience

Teddy bear stick puppet:
1. Precut one teddy bear shape for each child (use Pattern 5.1).
2. Tape or glue the shapes to craft sticks for a handle.
3. Invite children to decorate the bear with crayons, color pens, or paint.

Bonus Storytime Resources

More Books

Bears on Chairs by Shirley Parenteau, illustrated by David Walker
Hush Little Polar Bear by Jeff Mack
Mama's Little Bears by Nancy Tafuri
My Little Polar Bear by Claudia Rueda
One Bear, One Dog by Paul Stickland

Extra Action Chant

I Know a Bear

I know a tall bear, (*Put hands high in the air.*)
With a large round head, (*Circle arms over head.*)
And a medium round nose, (*Circle nose with both hands.*)
With two small round ears, (*Cover ears with hands.*)
And two round black eyes. (*Circle eyes with hands.*)
When he sees me he greets me by waving his two large paws, (*Wave both hands as paws.*)
With a great big, "Rawr!" (*Roar.*)

Extra Action Song

"Going on a Bear Hunt" action song from *Kids in Action* by Greg & Steve

Additional Art Experience

Fuzzy polar bear:

1. Print out polar bear drawing (use Pattern 5.2).
2. Invite children to glue cotton balls or cotton fiberfill onto the bear.

Pattern 5.1 **Teddy bear stick puppet**

Pattern 5.2 **Polar bear**

Berry Delicious

Opening Song and Rhyme

Book #1 *Jamberry* by Bruce Degen

Stand-Up Activity

Sung to the tune of "I'm a Little Teapot"

I'm a Tasty Berry

I'm a tasty blueberry, (*Point to self.*)

Nice and round. (*Make circle with arms in front of body.*)

I grow on a bush, (*Raise arms slowly upward.*)

When the sun is bright. (*Make circle with arms over head.*)

When I get all blue, then it's time to be picked. (*Use sign language for "blue."*)

Just pop me in your mouth, (*Point to mouth.*)

For a yummy treat. (*Rub tummy.*)

(*Repeat with other berries, such as raspberries, blackberries, strawberries, etc.*)

Flannel Board

Count the berry circles on top of a plate:

Alternate: Or count on top of a canoe like the canoe in *Jamberry*

Pieces: Circles of various berry colors, plate (use Pattern 6.1)

Directions: Place the plate on the flannel board. Add some circles and count them as a group. Take the circles down and add some more for counting. Repeat as many times as necessary.

Book #2 *Little Mouse, the Red Ripe Strawberry, and the Big Hungry Bear* by Don and Audrey Wood

Action Song

Sung to the tune of "Ring around the Rosie"

Ring around the Strawberry Patch

Ring around the strawberry patch, basket full of strawberries. (*Spin around.*)

Skipping, (*Skip around.*)

Jumping, (*Jump.*)

We all fall down. (*Fall to the ground.*)

Picking lots of strawberries, (*Pretend to pick stuff off the ground.*)

Making a tasty treat. (*Roll hands over each other.*)

Yummy! Yummy! (*Rub tummy.*)

We all jump up. (*Jump up to standing.*)

Closing Song

Art Experience

Berries on a plate/canoe:

1. Print out the plate/canoe drawing (use Pattern 6.1).
2. Precut a supply of circles in different berry colors or purchase some foam circles.
3. Invite children to glue these "berries" onto the plate or canoe.

Bonus Storytime Resources

More Books

All for Pie, Pie for All by David Martin, illustrated by Valeri Gorbachev

Bear Wants More by Karma Wilson, illustrated by Jane Chapman

Blackberry Banquet by Terry Pierce, illustrated by Lisa Downey

One Little Blueberry by Tammi Salzano, illustrated by Kat Whelan

Pie in the Sky by Lois Ehlert

Extra Action Rhyme

Sung to the tune of "Peas Porridge Hot"

Pick Berries High

Pick berries high. (*Reach hands high.*)

Pick berries low. (*Reach low.*)

Pick berries on the bush, nine in a row. (*Clap nine times.*)

Some like them red. (*Use sign language for "red."*)

Some like them blue. (*Use sign language for "blue."*)

Some like them on the bush, nine in a row. (*Clap nine times.*)

Additional Art Experience

Strawberry seeds:

1. Print out the strawberry drawing (use Pattern 6.2).
2. Invite children to paint on strawberry seeds using bingo bottle paints or Q-tips.

Pattern 6.1 **Plate or canoe**

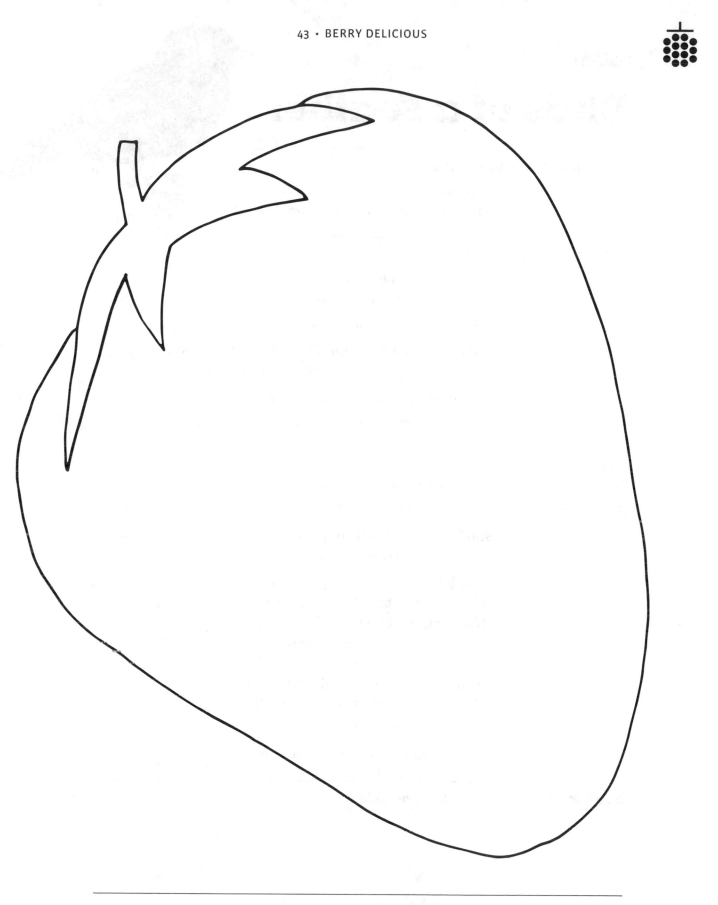

Pattern 6.2 **Strawberry**

Birds of a Feather

Opening Song and Rhyme

Book #1 *Birds* by Kevin Henkes, illustrated by Laura Dronzek

Stand-Up Activity

Little Bird
(Traditional)

I saw a little bird go hop, hop, hop. *(Jump.)*

I told the little bird to stop, stop, stop. *(Hold up hand, palm out.)*

I went to the tree to say "How do you do?" *(Bow.)*

He shook his little tail, *(Wiggle bottom.)*

And flew away. *(Flap arms as wings straight out to the sides.)*

Flannel Board
Pieces: One blue bird, one red bird, other colored birds
Favorite source: Preschool Songs by Cedarmont Kids

Bluebird, Bluebird through My Window
(Traditional)

Blue bird, blue bird through my window.
Blue bird, blue bird through my window.
Blue bird, blue bird through my window.
Oh Johnny, I'm so tired.
Red bird, red bird through my window.
Red bird, red bird through my window.
Red bird, red bird through my window.
Oh Johnny, I'm so tired.

(Continue with other colored birds.)

Book #2 *Feathers for Lunch* by Lois Ehlert

Fingerplay

Two Little Blackbirds

(Nursery rhyme)

Two little blackbirds sitting on a fence, *(Show two thumbs.)*

One named Jack, *(Wiggle one thumb.)*

The other named Jill. *(Wiggle other thumb.)*

Fly away, Jack. *(Move first thumb behind back.)*

Fly away, Jill. *(Move the other thumb behind back.)*

Come back, Jack. *(Move first thumb back up front.)*

Come back, Jill. *(Move second thumb back up front.)*

Two little blackbirds sitting on a fence. *(Wiggle both thumbs.)*

One named Jack, *(Wiggle one thumb.)*

The other named Jill. *(Wiggle other thumb.)*

Fly high, Jack. *(Move first thumb high into the air.)*

Fly low, Jill. *(Move second thumb low toward the ground.)*

Come back, Jack. *(Move first thumb to starting position.)*

Come back, Jill. *(Move second thumb to starting position.)*

Two little blackbirds sitting on a fence. *(Wiggle both thumbs.)*

Closing Song

Art Experience

Triangle bird:

1. Precut a large triangle, a small circle, and a small triangle from colored paper; different colored paper is best (use Pattern 7.1).
2. Precut a large tissue paper rectangle, approximately three inches by six inches.
3. Cut a four-inch slit in the middle of the large triangle.
4. Precut a length of yarn, approximately six inches long.
5. Invite children to pull the tissue paper halfway through the slit for the body and wings of a bird.
6. Add a circle head and a triangle beak with glue.
7. Decorate the bird with color pens.
8. Tape a length of yarn to the top of the bird to see it fly through the air.

Bonus Storytime Resources

More Books

All My Little Ducklings by Monica Wellington

Grumpy Bird by Jeremy Tankard

Have You Seen Birds? by Joanne Oppenheim and Barbara Reid

Seven Hungry Babies by Candace Fleming, illustrated by Eugene Yelchin

What's the Magic Word? by Kelly S. DiPucchio, illustrated by Marsha Winborn

Extra Action Rhyme

Little Duck, Little Duck

(Suit actions to words.)

Little duck, little duck waddle around.
Little duck, little duck, touch the ground.
Little duck, little duck, wings go flap.
Little duck, little duck, beak goes "Quack! Quack!"
Little duck, little duck, jump into the river.
Little duck, little duck, give a little shiver.
Little duck, little duck, shake your feet.
Little duck, little duck, find your seat.

Extra Action Song

"Six Little Ducks" action song from *More Singable Songs* by Raffi

Additional Art Experiences

Bird-watching binoculars:

1. Precut paper towel tubes into thirds, approximately 3½ inches long.
2. Tie or tape two tubes together.
3. Invite children to decorate these pretend binoculars with color pens or stickers or by gluing on tissue paper squares and foam shapes.

Feather painting:

1. Provide each child with a large feather, paint, and paper.
2. Invite children to paint a picture using the feather as a paintbrush.

Pattern 7.1 **Triangle bird body, head, and beak**

Boats in the Water

Opening Song and Rhyme

Book #1 *I'm Mighty* by Kate and Jim McMullan

Stand-Up Activity
Sung to the tune of "Mary Had a Little Lamb"

My Little Boat in the Wavy Sea

The wavy sea goes up and down, up and down, up and down.
(Raise hands up high, then move them down low.)

The wavy sea goes up and down, with my little boat.
(Cup hands like a boat.)

The fishing poles move side to side, side to side, side to side.
(Put hands together in front of body, then move them together left and right.)

The fishing poles move side to side, in my little boat.
(Cup hands like a boat.)

All the fishies just wiggle their tails, wiggle their tails, wiggle their tails.
(Wiggle bottom.)

All the fishies just wiggle their tails, but I never catch a fish.
(Shake head and one finger.)

Flannel Board
Pieces: One boat bottom, one white sail, one pink sail, one blue sail, one green sail
(use Pattern 8.1)

Sails on a Sailboat

My sailboat now has one sail, a white sail, a pretty sail.
My sailboat now has one sail, sailing in the wind.
My sailboat now has two sails, a white sail and a pink sail.
My sailboat now has two sails, sailing in the wind.
My sailboat now has three sails, a white sail, a pink sail, and a blue sail.
My sailboat now has three sails, sailing in the wind.
My sailboat now has four sails, a white sail, a pink sail, a blue sail, and a green sail.
My sailboat now has four sails, and now it's ready to go!

Book #2 *Boats* by Anne Rockwell

Action Song

Favorite source: Songs for Wiggleworms produced by Old Town School Music

Row, Row, Row Your Boat
(Traditional)

Row, row, row your boat,
(Pretend to row a boat.)

Gently down the stream.

Merrily, merrily, merrily, merrily,

Life is but a dream.

Sway, sway, sway your boat,
(Sway body left to right.)

Gently down the stream.

Merrily, merrily, merrily, merrily,

Life is but a dream.

(Continue with other action words for more verses, such as stretch, nod, twist, etc.)

Closing Song

Art Experience

Sailboat:
1. Precut one colorful boat bottom for each child (use Pattern 8.1).
2. Precut a good number of colorful triangular-shaped sails for each child.
3. Give each child a regular piece of white paper.
4. Invite children to glue the boat bottom onto the regular paper, and then glue the sails onto the ship bottom in any pattern.

Bonus Storytime Resources

More Books

Boats by Byron Barton
Boats for Bedtime by Olga Litowinsky, illustrated by Melanie Hope Greenberg
Four Brave Sailors by Mira Ginsburg, illustrated by Nancy Tafuri
Harbor by Donald Crews
One Dog Canoe by Mary Casanova, illustrated by Ard Hoyt

Extra Fingerplay

People Row a Boat

Five little people climbed into a boat.
(*Count five fingers on one hand.*)

The boat tilted right.
(*Lean body to the right.*)

The boat tilted left.
(*Lean body to the left.*)

They rowed and rowed and rowed,
(*Pretend to row a boat.*)

But the boat went very, very slow.
(*Roll hands slowly over each other.*)

Five more people climbed into the boat.
(*Count five fingers on the other hand.*)

The boat tilted left.
(*Lean body to the left.*)

The boat tilted right.
(*Lean body to the right.*)

Everyone began to row,
(*Pretend to row a boat.*)

And now the boat is going very, very fast.
(*Roll hands quickly over each other.*)

Additional Art Experience

Paper plate tugboat:

1. Precut a paper plate in half for the bottom of the boat.
2. Precut a square for the cabin of the boat and a small rectangle for the smokestack.
3. Invite children to glue their tugboat pieces together and then decorate with color pens or crayons (see Figure 8.1).

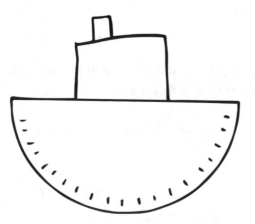

Figure 8.1 **Paper plate tugboat**

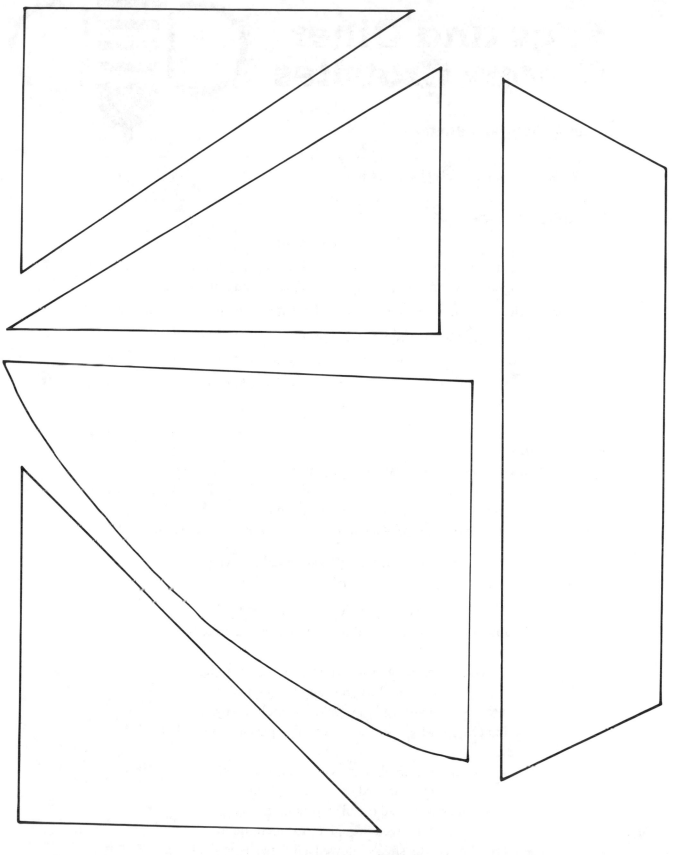

Pattern 8.1 **Sailboat bottom and sails**

Bugs and Other Creepy Crawlies

Opening Song and Rhyme

Book #1 *Very Quiet Cricket* by Eric Carle

Stand-Up Activity

Little Wiggle Worm

I'm a little wiggle worm wiggling all around. (*Wiggle body.*)
First I wiggle down to the ground. (*Keep wiggling and touch the ground.*)
Then I wiggle upright. (*Keep wiggling and stand with hands high in the air.*)
Now I wiggle to the right. (*Keep wiggling and move to the right.*)
Now I wiggle to the left. (*Keep wiggling and move to the left.*)
Now I stop and jump up and down! (*Jump.*)
Finally I wiggle spinning around and around. (*Spin around.*)

Flannel Board

Pieces: Old lady, fly, spider, bird, cat, dog, cow, horse
Directions: Don't worry about making the old lady actually swallow anything. Focus on showing a picture of the animal to be swallowed.
Favorite source: Magical World of Nursery Rhymes by Sarah J. MacDonald

There Was an Old Lady Who Swallowed a Fly
(Traditional)

There was an old lady who swallowed a fly,
I don't know why she swallowed a fly—perhaps she'll die!

There was an old lady who swallowed a spider,
That wriggled and wiggled and tickled inside her.
She swallowed the spider to catch the fly,
I don't know why she swallowed a fly—perhaps she'll die!

There was an old lady who swallowed a bird,
How absurd to swallow a bird.
She swallowed the bird to catch the spider,
She swallowed the spider to catch the fly,
I don't know why she swallowed a fly—perhaps she'll die!

There was an old lady who swallowed a cat,
Fancy that, to swallow a cat!
She swallowed the cat to catch the bird,
She swallowed the bird to catch the spider,
She swallowed the spider to catch the fly,
I don't know why she swallowed a fly—perhaps she'll die!

There was an old lady who swallowed a dog,
What a hog, to swallow a dog.
She swallowed the dog to catch the cat,
She swallowed the cat to catch the bird,
She swallowed the bird to catch the spider,
She swallowed the spider to catch the fly,
I don't know why she swallowed a fly—perhaps she'll die!

There was an old lady who swallowed a cow,
I don't know how she swallowed a cow.
She swallowed the cow to catch the dog,
She swallowed the dog to catch the cat,
She swallowed the cat to catch the bird,
She swallowed the bird to catch the spider,
She swallowed the spider to catch the fly,
I don't know why she swallowed a fly—perhaps she'll die!

There was an old lady who swallowed a horse . . .
She died, of course!
Because she swallowed the horse to catch the cow.
She swallowed the cow to catch the dog,
She swallowed the dog to catch the cat,
She swallowed the cat to catch the bird,
She swallowed the bird to catch the spider,
She swallowed the spider to catch the fly,
I don't know why she swallowed a fly—perhaps she'll die!

Book #2 *Bugs, Bugs, Bugs!* by Bob Barner

Action Song
Favorite source: Toddler Action Songs by Cedarmont Kids

Baby Bumblebee
(Traditional)

I'm bringing home a baby bumblebee. Won't my mommy be so proud of me?
(Walk in place while pretending to hold something in cupped hands.)

I'm bringing home a baby bumblebee. Ouch, it stung me!

I'm squishing up my baby bumblebee. Won't my mommy be so proud of me?
(Clap hands together and pretend to squish something in hands.)

I'm squishing up my baby bumblebee. Eew, it's messy!

I'm wiping off my baby bumblebee. Won't my mommy be so proud of me?
(Wipe hands on your clothes.)

I'm wiping off my baby bumblebee. Now my mommy won't be mad at me!

Closing Song

Art Experience

Butterfly:
1. Print out the butterfly drawing (use Pattern 9.1).
2. Precut a variety of sewing notions, lace, and ribbon into one-inch pieces.
3. Invite children to glue the sewing notions onto the butterfly.

Bonus Storytime Resources

More Books
Butterfly, Butterfly: A Book of Colors by Petr Horáček
I Love Bugs! by Philemon Sturges, illustrated by Shari Halpern
In the Tall, Tall Grass by Denise Fleming
Pattern Bugs by Trudy Harris, illustrated by Anne Canevari Green
Tiny Little Fly by Michael Rosen, illustrated by Kevin Waldron

Extra Action Chant

Two Moths

I see two moths flying toward the light. *(Use one finger on each hand for the moths.)*

They fly around in circles. *(Circle fingers around each other.)*

Sometimes they fly fast. *(Circle fingers fast.)*

Sometimes they fly slow. *(Circle fingers slowly.)*

But never do they touch that light as they fly away. *(Move fingers behind back.)*

Additional Art Experiences

Ants on a log:

1. Prepare a stick of celery, a glob of peanut butter or cream cheese, and five raisins for each child.
2. Invite children to smear the peanut butter or cream cheese onto the celery log. Then place five raisin ants onto the log.

Paper plate bee:

1. Purchase one yellow paper plate for each child.
2. Precut one black circle and two blue circles for each child, approximately four-inch diameter.
3. Precut a length of black crepe paper for each child, approximately five inches.
4. Invite children to use a pen to add black stripes to the yellow paper plate body of the bee. Then glue on the black head, the blue wings, and the long stinger (see Figure 9.1). Optional: Glue on two eyes with dot stickers, buttons, or pom-poms.

Figure 9.1 **Paper plate bee**

Pattern 9.1 **Butterfly**

Cats and Kittens

Opening Song and Rhyme

Book #1 *Cats Sleep Anywhere* by Eleanor Farjeon,
illustrated by Anne Mortimer

Stand-Up Activity

Kitty Cats Like

Kitty cats like to say hello.
(Use sign language for "cat" and then meow.)

Kitty cats like to drink milk.
(Pretend to drink milk from a bowl made by hands.)

Kitty cats like to growl when they play. *(Growl.)*

Kitty cats like to run after mice. *(Run in place.)*

Kitty cats like to jump to high places. *(Jump.)*

Kitty cats like to climb trees. *(Pretend to climb.)*

Kitty cats like to purr when they are happy. *(Make purring sound.)*

And some kitty cats like to find sunny spots to sleep in.
(Put hands together on the side of the face.)

Flannel Board

Pieces: Four cats (use Pattern 10.1)

Four Kittens on a Fence

Four little kittens were sitting on a fence.
The first one said, "I see a mouse."
So she pounced to the ground.
The second one said, "I see a bird."
So she climbed a tree.
The third one said, "I smell some catnip."
So she jumped into the garden to eat some tasty greens.
The fourth one said, "I think it's time for a nap."
So he found a sunny spot to curl up and sleep.
Four little kittens are no longer sitting on a fence.

Book #2 *Cookie's Week* by Cindy Ward and Tomie DePaola

Fingerplay

Five Kittens
(Traditional)

Five little kittens standing in a row,
(Hold up five fingers.)

They nod their heads to the children like so.
(Bend fingers.)

They run to the left.
(Run fingers to the left.)

They run to the right.
(Run fingers to the right.)

They stand up and stretch in the bright sunlight.
(Stretch fingers out tall and high.)

Along comes a dog who's looking for some fun.
(Hold up one finger from opposite hand.)

MEOW! See those little kittens run away.
(Put first five fingers behind back.)

Closing Song

Art Experience

Cat whiskers:

1. Print out the cat drawing (use Pattern 10.1).
2. Precut a supply of yarn approximately three inches long.
3. Invite children to glue yarn whiskers onto the cat. (Optional: Glue on dried spaghetti noodles as the whiskers.)

Bonus Storytime Resources

More Books

Come Here, Cleo! by Caroline Mockford
I Don't Want a Cool Cat! by Emma Dodd
I Love Cats by Barney Saltzberg
A Kitten's Year by Nancy Raines Day, illustrated by Anne Mortimer
Kitty's Cuddles by Jane Cabrera

Extra Action Rhyme

Pussy Cat, Pussy Cat
(Suit actions to words.)

Pussy cat, pussy cat, turn around.
Pussy cat, pussy cat, touch the ground.
Pussy cat, pussy cat, walk on your toes.
Pussy cat, pussy cat, paw your nose.
Pussy cat, pussy cat, stretch up high.
Pussy cat, pussy cat, jump to the sky.
Pussy cat, pussy cat, start to eat.
Pussy cat, pussy cat, find your seat.

Additional Art Experience

Paper plate cat mask:

1. Precut a paper plate in half.
2. In one half, cut out eye holes and tape on a craft stick as a handle.
3. Cut the other half in half again to make fourths.
4. Invite children to glue the triangular fourths onto the eye hole half for cat ears, and then decorate with crayons or color pens (see Figure 10.1).

Figure 10.1 **Paper plate cat mask**

Pattern 10.1 **Cat**

Chickens

Opening Song and Rhyme

Book #1 *Big Fat Hen* illustrated by Keith Baker

Stand-Up Activity

This Is the Way the Chicken Moves
(Suit actions to words.)

This is the way the chicken walks,
Bob the head, chin in front,
Bob the head, chin in front.
This is the way the chicken stretches,
Flap, flap, flap your wings,
Flap, flap, flap your wings.

This is the way the chicken dances,
Move your tail feathers to the left,
Move your tail feathers to the right.
This is the way the chicken sits,
Fold your legs on the nest like so,
Fold your legs on the nest like so.

Flannel Board

Pieces: One violet chicken, two indigo chickens, three blue chickens, four green chickens, five yellow chickens, six orange chickens (use Pattern 11.1), one large red chicken coop

Many Hens of Different Colors

I have one little violet hen,
Two little indigo hens,
Three little blue hens,
Four little green hens,
Five little yellow hens,
Six little orange hens,
And they all live together in a big red chicken coop.

Book #2 *Charlie Chick* by Nick Denchfield and Ant Parker (pop-up)

Fingerplay

Two Little Chickens Sitting on a Fence

Two little chickens sitting on a fence, *(Show two thumbs.)*
One named Jack, *(Wiggle one thumb.)*
The other named Jill. *(Wiggle other thumb.)*
Fly away, Jack. *(Move first thumb behind back.)*

(Continued on page 62)

Fly away, Jill. (*Move second thumb behind back.*)

Come back, Jack. (*Bring first thumb to the front.*)

Come back, Jill. (*Bring second thumb to the front.*)

Two little chickens sitting on a fence. (*Wiggle both thumbs.*)

Closing Song

Art Experience

Modern art circle chicken:

1. Cut out a large circle from colorful paper (use Pattern 11.2).
2. Cut the circle into halves.
3. Cut one half into quarters.
4. Cut one quarter into eighths.
5. Give all of these circle pieces to a child along with one or two googly eyes, some glue, and another whole piece of paper of a different color.
6. Invite children to glue the pieces onto the whole paper in an imaginative chicken shape.

Bonus Storytime Resources

More Books

Chick: A Pop-Up Book by Ed Vere

Hurry! Hurry! by Eve Bunting, illustrated by Jeff Mack

I Bought a Baby Chicken by Kelly Milner Halls, illustrated by Karen Stormer Brooks

Maisy at the Farm by Lucy Cousins (lift-flap)

This Little Chick by John Lawrence

Extra Action Rhyme

Little Chick, Little Chick

(*Suit actions to words.*)

Little chick, little chick, turn around.

Little chick, little chick, scratch the ground.

Little chick, little chick, strut on your toes.

Little chick, little chick, touch your nose.

Little chick, little chick, reach up high.

Little chick, little chick, flap to the sky.

Little chick, little chick, wiggle your feet.

Little chick, little chick, find your nest seat.

Extra Action Song

"I Know a Chicken" action song from *Whaddaya Think of That* by Laurie Berkner

Additional Art Experience

Feathers on a chick:

1. Print out the baby chicken drawing (use Pattern 11.1).
2. Cut out a lot of tissue paper strips, approximately ¼ inch by three inches.
3. Invite children to glue the tissue paper strips as feathers onto the baby chick.

Pattern 11.1 **Baby chick**

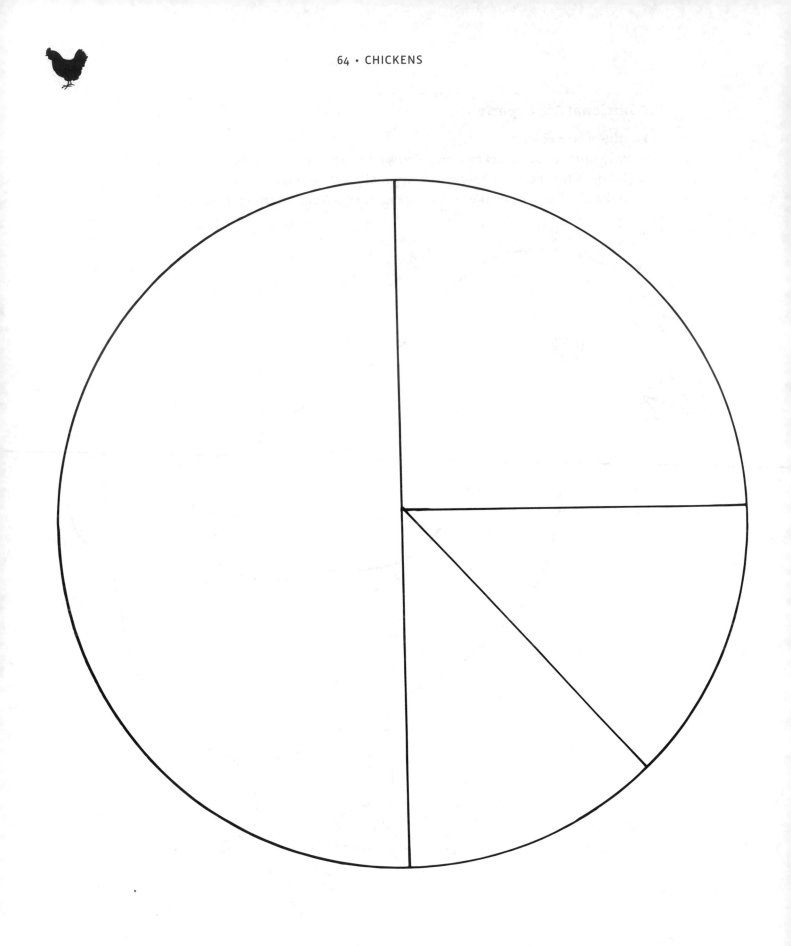

Pattern 11.2 **Modern art circle chicken**

Clothing and Hats

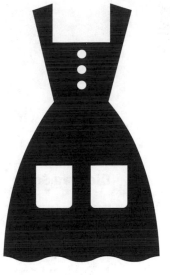

Opening Song and Rhyme

Book #1 *The Magic Hat* by Mem Fox, illustrated by Tricia Tusa

Stand-Up Activity
Sung to the tune of "Mary Had a Little Lamb"

Jumping Shoes
(Suit actions to words.)

Today I have my jumping shoes, jumping shoes, jumping shoes,
Today I have my jumping shoes, all day long.
Today I have my running shoes, running shoes, running shoes,
Today I have my running shoes, all day long.

(Continue with more action words, such as spinning, tiptoe, sitting, etc.)

Flannel Board

Graph favorite hat color:

Pieces: Several copies of a hat in three different colors
Directions: Hand out three different colored hat pictures. Let each child pick one favorite color. Tape these pictures onto the wall or flannel board in the form of a simple pictorial bar graph. Count how many hats are chosen for each color. Which color has the highest number of hats? Which has the smallest number?

Book #2 *Clothesline* by Jez Alborough

Action Song
Sung to the tune of "Skip to My Lou"

With Your Clothes

Slide with your socks, how about you? *(Slide feet side to side.)*
Slide with your socks, how about you? Slide with your socks, how about you?
Now slide in your clothes like I do.

Prance with your pants, how about you? *(March.)*
Prance with your pants, how about you? Prance with your pants, how about you?
Now prance in your clothes like I do.

Slither with your shirt, how about you? *(Move your arms and slither.)*
Slither with your shirt, how about you? Slither with your shirt, how about you?

(Continued on page 66)

Now slither in your clothes like I do.

Hop with your hat, how about you? (*Jump.*)
Hop with your hat, how about you? Hop with your hat, how about you?
Now hop in your clothes like I do.

Closing Song

Art Experience

Newspaper sailor hat:

1. Fold and prepare one newspaper sailor hat per child (go to www.dltk-kids.com /crafts/columbus/newspaper_sailors_hats.htm for simple folding directions).
2. Invite children to decorate the hat with stickers or by gluing on foam shapes.

Bonus Storytime Resources

More Books

Ella Sarah Gets Dressed by Margaret Chodos-Irvine

Hats, Hats, Hats by Ann Morris, illustrated by Ken Heyman

How Do I Put It On? by Shigeo Watanabe, illustrated by Yasuo Ohtomo

Mrs. McNosh Hangs Up Her Wash by Sarah Weeks, illustrated by Nadine Bernard Westcott

Two Shoes, Blue Shoes, New Shoes by Sally Fitz-Gibbon, illustrated by Farida Zaman

Extra Action Song #1

Sung to the tune of "If You're Happy and You Know It"

I'm Getting Ready to Go Outside

Oh my hat goes on my head, on my head.
(*Point to head and pretend to put on a hat.*)
Oh my hat goes on my head, on my head.
I'm getting ready now, to go outside and play.
Oh my hat goes on my head, on my head.

Oh my jacket goes on my arms, on my arms.
(*Point to arms and pretend to put on a jacket.*)
Oh my jacket goes on my arms, on my arms.
I'm getting ready now, to go outside and play.
Oh my jacket goes on my arms, on my arms.

Oh my boots go on my feet, on my feet.
(*Point to feet and pretend to put on boots.*)
Oh my boots go on my feet, on my feet.
I'm getting ready now, to go outside and play.
Oh my boots go on my feet, on my feet.

Oh my gloves go on my hands, on my hands.
(*Wave hands and pretend to put on gloves.*)
Oh my gloves go on my hands, on my hands.
I'm getting ready now, to go outside and play.
Oh my gloves go on my hands, on my hands.

Extra Action Song #2

"I Like My Hat" action song from *Stinky Cake* by Carole Peterson

Additional Art Experience

Felt mitten:

1. Precut one mitten shape on white felt fabric for each child (use Pattern 12.1).
2. Invite children to decorate the mitten using color pens.

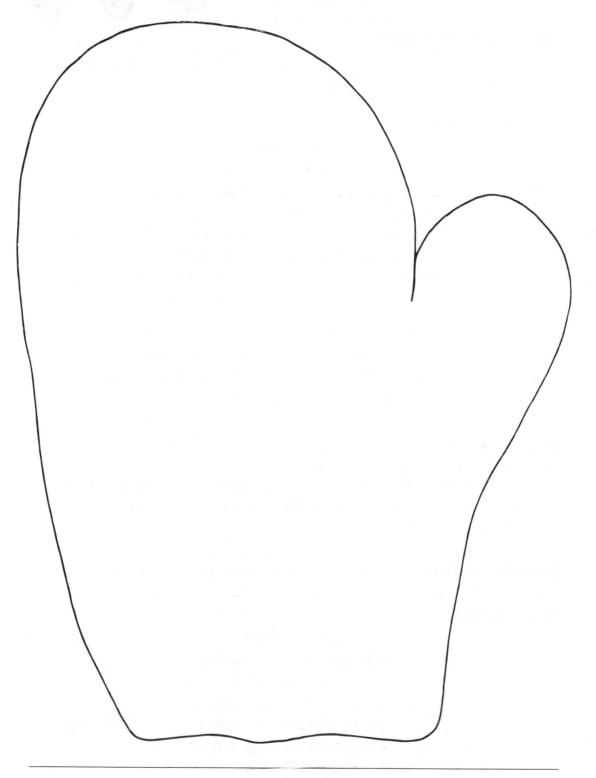

Pattern 12.1 **Mitten**

Colors and Patterns

Opening Song and Rhyme

Book #1 *Mouse Paint* by Ellen Stoll Walsh

Stand-Up Activity

Colored Shoes
(Suit actions to words.)

Stomping in my red shoes, red shoes, red shoes,
Stomping in my red shoes, here at storytime.
Running in my blue shoes, blues shoes, blue shoes,
Running in my blue shoes, here at storytime.
Sliding in my green shoes, green shoes, green shoes,
Sliding in my green shoes, here at storytime.
Twirling in my pink shoes, pink shoes, pinks shoes,
Twirling in my pink shoes, here at storytime.
Sitting in my white shoes, white shoes, white shoes,
Sitting in my white shoes, here at storytime.

Flannel Board

Pattern squares:
Pieces: Squares of three different colors
Directions: Place colored squares into a pattern on the flannel board. Be sure the children help re-create the pattern as it repeats, for example, blue, red, red, blue, red, red, blue, red, red.

Book #2 *Zoe's Hats: A Book of Colors and Patterns* by Sharon Lane Holm

Action Rhyme

I Look and Look
I look and look and what do I see?
(Make circles with hands around eyes.)

A bright red apple hanging in the tree.
(Use sign language for "apple.")

I look and look and what do I see?
(Make circles with hands around eyes.)

A yellow sun shining right on me.
(Form circle over head with arms.)

I look and look and what do I see?
(Make circles with hands around eyes.)

A great orange fruit, shiny and round.
(Form circle with hands.)

I look and look and what do I see?
(Make circles with hands around eyes.)

Some green grass growing on the ground.
(Touch ground.)

I look and look and what do I see?
(Make circles with hands around eyes.)

The blue waves on the ocean and sea.
(Make wave motions with one arm.)

I look and look and what do I see?
(Make circles with hands around eyes.)

All of the colors around you and me!
(Point to other person, then point to self.)

Closing Song

Art Experience

Pattern squares:

1. Precut long strips of paper or use receipt paper.
2. Precut small colored squares in two or three different colors, approximately two inches square.
3. Invite children to glue the squares in any pattern on the long strip of paper (see Figure 13.1). Tip: Try to use the same color squares as used in the flannel board activity.

Figure 13.1 **Pattern squares**

Bonus Storytime Resources

More Books

Cat's Colors by Jane Cabrera

Dog's Colorful Day: A Messy Story about Colors and Counting by Emma Dodd

Maisy's Rainbow Dream by Lucy Cousins

A Piece of Chalk by Jennifer A. Ericsson, illustrated by Michelle Shapiro

Snappy Little Colors by Kate Lee and Caroline Repchuk, illustrated by Derek Matthews (pop-up)

Extra Fingerplay

Shake the Bottle

Here is an empty bottle.
(Cup hands in front of body.)

Into it I pour some red.
(Use sign language for "red.")

Then I pour some blue.
(Use sign language for "blue.")

Now I shake, shake, shake the bottle.
(Close hands and shake them together.)

Shake, shake, shake the bottle.

Shake, shake, shake the bottle.

And now I have purple.
(Use sign language for "purple" and open up hands.)

(Repeat while combining blue and yellow to make green or red and yellow to make orange.)

Additional Art Experience

Rainbow:

1. Print out the rainbow drawing (use Pattern 13.1).
2. Invite children to place colorful dot stickers along the bands of the rainbow.

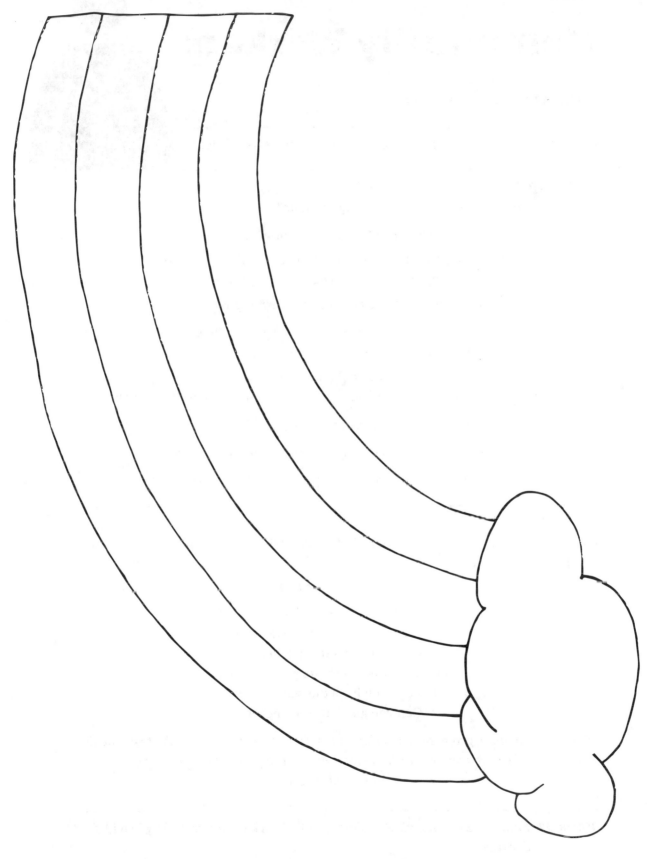

Pattern 13.1 **Rainbow**

Community Workers

Opening Song and Rhyme

Book #1 *When Poppy and Max Grow Up* by Lindsey Gardiner

Stand-Up Activity
Sung to the tune of "Do You Know the Muffin Man?"

Can You When You Grow Up?

Can you paint like an artist, like an artist, like an artist?
(Pretend to paint with wide sweeps of the arm.)

Can you paint like an artist, when you grow up?

Can you spin like a dancer, like a dancer, like a dancer. *(Spin around.)*

Can you spin like a dancer, when you grow up?

Can you cook like a chef . . .
(Make a circle with one arm, then pretend to stir in the circle with the other hand.)

Can you swim like a diver . . . *(Pretend to swim.)*

Can you ride like a cowboy . . . *(Pretend to ride a horse.)*

Can you fly like a pilot . . . *(Make airplane arms.)*

Flannel Board
Pieces: Doctor, plumber, mail carrier, chef, veterinarian, teacher, police officer, and
other professions

Can You Guess My Job?

Community workers work far and near.
This person helps people get well,
Can you guess this job here?
Community workers work far and near.
This person fixes the water pipes,
Can you guess this job here?

*(Repeat with more profession descriptions, such as deliver letters, make tasty meals,
keep your pets healthy, teach you new things, keep the city safe,
catch bad guys, etc.)*

Book #2 *Shhhhh! Everybody's Sleeping* by Julie Markes, illustrated by David
Parkins

Action Chant

Busy Family of Workers

My father is a firefighter, my father is a firefighter,

He goes like this: Hurry, hurry put the fire out.
(Run in place.)

We all go like this: Hurry, hurry.
(Run.)

My mother is a librarian, my mother is a librarian,

She goes like this: Read a book, please.
(Put hands together and open them like a book.)

We all go like this: Hurry, hurry—Read a book.
(Run, then open hands like a book.)

My sister is a baker, my sister is a baker,

She goes like this: Mix, mix, mix the cake together.
(Curl one arm in a circle, then pretend to stir a spoon in this circle with the other hand.)

We all go like this: Hurry, hurry—Read a book—Mix, mix, mix.
(Run, then open hands like a book, then stir spoon.)

My brother is a carpenter, my brother is a carpenter,

He goes like this: Hammer, hammer, bang the nail.
(Hammer one fist against the other hand.)

We all go like this: Hurry, hurry—Read a book—Mix, mix—
Hammer, hammer, hammer.
(Run, then open hands like a book, then stir spoon, then hammer hand.)

Whew!
(Wipe brow.)

We are a very busy family!

Closing Song

Art Experience

A little book that a librarian might find at the library:

1. Fold or staple a small book for each child (go to www.teacherhelp.org/bookdir
.htm for directions on a staple-free folded book).
2. Invite children to decorate this book with stickers or rubber stamps.

Bonus Storytime Resources

More Books

Bugs at Work by David A. Carter (board book)

Goodnight Piggywiggy by Christyan and Diane Fox

I Am Me! by Alexa Brandenberg

Kitten Red Yellow Blue by Peter Catalanotto

When I Grow Up by Jo S. Kittinger, illustrated by Margeaux Lucas

Extra Action Song

Sung to the tune of "Bluebird, Bluebird through My Window"

Police Officer, Police Officer

Police officer, police officer with his police badge.
(Place hands over heart.)

Police officer, police officer helping people.
(Use sign language for "help.")

Police officer, police officer if you have a problem,
(Place hands on cheeks.)

Just pick up a phone and call 9-1-1!
(Use sign language for the numbers 9, 1, and 1.)

Additional Art Experiences

Postcard that a mail carrier might deliver in the mail:

1. Precut postcards on cardstock. If you plan to mail these postcards, be sure the paper thickness and size fit in the guidelines for postcard postal rates.
2. Invite children to decorate the back side of the postcard (the side without the address lines) with crayons or color pens.

Police badge that a police officer might wear:

1. Precut police badge shapes (use Pattern 14.1).
2. Precut strips of aluminum foil, approximately ½ inch by two inches.
3. Invite children to glue on the strips of foil to create a shiny badge.
4. Use double-sided tape to stick the badge to the children's clothing.

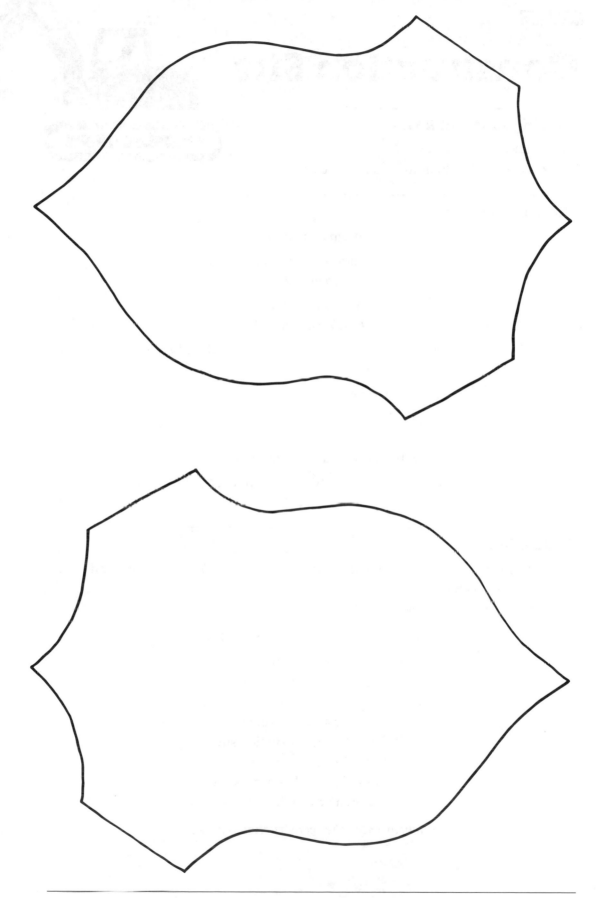

Pattern 14.1 **Police badge**

Construction Site

Opening Song and Rhyme

Book #1 *I'm Dirty* by Kate and Jim McMullan

Stand-Up Activity

Cranes Reach

Cranes reach up high,
(*Reach high.*)

Cranes reach down low,
(*Touch the ground.*)

Cranes reach really, really far, picking up their load.
(*Stretch arms out.*)

Cranes turn to the right,
(*With arms out, turn to the right.*)

Cranes turn to the left,
(*With arms out, turn to the left.*)

Cranes reach up really, really high, dropping off their load.
(*Reach high.*)

Flannel Board

Pieces: Dump truck, bulldozer, cement mixer, excavator, front-end loader, and other
   construction vehicles
Sung to the tune of "Pop Goes the Weasel"

All around the Construction Site

All around the construction site,
I see lots of busy trucks.
Here's one coming down the street,
Hey, it's a dump truck!
All around the construction site,
I see lots of busy trucks.
Here's one coming down the street,
Hey, it's a bulldozer!

(*Repeat with other construction trucks.*)

Book #2 *Tip Tip Dig Dig* by Emma Garcia

Action Song

Sung to the tune of "Wheels on the Bus"

The Wheels on the Dump Truck

The wheels on the dump truck go round and round,
round and round, round and round,
(Roll hands over each other.)
The wheels on the dump truck go round and round, driving to the work site.

The driver in the dump truck goes steer-steer-steer,
steer-steer-steer, steer-steer-steer,
(Pretend to drive with hands on a steering wheel.)
The driver in the dump truck goes steer-steer-steer, driving to the work site.

The box on the dump truck tips up and down, up and down, up and down,
(Put arms together in front of the body; move one arm up and down at the elbow.)
The box on the dump truck tips up and down, now at the work site.

The horn on the dump truck goes beep-beep-beep,
beep-beep-beep, beep-beep-beep,
(Pretend to honk horn.)
The horn on the dump truck goes beep-beep-beep, driving from the work site.

Closing Song

Art Experience

Dirty dump truck:
1. Print out the dump truck drawing (use Pattern 15.1).
2. Invite children to glue sand or dirt onto the dump truck.

Bonus Storytime Resources

More Books

Big Machines! Big Buildings! by Kevin Lewis, illustrated by Reg Cartwright
Construction Countdown by K. C. Olson, illustrated by David Gordon
I Love Trucks! by Philemon Sturges, illustrated by Shari Halpern
Machines at Work by Byron Barton
One Big Building: A Counting Book about Construction by Michael Dahl, illustrated by Todd Ouren

Extra Action Song

Favorite sources: Little Songs for Little Me by Nancy Stewart or "Joannie Works with One Hammer" from *Here Comes the Big Red Car* by The Wiggles

Peter Hammers
(Traditional)

Peter hammers with one hammer, one hammer, one hammer,
(Make up-and-down motion with one fist.)
Peter hammers with one hammer all day long.

Peter hammers with two hammers, two hammers, two hammers,
(Make up-and-down motion with both fists.)
Peter hammers with two hammers all day long.

Peter hammers with three hammers, three hammers, three hammers,
(Make up-and-down motion with both fists and one leg.)
Peter hammers with three hammers all day long.

Peter hammers with four hammers, four hammers, four hammers,
(Make up-and-down motion with both fists and both legs.)
Peter hammers with four hammers all day long.

Peter hammers with five hammers, five hammers, five hammers,
(Make up-and-down motion with both fists, both legs, and nod head.)
Peter hammers with five hammers all day long.

Peter's getting sleepy now, sleepy now, sleepy now,
(Put hands together on the side of the face.)
Peter's getting sleepy now, off to bed he goes.

Additional Art Experience

Building blueprint:

1. Give each child a large sheet of dark blue construction paper, white chalk, and a ruler.
2. Invite children to draw with the chalk and rulers to make lines similar to those on a blueprint.

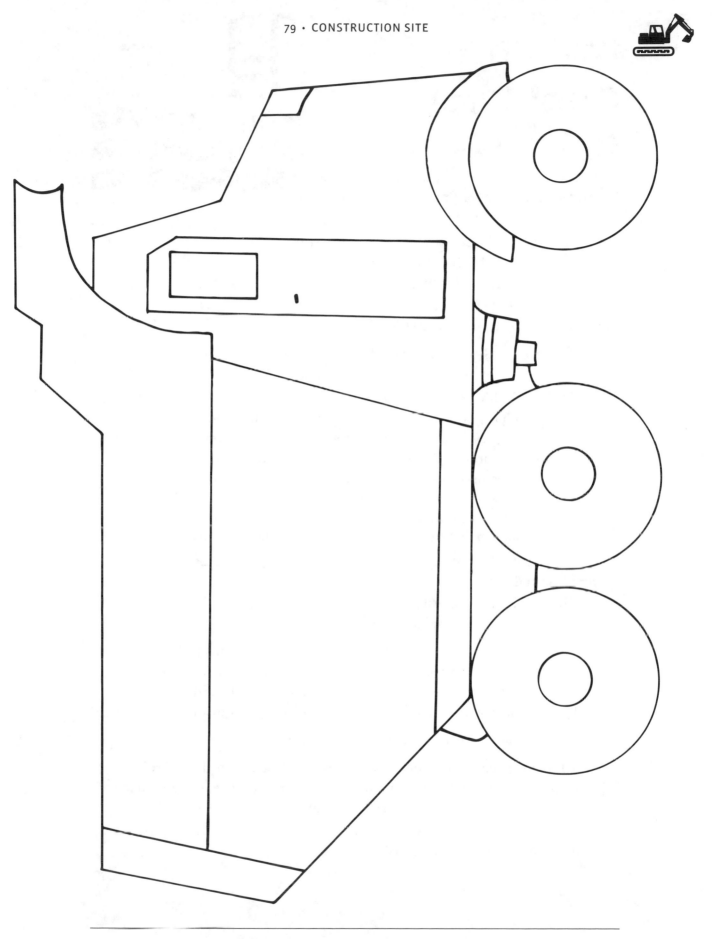

Pattern 15.1 **Dump truck**

Cool Pool of Water

Opening Song and Rhyme

Book #1 *Down by the Cool of the Pool* by Tony Mitton,
illustrated by Guy Parker-Rees

Stand-Up Activity

Sung to the tune of "London Bridge Is Falling Down"

Around the Cool Water

(Suit actions to words.)

Splashing around the cool water, cool water, cool water.
Splashing around the cool water, I can play in the pond all day.
Jumping around the cool water, cool water, cool water.
Jumping around the cool water, I can play in the pond all day.
Swimming around the cool water, cool water, cool water.
Swimming around the cool water, I can play in the pond all day.
Sitting next to the cool water, cool water, cool water.
Sitting next to the cool water, I can play in the pond all day.

Flannel Board

Pieces: Five turtles (use Pattern 16.1)

Turtles Went Out to Play

One little turtle went out to play upon a lily pad one day.
He had such a marvelous time, he asked for another to join the fun.
Two little turtles went out to play upon a lily pad one day.
They had such a marvelous time, they asked for another to join the fun.

(Repeat counting up to five turtles.)

Five little turtles went out to play upon a crowded lily pad one day.
They jumped into the water and started to swim, and that's how they continued to
have some fun.

Book #2 *Maisy's Pool* by Lucy Cousins

Action Rhyme

Sung to the tune of "She'll Be Coming around the Mountain When She Comes"

We'll Be Swimming in the Pool

We'll be swimming in the pool when it's hot.
(Pretend to swim.)

We'll be swimming in the pool when it's hot.

We'll be swimming the backstroke,
(Pretend to backstroke swim.)

The side stroke,
(Pretend to swim on side.)

And some diving.
(Make diving motion with hands together.)

We'll be swimming in the pool when it's hot.
(Pretend to swim.)

Closing Song

Art Experience

Paint a pond:

1. Provide each child with paper, blue paint, and a paintbrush.
2. Invite children to paint their own pond or pool of water with the blue paint.

Bonus Storytime Resources

More Books

In the Small, Small Pond by Denise Fleming

Little White Duck by Walt Whippo, illustrated by Joan Paley

Lovely Day for Amelia Goose by Yu Rong

Splash! by Ann Jonas

Water, Water by Eloise Greenfield, illustrated by Jan Spivey Gilchrist

Extra Action Rhyme

Down by the Pool

Down by the pool in the bright clear water,
Swam a little turtle boy and his mama turtle too.
"Swim," says the turtle. (*Pretend to swim.*)
"We swim," says the mama.
And they swim around the water in the bright sunlight.

Down by the pool in the bright clear water,
Jumped a little frog girl and her papa frog too.
"Jump," says the frog. (*Jump.*)
"We jump," says the papa.
And they jump around the water in the bright sunlight.

Down by the pool in the bright clear water,
Waddles a little duck boy and his mama duck too.
"Waddle," says the duck. (*Waddle walk.*)
"We waddle," says the mama.
And they waddle around the water in the bright sunlight.

Down by the pool in the bright clear water,
Flew a little dragonfly girl and her papa dragonfly too.
"Fly," says the dragonfly. (*Fly around with airplane arms.*)
"We fly," says the papa.
And they fly around the water in the bright sunlight.

Extra Action Song

"Listen to the Water" action song from *More Tickles and Tunes* by Kathy Reid-Naiman

Additional Art Experience

Turtle shell:

1. Print out the turtle drawing (use Pattern 16.1).
2. Invite children to decorate the shell of the turtle by gluing on small pieces of paper, craft foam shapes, dot stickers, or sewing trim.

Pattern 16.1 **Turtle**

Counting

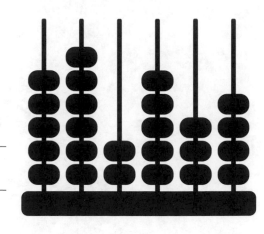

Opening Song and Rhyme

Book #1 *1, 2, Buckle My Shoe* by Anna Grossnickle Hines

Stand-Up Activity
Sung to the tune of "Hokey Pokey"

Number Pokey
(Suit actions to words.)

You put one finger in. You put one finger out.
You put one finger in and you shake it all about.
You do the number pokey and you turn yourself about.
That's how we count to one.

You put two fingers in. You put two fingers out.
You put two fingers in and you shake them all about.
You do the number pokey and you turn yourself about.
That's how we count to two.

(Repeat up to five fingers.)

Flannel Board
Pieces: Numerals 1 through 12, gift, cake, elves

The Little Elves Are Coming Right In

One, two, three, four, I see a present at the garden door.
Five, six, seven, eight, I see a cake at the garden gate.
Nine, ten, eleven, twelve, the little elves are coming right in!

Book #2 *Ten Black Dots* by Donald Crews

Fingerplay

Hickory Dickory Dock
(Nursery rhyme)
Hickory dickory dock, a mouse ran up the clock. *(Run one hand up the other arm.)*
The clock struck one. *(Clap once.)*
The mouse ran down. *(Run one hand down the other arm.)*
Hickory dickory dock.

Hickory dickory dock, a mouse ran up the clock.
(*Run one hand up the other arm.*)
The clock struck two. (*Clap twice.*)
The mouse said "BOO!"
Hickory dickory dock.

Hickory dickory dock, a mouse ran up the clock.
(*Run one hand up the other arm.*)
The clock struck three. (*Clap three times.*)
The mouse said "Wheee!"
(*Slide one hand down the other arm and then down to the floor as if on a slide.*)
Hickory dickory dock.

Hickory dickory dock, a mouse ran up the clock.
(*Run one hand up the other arm.*)
The clock struck four. (*Clap four times.*)
There is no more. (*Shake head, then show empty hands.*)
Hickory dickory dock.

Closing Song

Art Experience

Count to 5 book:

1. Prefold three pieces of paper in half together. Staple along the fold to make a small book.
2. On the cover write the words "My Count to 5 Book." On each right side page write the numerals 1 through 5.
3. Invite children to put dot stickers or stamps on each page to match the number written on the page.

Bonus Storytime Resources

More Books

Count! by Denise Fleming
Counting Kisses by Karen Katz
Mouse Count by Ellen Stoll Walsh
1, 2, 3 to the Zoo: A Counting Book by Eric Carle
Ten Terrible Dinosaurs by Paul Stickland

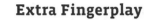

Extra Fingerplay

Beehive

(Traditional)

Here is the beehive, where are the bees?
(Show closed hand in a fist.)

Hidden away where nobody sees.

Watch and you will see them come out of their hive,
(Bring out fingers one at a time.)

One, two, three, four, five,

Buzz, buzz, buzz.

Extra Action Song

"Count the Bells" action song from *Sing It! Say It! Stamp It! Sway It! Volume 3* by Peter & Ellen Allard (As you count the bells, make this a movement activity by doing a large body motion for each bell sound, such as sweeping arms above the head and down again.)

Additional Art Experience

A row of ten:

1. At the top of a long strip of paper or receipt paper write the number 10.
2. Invite children to glue buttons or craft foam shapes onto the paper to create a row of ten objects (see Figure 17.1).

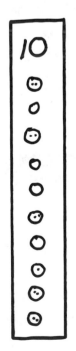

Figure 17.1 **A row of ten**

Dinosaurs

Opening Song and Rhyme

Book #1 *How Do Dinosaurs Say Goodnight?* by Jane Yolen and Mark Teague

Stand-Up Activity

Dinosaur, Dinosaur

(Suit actions to words.)

Dinosaur, dinosaur, turn around. Dinosaur, dinosaur, dig in the ground.

Dinosaur, dinosaur, walk on your toes. Dinosaur, dinosaur, scratch your nose.

Dinosaur, dinosaur, reach up high. Dinosaur, dinosaur, fly in the sky.

Dinosaur, dinosaur, stomp your feet. Dinosaur, dinosaur, show your teeth.

Dinosaur, dinosaur, give a roar. Dinosaur, dinosaur, sit on the floor.

Flannel Board

Pieces: Five or more dinosaurs (use Pattern 18.1)

Directions: Start with one dinosaur on the board. Add two more at the end of the song. Count the dinosaurs. Repeat the singing, adding, and counting as many times as necessary.

Sung to the tune of "Row, Row, Row Your Boat"

Dino, Dino, Dinosaur

Dino, dino, dinosaur, stomping on the ground.
Now we add one and two, till we have a herd.

Book #2 *Dinosaur Stomp! A Monster Pop-Up Book* by Paul Stickland

Action Chant

A Dinosaur Goes

(Adapted traditional)

A dinosaur goes like this and that. *(Sway side to side.)*

He's terribly big, *(Raise hands up high.)*

And he's terribly fat. *(Make large circle with arms in front of body.)*

He has two eyes, *(Circle eyes with fingers.)*

Yet he makes you pause. *(Use sign language for "stop.")*

Goodness gracious, what sharp claws! *(Move hands as if they are claws.)*

Closing Song

Art Experience

Scales on a dinosaur:
1. Print out the dinosaur drawing (use Pattern 18.2).
2. Precut colorful one-inch tissue paper squares.
3. Invite children to glue square scales onto the dinosaur.

Bonus Storytime Resources

More Books

Dinosaur Bones by Bob Barner

Dinosaurs, Dinosaurs by Byron Barton

Dinosaur Train by John Steven Gurney

Dinosaurumpus by Tony Mitton, illustrated by Guy Parker-Rees

Snappy Little Dinosaurs by Dugald Steer, illustrated by Derek Matthews

Extra Action Song #1

Sung to the tune of "Shake My Sillies Out"

Shake My Dino Head

I'm going to shake, shake, shake my dino head, *(Shake head.)*
Shake, shake, shake my dino head, Shake, shake, shake my dino head,
And then go stomping about. *(Stomp feet.)*

I'm going to scratch, scratch, scratch my dino claws,
(Shape hands like claws and then scratch them in the air.)
Scratch, scratch, scratch my dino claws, Scratch, scratch, scratch my dino claws,
And then go stomping about. *(Stomp feet.)*

I'm going to wiggle, wiggle, wiggle my dino foot,
(Wiggle one foot.)
Wiggle, wiggle, wiggle my dino foot, Wiggle, wiggle, wiggle my dino foot,
And then go stomping about. *(Stomp feet.)*

I'm going to wag, wag, wag my dino tail,
(Move bottom side to side.)
Wag, wag, wag my dino tail, Wag, wag, wag my dino tail,
And then go stomping about. *(Stomp feet.)*

Extra Action Song #2

"We Are the Dinosaurs" action song from *Whaddaya Think of That* by Laurie Berkner

Additional Art Experience

Dinosaur stick puppet:

1. Precut dinosaur shapes (use Pattern 18.1).
2. Glue or tape a craft stick to the back of each dinosaur shape.
3. Invite children to decorate their dinosaur puppets with crayons, color pens, or paints.

Pattern 18.1 **Dinosaur stick puppets**

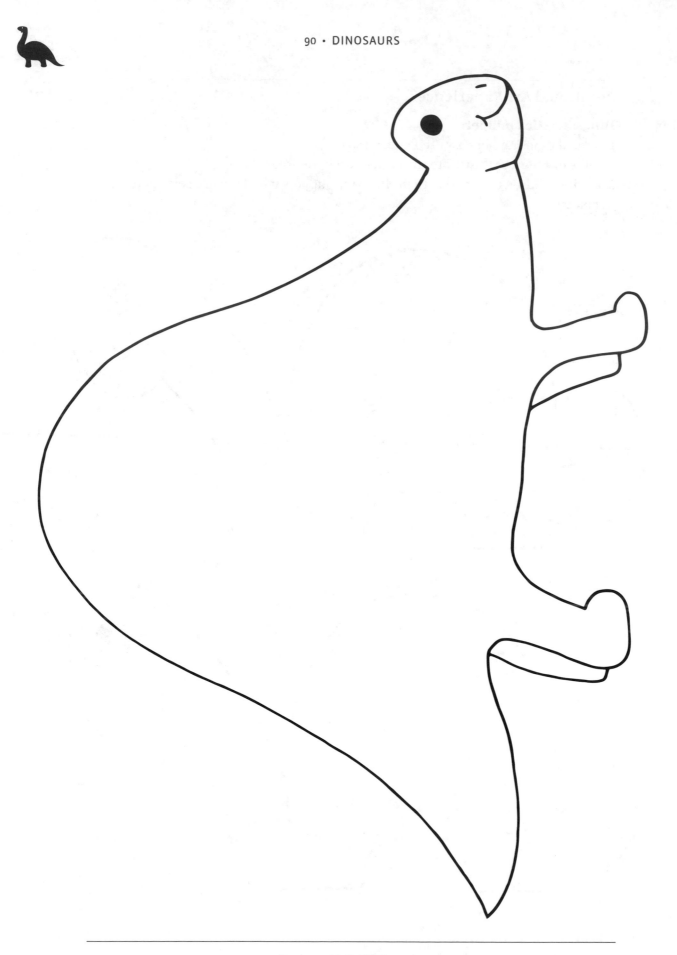

Pattern · 18.2 **Dinosaur**

Dogs and Puppies

Opening Song and Rhyme

Book #1 *Dogs* by Emily Gravett

Stand-Up Activity

Some Dogs
(Suit actions to words.)

Some dogs run.
Some dogs bark.
Some dogs jump.
Some dogs growl.
Some dogs roll in the grass.
Some dogs yip.
Some dogs sniff.
Some dogs howl.
And some dogs just wag their tails all day long.

Flannel Board
Pieces: Five dogs (use Pattern 21.1, p. 102)

Little Doggies

One little doggie going for a walk,
Along came another and now there are two.
Two little doggies playing with a ball,
Along came another and now there are three.
Three little doggies catching a Frisbee,
Along came another and now there are four.
Four little doggies digging up some bones,
Along came another and now there are five.
Five little doggies playing all day long,
The sun goes down, the moon comes up, and they all go home.

Book #2 *Bark, George* by Jules Feiffer

Fingerplay

Ten Little Puppies

Ten little puppies coming to play. (*Show ten fingers.*)

Happy little puppies, what a good day. (*Wave fingers.*)

They run to the left. (*Move hands to the left.*)

They run to the right. (*Move hands to the right.*)

They roll in the grass in the bright sunlight. (*Roll hands over each other.*)

As the sun goes down and the stars shine bright,
(*Circle arms over head for sun.*)

They stop to find their food bowls to eat, eat, eat.
(*Cup hands together and pretend to lick.*)

Closing Song

Art Experience

Dog face:

1. Precut one large triangle for each child.
2. Fold over two corners of the triangle to create a dog face with floppy ears (see Figure 19.1).
3. Invite children to decorate this face with dot stickers for eyes and nose, as well as with crayons.

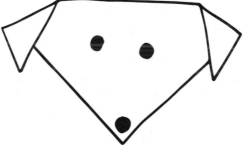

Figure 19.1 **Dog face**

Bonus Storytime Resources

More Books

Along Came Toto by Ann Axworthy

Dog's Day by Jane Cabrera

Here Come Poppy and Max by Lindsey Gardiner

Rrralph by Lois Ehlert

Where's Spot? by Eric Hill

Extra Action Song

Sung to the tune of "This Old Man"

This Little Puppy

This little puppy began to run when she chased a rabbit in the sun. *(Run in place.)*

With a woof-woof, *(Bark.)* Wag the tail, *(Wiggle bottom.)*

Give the dog a bone. *(Cup hands together in front of body.)*

This little puppy began to run. *(Run in place.)*

This little puppy began to fly when she saw a butterfly.

(Flap arms as wings straight out to the sides.)

With a woof-woof, *(Bark.)* Wag the tail, *(Wiggle bottom.)*

Give the dog a bone. *(Cup hands together in front of body.)*

This little puppy began to fly.

(Flap arms as wings straight out to the sides.)

This little puppy began to jump when she found a cat on a stump. *(Jump.)*

With a woof-woof, *(Bark.)* Wag the tail, *(Wiggle bottom.)*

Give the dog a bone. *(Cup hands together in front of body.)*

This little puppy began to jump. *(Jump.)*

This little puppy turned all around when she chased her tail on the ground.

(Spin around.)

With a woof-woof, *(Bark.)* Wag the tail, *(Wiggle bottom.)*

Give the dog a bone. *(Cup hands together in front of body.)*

This little puppy turned all around. *(Spin around.)*

This little puppy fell asleep when she saw the little white sheep.

(Put hands together on the side of the face.)

With a woof-woof, *(Bark.)* Wag the tail, *(Wiggle bottom.)*

Give the dog a bone. *(Cup hands together in front of body.)*

This little puppy fell asleep.

Additional Art Experience

Dog collar:

1. Precut one strip of white felt for each child, approximately two inches by eight inches.
2. Glue or sew the hook side of a small piece of Velcro to one end of each white felt strip.
3. Invite children to decorate the felt collar with color pens.

Farm Animals

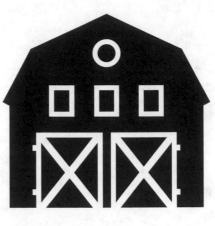

Opening Song and Rhyme

Book #1 *Barnyard Banter* by Denise Fleming

Stand-Up Activity

Clippity, Clippity Clop

Clippity, clippity clop, the horses go clip clop.
(*Make horse hoof sound by clapping hands on legs.*)

They gallop to the right. (*Gallop right.*)

They gallop to the left. (*Gallop left.*)

They gallop all around. (*Gallop in a small circle.*)

And they come to a stop. (*Use sign language for "stop."*)

Clippity, clippity clop. (*Make horse hoof sound.*)

Flannel Board

Pieces: Cow, sheep, horse, pig, chicken, other farm animals

Favorite sources: Animal Songs by Bob McGrath and *Little Songs for Little Me* by Nancy Stewart

Old MacDonald Had a Farm

Old MacDonald had a farm, Ee-i-ee-i-oh!
And on that farm he had some cows, Ee-i-ee-i-oh!
With a moo-moo here, And a moo-moo there,
Here a moo, there a moo,
Everywhere a moo-moo.
Old MacDonald had a farm, Ee-i-ee-i-oh!

And on that farm he had some sheep, Ee-i-ee-i-oh!
With a baa-baa here, And a baa-baa there,
Here a baa, there a baa,
Everywhere a baa-baa.
Old MacDonald had a farm, Ee-i-ee-i-oh!

(*Repeat with other animals, such as horse, pig, chicken, etc.,
and the sounds they make.*)

Book #2 *I Went Walking* by Sue Williams, illustrated by Julie Vivas

Action Chant

I Went to the Farm to See the Animals

I went to the farm to see the animals, see the animals, see the animals.
I went to the farm to see the animals, and this is what they did.

The cows I saw went walking, walking, walking.
(Walk in place.)
The cows I saw went walking, and then I saw the sheep.

The sheep I saw went sliding, sliding, sliding.
(Slide feet side to side.)
The sheep I saw went sliding, and then I saw the ducks.

The ducks I saw went waddling, waddling, waddling.
(Pretend to waddle like a duck.)
The ducks I saw went waddling, and then I saw the chickens.

The chickens I saw went scratching, scratching, scratching.
(Scratch ground with feet.)
The chickens I saw went scratching, and then I saw the pigs.

The pigs I saw went rolling, rolling, rolling.
(Roll hands over each other.)
The pigs I saw went rolling in the mud, and that is what I saw.

Closing Song

Art Experience

Spotted cow:
1. Print off the cow drawing (use Pattern 20.1).
2. Invite children to add fingerprint spots to the cow.

Bonus Storytime Resources

More Books

Can You Moo? by David Wojtowycz
I Heard a Little Baa by Elizabeth MacLeod and Louise Phillips
I Love Animals by Flora McDonnell
Snappy Little Farmyard by Dugald Steer, illustrated by Derek Matthews
Spots, Feathers, and Curly Tails by Nancy Tafuri

Extra Action Rhyme

Little Sheep

(Suit actions to words.)

Little sheep, little sheep, turn around.
Little sheep, little sheep, graze on the ground.
Little sheep, little sheep, frolic on your toes.
Little sheep, little sheep, wiggle your nose.
Little sheep, little sheep, fluff your wool.
Little sheep, little sheep, jump to keep cool.
Little sheep, little sheep, scratch your feet.
Little sheep, little sheep, find your seat.

Extra Action Songs

"Six Little Ducks" action song from *More Singable Songs* by Raffi or *Toddler Tunes* by Cedarmont Kids Classics

Additional Art Experience

Fluffy sheep:

1. Print out the sheep drawing on white paper or cut out a sheep shape on black construction paper (use Pattern 20.2).
2. Invite children to glue cotton balls or cotton fiberfill as wool on the sheep.

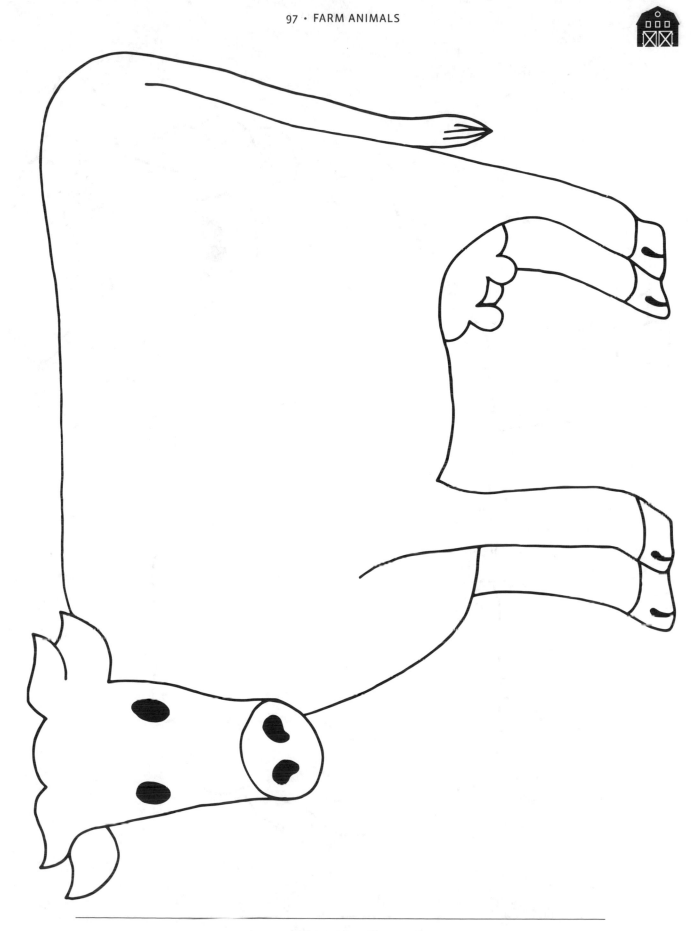

Pattern 20.1 **Cow**

Pattern 20.2 **Sheep**

Fire Trucks and Firefighters

Opening Song and Rhyme

Book #1 *Fire Fighter Piggywiggy* by Christyan and Diane Fox

Stand-Up Activity

Sung to the tune of "Bumpin' Up and Down in My Little Red Wagon"

Little Red Fire Truck

Bumping up and down in my little red fire truck.
(Bend knees up and down.)

Bumping up and down in my little red fire truck.

Bumping up and down in my little red fire truck, hurry to the fire.

The wheels on the truck go round and around.
(Roll hands over each other.)

The wheels on the truck go round and around.

The wheels on the truck go round and around, hurry to the fire.

The lights on the truck go blink-blink-blink.
(Flick open fingers.)

The lights on the truck go blink-blink-blink.

The lights on the truck go blink-blink-blink, hurry to the fire.

The siren on the truck goes woo-woo.
(Turn one hand in a small circle high in the air.)

The siren on the truck goes woo-woo.

The siren on the truck goes woo-woo, hurry to the fire.

The ladder on the truck goes up-up-up.
(Reach both arms high in the air.)

The ladder on the truck goes up-up-up.

The ladder on the truck goes up-up-up, hurry to the fire.

The water from the hose goes whoosh-whoosh.
(Pretend to spray a water hose.)

The water from the hose goes whoosh-whoosh.

The water from the hose goes whoosh-whoosh, now the fire is all out!

Flannel Board

Pieces: Six different colored fire stations, one Dalmatian dog that fits under the fire stations

Directions: Set out all six fire stations. Hide the dog under one of these buildings. Say the little rhyme and let the children guess which station the dog is under. Continue saying the rhyme and guessing until the dog is found.

Fire Dog Hiding

Where is my fire dog, my Dalmatian puppy dog?

Which fire station is he hiding at?

Can you spot him now?

Book #2 *Maisy's Fire Engine* by Lucy Cousins (board book)

Action Song

Sung to the tune of "Row, Row, Row Your Boat"

Driving the Fire Truck

Drive, drive, drive the truck, driving the fire truck.

(Pretend to drive.)

Hurry now, let's go fast, put the fire out.

(Move arms back and forth in front of body as they cross each other.)

Ring, ring, ring the bell, ringing loud and clear.

(Pretend to ring bell with one hand.)

Hurry now, let's go fast, put the fire out.

(Move arms back and forth in front of body as they cross each other.)

Up, up, up the ladder, raising the ladder high.

(Roll hands over each other high in the air.)

Hurry now, let's go fast, put the fire out.

(Move arms back and forth in front of body as they cross each other.)

Spray, spray, spray the hose with a lot of water.

(Pretend to spray a water hose.)

Hurry now, let's go fast, put the fire out.

(Move arms back and forth in front of body as they cross each other.)

Closing Song

Art Experience

Paper firefighter hat:

1. Precut one firefighter hat for each child (use Pattern 21.2). To make a paper firefighter hat:

a. Cut along the outside edge to create an oval-like shape.

b. Next, cut along the black lines inside the hat to make an oval-like hole.

c. Cut off and discard the blackened part, and then fold up the half-oval at the dotted line (see Figure 21.1). This creates a space for the child's head. The head space can be cut larger if needed.

2. Invite children to decorate the hats with color pens.

Figure 21.1 **Paper firefighter hat**

Bonus Storytime Resources

More Books

Fire Truck by Peter Sís

Firefighters! Speeding! Spraying! Saving! by Patricia Hubbell, illustrated by Viviana Garofoli

Flashing Fire Engines by Tony Mitton and Ant Parker

Night Fire by Lori Lukasewich

This Is the Firefighter by Laura Godwin, illustrated by Julian Hector

Extra Action Song #1

Sung to the tune of "I'm a Little Teapot"

I'm a Little Firefighter

I'm a little firefighter, off I go. *(Point to self.)*

Here is my helmet, *(Put hands on head.)*

Here is my truck. *(Point to the side.)*

When my clothes catch on fire I know what to do. *(Wipe hands on clothes.)*

I stop, drop, and roll to put the fire out! *(Roll on ground.)*

Extra Action Song #2

"Drive the Fire Truck" from *Songs for Wiggleworms* by Old Town School of Music

Additional Art Experience

Dalmatian fire dog:

1. Print out the Dalmatian drawing (use Pattern 21.1).
2. Invite children to add spots to the dog using dot stickers or bingo dabber paints.

Pattern 21.1 **Dalmatian fire dog**

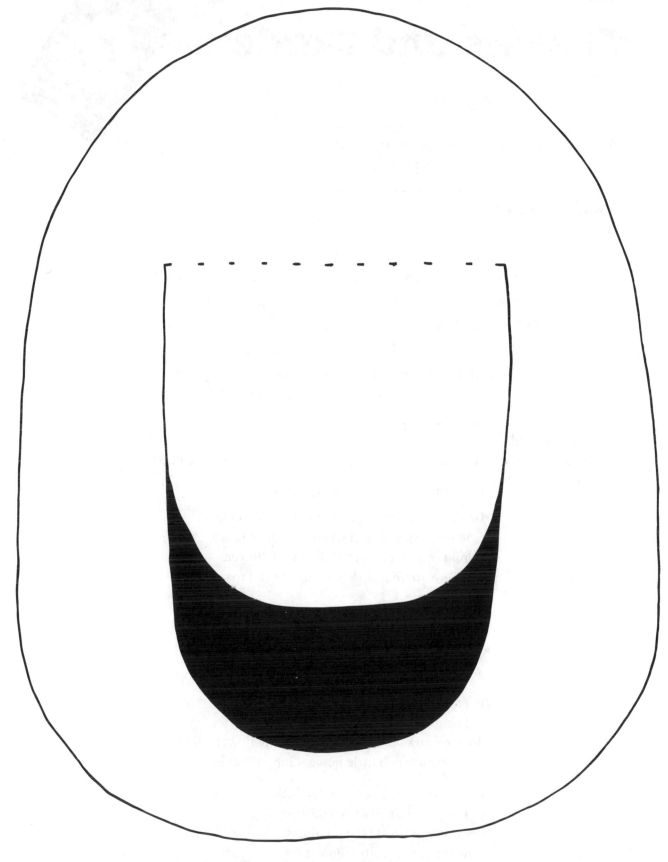

Pattern 21.2 **Paper firefighter hat**

Flowers and Gardens

Opening Song and Rhyme

Book #1 *Mrs. McNosh and the Great Big Squash* by Sarah Weeks, illustrated by Nadine Bernard Westcott

Stand-Up Activity

A Little Seed
(Traditional)

A tiny seed lies asleep in the ground. *(Crouch on the ground.)*

"Awake," says the sun, "I am giving you warmth." *(Circle arms overhead.)*

"Awake," says the rain, "I am giving you water." *(Flutter fingers down.)*

The little seed heard and loved what it felt, *(Hug self.)*

It came up through the earth, *(Open hands and turn up fingers.)*

And grew up to the sky. *(Raise hands high.)*

Flannel Board
Pieces: Red flower, yellow flower, purple flower, white flower, orange flower

Flowers in a Terra-Cotta Pot

In a terra-cotta pot grew five little flowers.
The prettiest flowers, you ever did see.
Along came a child to pick the red flower.
Now there are four little flowers for you to see.

In a terra-cotta pot grew four little flowers.
The prettiest flowers, you ever did see.
Along came a child to pick the yellow flower.
Now there are three little flowers for you to see.

In a terra-cotta pot grew three little flowers.
The prettiest flowers, you ever did see.
Along came a child to pick the purple flower.
Now there are two little flowers for you to see.

In a terra-cotta pot grew two little flowers.
The prettiest flowers, you ever did see.
Along came a child to pick the white flower.
Now there is one little flower for you to see.

In a terra-cotta pot grew one little flower.
The prettiest flower, you ever did see.
Along came a child to pick the orange flower.
Now there are no more flowers for you to see.

Book #2 *Jasper's Beanstalk* by Nick Butterworth and Mick Inkpen

Fingerplay

Ten Little Flowers

Ten little flowers standing in the sun. (*Show and count your ten fingers.*)

Ten thirsty flowers begin to droop. (*Bow down fingers.*)

Along come the clouds, (*Point to the sky.*)

And the rain begins to fall. (*Flutter hands down.*)

Ten little flowers lift their heads to the sun again. (*Lift fingers up.*)

Closing Song

Art Experience

Beanstalk:

1. Precut a bunch of heart shapes out of green paper.
2. Precut one length of green yarn for each child, approximately six inches.
3. Hand each child one large white piece of paper, a piece of yarn, and some heart-shaped green leaves.
4. Invite children to glue the yarn onto the paper and then glue the leaves around the yarn to create a beanstalk (see Figure 22.1).

Figure 22.1 **Beanstalk**

Bonus Storytime Resources

More Books

The Carrot Seed by Ruth Krauss, illustrated by Crockett Johnson
Growing Vegetable Soup by Lois Ehlert
My Garden by Kevin Henkes
The Surprise Garden by Zoe Hall, illustrated by Shari Halpern
Vegetable Garden by Douglas Florian

Extra Action Song

Sung to the tune of "Twinkle, Twinkle, Little Star"

Little Flower Open Up

Little flower begin to grow. *(Start crouched on the ground, then pretend to grow up.)*

Open up your petals bright. *(Open up arms to the sides.)*

Swaying in the sunshine light, *(Sway from side to side.)*

Come and let the bees buzz right. *(Put fingers together to make bee.)*

Little flowers in the night, *(Put arms back out to the sides.)*

Closing up your petals tight. *(Bring arms back in and hug self.)*

Additional Art Experience

Sunflower wind catcher:

1. Precut a supply of large yellow triangles.
2. Invite children to glue these triangles along the outside edge of a yellow paper plate for petals.
3. Glue some sunflower seeds (in their shells) to the center of the paper plate. Add a green crepe paper streamer on the bottom for a stem. Attach a length of yarn at the top so the flower can dance in the wind (see Figure 22.2).

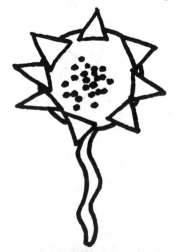

Figure 22.2 **Sunflower wind catcher**

Food, Yummy Food

Opening Song and Rhyme

Book #1 *Lunch* by Denise Fleming

Stand-Up Activity
Sung to the tune of "Baa, Baa, Black Sheep"

Yummy Fruit Salad

Yum, yum fruit salad, *(Rub belly.)*
Can I have some more? *(Use sign language for "more.")*
Apples, *(Use sign language for "apple.")*
Bananas, *(Use sign language for "banana.")*
Pineapples too. *(Use sign language for "pineapple.")*

Throw it in a bowl, *(Put arms in a circle in front of body.)*
Mix it up good, *(Spin around in place.)*
Dish it out to your friends, *(Pretend to spoon out the salad.)*
Then eat it all up! *(Pretend to eat.)*

Yum, yum fruit salad, *(Rub belly.)*
Can I have some more? *(Use sign language for "more.")*
Apples, *(Use sign language for "apple.")*
Bananas, *(Use sign language for "banana.")*
Pineapples too. *(Use sign language for "pineapple.")*

Flannel Board
Pieces: Ten cupcakes (use Pattern 23.1)
Sung to the tune of "Ten Little Indians"

Ten Little Cupcakes

One little, two little, three little cupcakes,
Four little, five little, six little cupcakes,
Seven little, eight little, nine little cupcakes,
Ten little cupcakes for us to eat!

Book #2 *Maisy Bakes a Cake* by Lucy Cousins

Fingerplay

Pat-a-Cake
(Nursery rhyme)

Pat-a-cake, pat-a-cake baker's man. *(Clap.)*
Bake me a cake as fast as you can.

Roll it, *(Roll hands over each other.)*
And pat it, *(Pat hands together softly.)*
And mark it with a "B." *(Write the letter "B" on chest.)*

Put it in the oven for baby and me. *(Push hands away from the body.)*

Closing Song

Art Experience

Colorful cupcake:

1. Print out the cupcake drawing (use Pattern 23.1).
2. Invite children to glue fruity breakfast cereal pieces or small pieces of sewing notions as sprinkles on a cupcake.

Bonus Storytime Resources

More Books

"Hi, Pizza Man!" by Virginia Walter, illustrated by Ponder Goembel
If You Give a Moose a Muffin by Laura Joeffe Numeroff, illustrated by Felicia Bond
My Pop Pop and Me by Irene Smalls, illustrated by Cathy Ann Johnson
Ruby's Tea for Two by Rosemary Wells (board book)
The Very Hungry Caterpillar by Eric Carle

Extra Action Song #1

"I'm a Little Teapot" action song from *This Little Piggy & Other Rhymes to Sing & Play* by Jane Yolen and Will Hillenbrand

Extra Action Song #2

"Milkshake" action song from *Songs for Wiggleworms* by Old Town School of Folk Music

Extra Action Song #3

Sung to the tune of "Three Blind Mice"

Three Round Pizzas

Small, medium, large,
(Circle arms in front of body in different sized circles.)

Small, medium, large,

Three round pizzas,
(Circle arms above head.)

Three on the table.

I looked around for someone else.
(Look from side to side.)

I snuck a piece for myself.
(Pretend to grab a piece of pizza.)

I ate it up really fast.
(Pretend to eat.)

It was yummy.
(Rub belly.)

It was yummy.

Additional Art Experiences

Watermelon wedge:

1. Print out the watermelon wedge drawing (use Pattern 23.2).
2. Invite children to use black dot stickers or bingo dabber paints to add seeds to the watermelon.

Alphabet soup:

1. Print out or precut a circle soup bowl (use Pattern 23.3).
2. Invite children to glue alphabet pasta or alphabet cereal onto the circle to create alphabet soup.

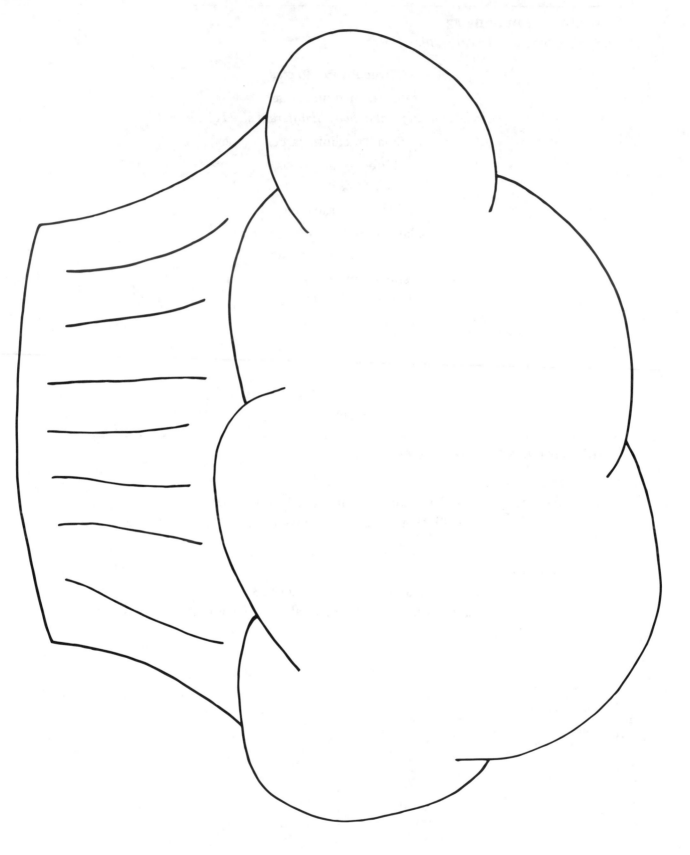

Pattern 23.1 **Cupcake**

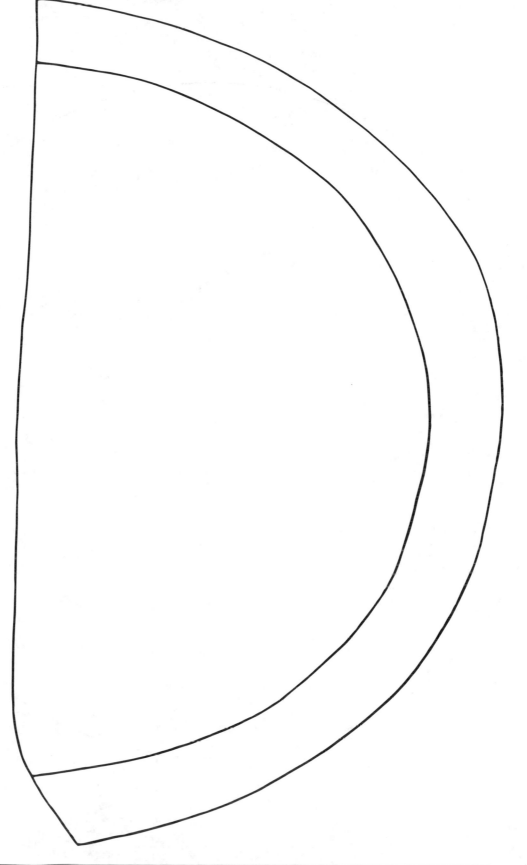

Pattern 23.2 **Watermelon wedge**

Pattern 23.3 **Soup bowl**

Frogs and Toads

Opening Song and Rhyme

Book #1 *Toad* by Ruth Brown

Stand-Up Activity

Little Toad

(Traditional)

I am a little toad, hopping down the road.
(Jump.)

Listen to my song.
(Cup hands to ears.)

I sleep all winter long.
(Put hands together on the side of the face.)

When spring comes, I peek out,
(Peek from behind hands.)

And then I jump about.
(Jump.)

And now I catch a fly.
(Stick out tongue.)

And now I wink my eye.
(Blink.)

And now and then I hop.
(Jump.)

And then I finally stop.
(Use sign language for "stop.")

Flannel Board

Pieces: Five frogs (use Pattern 24.1)
Favorite source: Singable Songs for the Very Young by Raffi

Five Green and Speckled Frogs

(Traditional)

Five green and speckled frogs,
Sat on a speckled log,
Eating some most delicious bugs,
Yum, yum.

(Continued on page 114)

One jumped into the pool,
Where it was nice and cool,
Then there were four green speckled frogs.

Four green and speckled frogs,
Sat on a speckled log,
Eating some most delicious bugs,
Yum, yum.

One jumped into the pool,
Where it was nice and cool,
Then there were three green speckled frogs.

(Continue counting down to zero frogs.)

Book #2 *Hop Jump* by Ellen Stoll Walsh

Action Rhyme

Sung to the tune of "Mr. Sun"

Mr. Frog and Toad

Oh, Mr. Frog-Toad, Mr. Frog and Toad, please jump along with me.
(Jump.)
Oh, Mr. Frog-Toad, Mr. Frog and Toad, come on out and play.
These little children want to jump with you.
Jump, jump, jumping is fun to do.
Oh, Mr. Frog-Toad, Mr. Frog and Toad, please jump along with me.

Oh, Mr. Frog-Toad, Mr. Frog and Toad, please run along with me.
(Run in place.)
Oh, Mr. Frog-Toad, Mr. Frog and Toad, come on out and play.
These little children want to run with you.
Run, run, running is fun to do.
Oh, Mr. Frog-Toad, Mr. Frog and Toad, please run along with me.

(Repeat with other action words, such as spin, tiptoe, sit, etc.)

Closing Song

Art Experience

Speckled frog:

1. Print out the frog drawing (use Pattern 24.1).
2. Invite children to use dot stickers or bingo-style paint dabbers to add speckles to the frog.

Bonus Storytime Resources

More Books

Bad Frogs by Thacher Hurd

Froggy Gets Dressed by Jonathan London, illustrated by Frank Remkiewicz

Jump Frog Jump! by Robert Kalan, illustrated by Byron Barton

Leap Back Home to Me by Lauren Thompson, illustrated by Matthew Cordell

The Wide-Mouthed Frog: A Pop-Up Book by Keith Faulkner, illustrated by Jonathan Lambert

Extra Action Rhyme

Frog Jumps over the Great Big Stick

Frog be nimble, frog be quick, frog jumps over the great big stick.

(Jump.)

Frog be nimble, frog be slick, frog swims under the great big stick.

(Pretend to swim.)

Frog be nimble, frog go click, frog runs around the great big stick.

(Run in a small circle.)

Additional Art Experience

Frog headband:

1. Print out one frog headband for each child (use Pattern 24.2).
2. Precut some green paper strips, approximately 2 inches by 14 inches.
3. Invite children to decorate the frog headbands with crayons or color pens.
4. To fit the headband around the child's head, tape or staple one paper strip to both sides of the frog, adjusting for the size of the child.

Pattern 24.1 **Speckled frog**

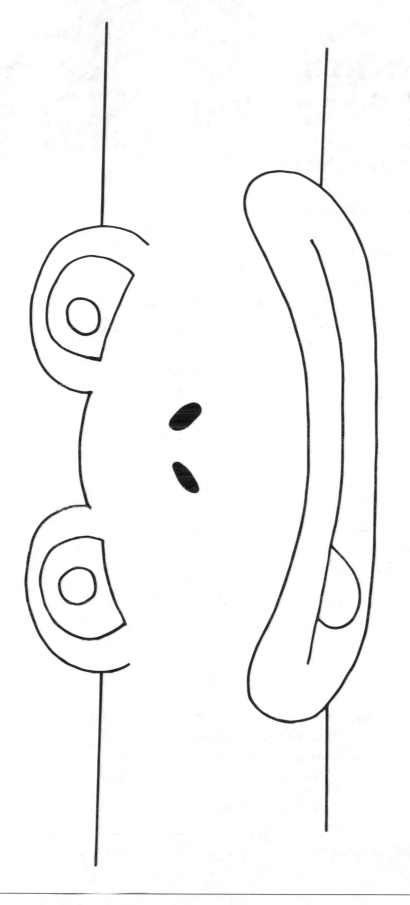

Pattern 24.2 **Frog headband**

Garbage and Recycling

Opening Song and Rhyme

Book #1 *I Stink* by Kate and Jim McMullan

Stand-Up Activity
Sung to the tune of "I'm a Little Teapot"

I'm a Little Garbage Truck

I'm a little garbage truck, watch me go.
(Point to self.)

Here is my hopper.
(Hold one arm out to the side.)

Here is my cab.
(Hold other arm out to the other side.)

When I get all filled up, to the dump I go.

Just tip me over and dump the garbage out.
(Tip to one side.)

Flannel Board
Pieces: Five recycling trucks (use Pattern 25.1)

Five Recycling Trucks

I see five recycling trucks going down the street,
Picking up plastic, glass, and cardboard.
Reusing trash is wise. Reusing trash is sweet.
Now one truck is full and drives away.

I see four recycling trucks going down the street,
Picking up plastic, glass, and cardboard.
Reusing trash is wise. Reusing trash is sweet.
Now one truck is full and drives away.

(Continue counting down to zero.)

Book #2 *Eco People on the Go!* by Jan Gerardi (board book)

Action Song

Sung to the tune of "Wheels on the Bus"

The Garbage Truck Drives down the Street

The garbage truck drives down the street, down the street, down the street.
(Pretend to drive.)
The garbage truck drives down the street, as it's picking up garbage.

The garbage truck stops and goes, stops and goes, stops and goes.
(Move arms forward, then bring them back.)
The garbage truck stops and goes, as it's picking up garbage.

The garbage truck goes smash-smash-smash,
smash-smash-smash, smash-smash-smash.
(Clap and twist palms together.)
The garbage truck goes smash-smash-smash, as it's picking up garbage.

The garbage truck has a stinky smell, stinky smell, stinky smell.
(Hold nose.)
The garbage truck has a stinky smell, as it's picking up garbage.

Closing Song

Art Experience

Recycling truck:
1. Print out the recycling truck drawing (use Pattern 25.1).
2. Collect a lot of shredded paper from a paper shredder.
3. Invite children to glue the shredded paper onto the recycling truck.

Bonus Storytime Resources

More Books

Big Earth, Little Me by Thom Wiley, illustrated by Kate Endle
Compost! Growing Gardens from Your Garbage by Linda Glaser, illustrated by
  Anca Hariton
The Earth Book by Todd Parr
Smash! Mash! Crash! There Goes the Trash! by Barbara Odanaka, illustrated by
  Will Hillenbrand
Trashy Town by Andrea Zimmerman and David Clemesha, illustrated by Dan
  Yaccarino

Extra Fingerplay

Sung to the tune of "Mary Had a Little Lamb"

If You See a Piece of Trash

If you see a piece of trash, piece of trash, piece of trash,
(Pretend to pick up a piece of garbage.)
If you see a piece of trash, pick it up right now.
Put it in a garbage can, garbage can, garbage can,
(Use sign language for "garbage can.")
Put it in a garbage can, do it right now.
If you can recycle it, recycle it, recycle it,
(Use sign language for "recycle.")
If you can recycle it, then recycle it right now.

Additional Art Experience

Garbage can:

1. Precut the garbage can shape on black or dark blue construction paper (use Pattern 25.2).
2. Invite children to decorate the garbage can with color chalk.

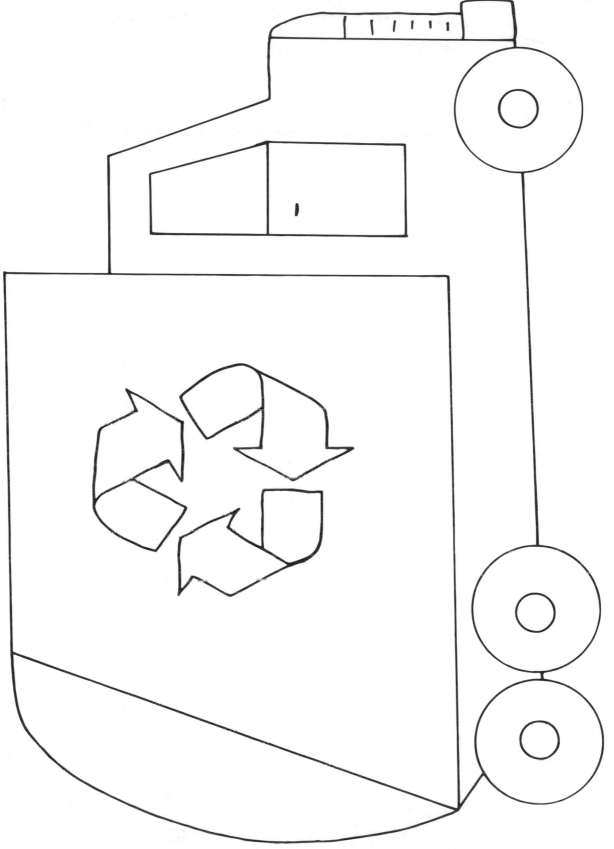

Pattern 25.1 **Recycling truck**

Pattern 25.2 **Garbage can**

Gingerbread and Other Cookies

Opening Song and Rhyme

Book #1 *The Cow Loves Cookies* by Karma Wilson, illustrated by Marcellus Hall

Stand-Up Activity
Sung to the tune of "Row, Row, Row Your Boat"

Baking Cookies

Stir, stir, stir the dough,
(Make a circle with one arm to the side of the body; pretend to stir a spoon inside this circle with the other hand.)
Stir the dough today. Baking cookies is so much fun.
Now they're good to eat.

Shape, shape, shape the cookies,
(Pat hands together.)
Shape the cookies today. Baking cookies is so much fun.
Now they're good to eat.

Sprinkle, sprinkle, sprinkle the cookies,
(Flutter hands.)
Sprinkle the cookies today. Baking cookies is so much fun.
Now they're good to eat.

Heat, heat, heat the oven,
(Place arms outstretched in front of body.)
Heat the oven today. Baking cookies is so much fun.
Now they're good to eat.

Eat, eat, eat the cookies,
(Pretend to eat.)
Eat the cookies today. Baking cookies is so much fun.
Now they're good to eat.

Flannel Board

Gingerbread man color pattern:

Pieces: Ten gingerbread men of one color; ten gingerbread men of a second color (use Pattern 26.1)

Directions: Start a pattern across the board using the two colors (e.g., blue, blue, red, blue, blue, red, blue, blue, red). Let the children help finish the pattern.

Book #2 *Maisy Makes Gingerbread* by Lucy Cousins

Action Song

Sung to the tune of "Head, Shoulders, Knees and Toes"

Gingerbread Head and Shoulders

Head, shoulders, knees and toes, knees and toes. *(Point to body parts.)*
Head, shoulders, knees and toes, knees and toes.
I use icing to finish these things, *(Shake finger.)*
On my gingerbread boys, *(Use sign language for "boy.")*
And girls. *(Use sign language for "girl.")*

Closing Song

Art Experience

Gingerbread boy or girl:

1. Print out the gingerbread cookie shape (use Pattern 26.1).
2. Precut a variety of sewing notions into one-inch chunks.
3. Invite children to decorate the gingerbread cookie by gluing the sewing notions onto the cookie shape.

Bonus Storytime Resources

More Books

Cookie Count: A Tasty Pop-Up by Robert Sabuda
If You Give a Mouse a Cookie by Laura Joffe Numeroff, illustrated by Felicia Bond
The Moon Might Be Milk by Lisa Shulman, illustrated by Will Hillenbrand
Mr. Cookie Baker by Monica Wellington
Who Ate All the Cookie Dough? by Karen Beaumont, illustrated by Eugene Yelchin

Extra Action Song #1

"I'm a Little Teapot" action song from *This Little Piggy & Other Rhymes to Sing & Play* by Jane Yolen and Will Hillenbrand

Extra Action Song #2

Sung to the tune of "Do You Know the Muffin Man?"

Gingerbread Friend

Oh yes, I have raisins for eyes, raisins for eyes, raisins for eyes,
(Circle eyes with fingers.)

Oh yes, I have raisins for eyes, because I'm a gingerbread friend.

I have buttons down my chest, down my chest, down my chest,
(Slide finger down chest.)

I have buttons down my chest, because I'm a gingerbread friend.

My little mouth is sweet and smiling, sweet and smiling, sweet and smiling,
(Point to mouth.)

My little mouth is sweet and smiling, because I'm a gingerbread friend.

I can run away from you, away from you, away from you,
(Run in place.)

I can run away from you, because I'm a gingerbread friend.

I like to yell, "Catch me if you can! Catch me if you can! Catch me if you can!"
(Wave.)

I like to yell, "Catch me if you can!" because I'm a gingerbread friend.

Additional Art Experience

Colorful cookie:

1. Precut or print out one large circle for each child (use Pattern 26.2).
2. Invite children to decorate this cookie shape with colorful dot stickers or bingo-style paint bottles.

Pattern 26.1 **Gingerbread boy or girl**

Pattern 26.2 **Cookie circle**

Green for St. Patrick's Day

Opening Song and Rhyme

Book #1 *Where Is the Green Sheep?* by Mem Fox and Judy Horacek

Stand-Up Activity

Leprechaun, Leprechaun

Leprechaun, leprechaun, turn around. (*Spin around.*)

Leprechaun, leprechaun, find gold on the ground.

(*Touch the ground and pretend to pick something up.*)

Leprechaun, leprechaun, jump on your toes. (*Jump.*)

Leprechaun, leprechaun, scratch your nose. (*Scratch nose.*)

Leprechaun, leprechaun, reach up high. (*Put hands up high.*)

Leprechaun, leprechaun, see a rainbow in the sky.

(*Sketch a rainbow arch with one hand.*)

Leprechaun, leprechaun, point to your feet. (*Touch feet.*)

Leprechaun, leprechaun, have a seat. (*Sit.*)

Flannel Board

Pieces: Shamrock (use Pattern 27.1), leprechaun, green bird, and other green objects
Sung to the tune of "The Farmer in the Dell"

Hi Ho for St. Patrick's Day

This shamrock is green, this shamrock is green,
Hi, ho for St. Patrick's Day, this shamrock is green.

This leprechaun wears green, this leprechaun wears green,
Hi, ho for St. Patrick's Day, this leprechaun wears green.

This bird is green, this bird is green,
Hi, ho for St. Patrick's Day, this bird is green.

(*Add other green objects, such as a green sheep, traffic light, snake, popsicle, etc.*)

Book #2 *St. Patrick's Day Countdown* by Salina Yoon

Fingerplay

Little Clover

Hey, little clover with four leaves, not three. (*Count four fingers.*)

I want to pick you to take home with me.

One leaf for wisdom. (*Point to one finger.*)

One leaf for love. (*Point to another finger.*)

One leaf for happiness. (*Point to another finger.*)

And one leaf for luck. (*Point to last finger.*)

Closing Song

Art Experience

Shamrock:

1. Precut one shamrock on green construction paper for each child (use Pattern 27.1).
2. Invite children to decorate this shamrock shape with color chalk.

Bonus Storytime Resources

More Books

Green Means Go by Susan Ring

It's St. Patrick's Day! by Rebecca Gómez, illustrated by Mary Morgan

Little Green by Keith Baker

The Night before St. Patrick's Day by Natasha Wing, illustrated by Amy Wummer

Stanley Mows the Lawn by Craig Frazier

Extra Action Song

Favorite source: Playtime: 49 Favorite Action and Sing-Along Songs from CEMA Special Markets

Did You Ever See a Lassie?

(*Traditional*)

Did you ever see a lassie, a lassie, a lassie,
(*Use sign language for "girl."*)

Did you ever see a lassie go this way and that?

Go this way and that way, and this way and that way.
(*Sway body and arms from side to side.*)

Did you ever see a lassie go this way and that?

(*Continued on page 130*)

Did you ever see a laddie, a laddie, a laddie,
(Use sign language for "boy.")

Did you ever see a laddie go this way and that?

Go this way and that way, and this way and that way.
(Sway body and arms from side to side.)

Did you ever see a laddie go this way and that?

Additional Art Experience

Green dancing streamer:

1. Precut the center out of a paper plate for each child.
2. Precut long pieces of green and white tissue paper or crepe paper. Each streamer should be about one-inch wide and two- to three-feet long. This looks best with two or more different shades of green. You will need five to ten streamers per child.
3. Invite children to glue the streamers onto the paper plate (see Figure 27.1).

Figure 27.1 **Green dancing streamer**

Pattern 27.1 **Shamrock**

Halloween

Opening Song and Rhyme

Book #1 *Snappy Little Halloween* by Derek Matthews
(pop-up)

Stand-Up Activity

Jack-O'-Lantern, Jack-O'-Lantern

Jack-o'-lantern, jack-o'-lantern, turn around. (*Spin around.*)

Jack-o'-lantern, jack-o'-lantern, roll on the ground.
(*Roll hands over each other.*)

Jack-o'-lantern, jack-o'-lantern, dance on your toes. (*Walk on tiptoes.*)

Jack-o'-lantern, jack-o'-lantern, light up your nose.
(*Touch nose.*)

Jack-o'-lantern, jack-o'-lantern, reach up high. (*Reach hands up high.*)

Jack-o'-lantern, jack-o'-lantern, jump to the sky. (*Jump.*)

Jack-o'-lantern, jack-o'-lantern, smile with heat. (*Point to smile.*)

Jack-o'-lantern, jack-o'-lantern, find your seat. (*Sit.*)

Flannel Board

Pieces: One pumpkin orange on one side and with a jack-o'-lantern face with a circle
mouth on the other side, one pumpkin orange on one side and with a silhouette
of a witch on the other side, one pumpkin orange on one side and with a sinister
jack-o'-lantern face on the other side, one pumpkin orange on one side and with a
happy jack-o'-lantern face on the other side, and one pumpkin orange on one side
with a silhouette of a person running on the other side

Directions: Start with pumpkins on the board showing only their orange sides. Flip
them over as you say the rhyme.

Five Little Pumpkins

(*Traditional*)

Five little pumpkins sitting on a gate,
The first one said, "Oh my, it's getting late!"
(*Turn over the jack-o'-lantern face with a circle mouth.*)

The second one said, "There are witches in the air!"
(*Turn over the silhouette of a witch.*)

The third one said, "But I don't care!"
(*Turn over the sinister jack-o'-lantern face.*)

The fourth one said, "I'm ready for some fun!"
(*Turn over the happy jack-o'-lantern face.*)

The fifth one said, "Let's run and run and run!"
(*Turn over the silhouette of a person running.*)

"Whooo" went the wind, and out went the lights,
(*Give a loud clap when the lights go out.*)

And the five little pumpkins rolled out of sight.
(*Remove the pumpkins from the board.*)

Book #2 *Halloween Countdown* by Jack Prelutsky, illustrated by Dan Yaccarino
(board book)

Action Rhyme

Pumpkins Over There

Pumpkins small,
(*Put hands low where a small pumpkin might stand.*)

And pumpkins tall,
(*Raise hands high in the air.*)

Pumpkins, pumpkins, everywhere.
(*Spin around.*)

Pumpkins fat,
(*Move hands out far to the sides.*)

And pumpkins thin,
(*Move hands close together in front of body.*)

Pumpkins, pumpkins, over there!
(*Point across room with both hands.*)

Closing Song

Art Experience

Triangle face pumpkins:

1. Precut or print out pumpkin shapes on orange paper (use Pattern 28.1).
2. Precut a large supply of small yellow triangles.
3. Invite children to glue the triangles onto the pumpkin shape to create jack-o'-lantern faces.

Bonus Storytime Resources

More Books

Biscuit Visits the Pumpkin Patch by Alyssa Satin Capucilli, illustrated by Pat Schories (board book)

Five Little Pumpkins by Dan Yaccarino (board book)

Halloween Night by Elizabeth Hatch, illustrated by Jimmy Pickering

Maisy's Halloween by Lucy Cousins (board book)

Where's Sam? A Lift-the-Flap Book by Yves Got

Extra Fingerplay

I Know a Little Pumpkin

I know a little pumpkin who sat on a wall.
(Make large circle with arms in front of body.)

I know this little pumpkin had a great fall.
(Lower arms to the ground.)

He rolled out the garden. He rolled down the street.
(Roll hands over each other.)

He rolled to a stop in front of a gate.
(Make stop motion with one hand.)

Along came a kid with a design update.
(Tap finger to side of head.)

Later that night as the kid trick or treated,

By the door sat the pumpkin with a smile that greeted.
(Point to your smile.)

Additional Art Experience

Mummy:

1. Print out a body shape on colored paper (use Pattern 28.2).
2. Precut a large supply of one-inch strips of white tissue paper (torn strips of tissue paper look best).
3. Invite children to glue these strips of tissue paper onto the body shape to create a mummy.

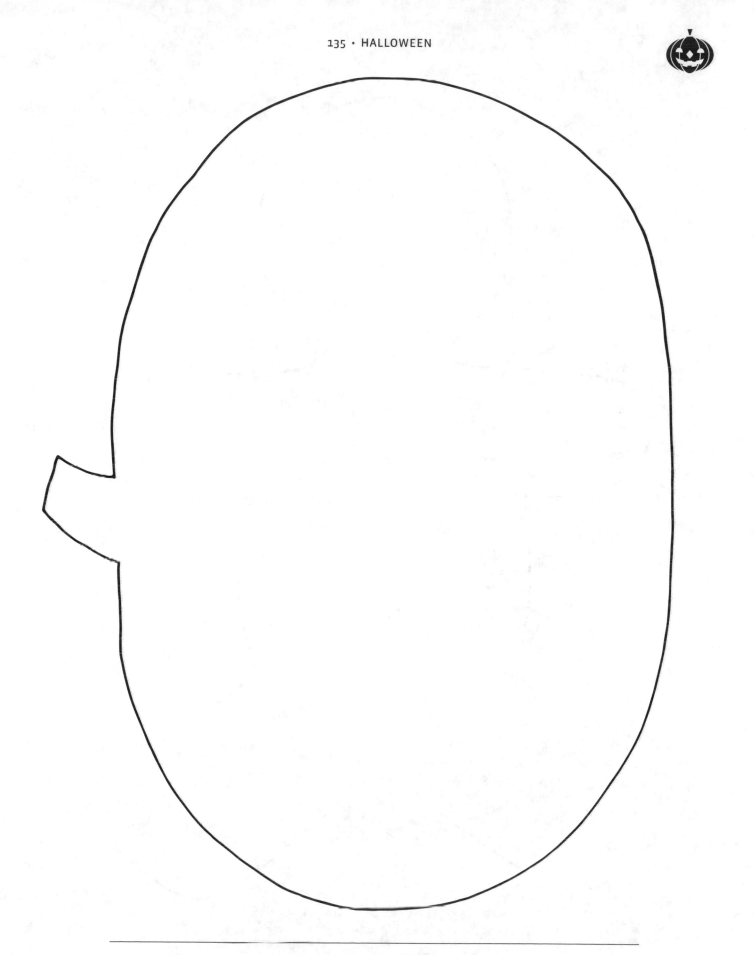

Pattern 28.1 **Pumpkin**

Pattern 28.2 **Mummy**

Lunar New Year

Opening Song and Rhyme

Book #1 *My First Chinese New Year* by Karen Katz

Stand-Up Activity
Sung to the tune of "The Farmer in the Dell"

A Marching We Will Go

A marching we will go. A marching we will go. *(March in place.)*

Let's all join the parade. A marching we will go.

A jumping we will go. A jumping we will go. *(Jump.)*

Let's all join the parade. A jumping we will go.

(Continue with other action words, such as spinning, running, sitting, etc.)

Flannel Board
Pieces: Five Chinese lions

Five Lions Dancing

Five lions dancing, moving down the street,
One left to mop the floor, now there are four.
Four lions dancing, moving down the street,
One left to chase a bee, now there are three.
Three lions dancing, moving down the street,
One stopped to eat bamboo, now there are two.
Two lions dancing, moving down the street,
One sat to watch the sun, now there is one.
One lion dancing, moving down the street,
She danced away to have some fun, and then there were none.

Book #2 *Ten Mice for Tet* by Pegi Deito Shea and Cynthia Weill, illustrated by Tô
Ngọc Trang, embroidery by Phạm Viết Đinh

Action Song
Sung to tune of "Baa, Baa, Black Sheep"

Rah, Rah, New Year

Rah, rah, new year, let's go celebrate.
(Cheer with one hand.)

(Continued on page 138)

Parties and dancing and parades go by.
(Sweep arms over head and then down to side while marching in place.)

Fireworks and firecrackers boom in the air.
(Raise arms high up while shaking hands.)

Lanterns and candles light up the street.
(Spin around.)

Rah, rah, new year, let's go celebrate.
(Cheer with one hand.)

Parties and dancing and parades go by.
(Sweep arms over head and then down to side while marching in place.)

Closing Song

Art Experience

Paper lantern:

1. Fold, cut, and tape together one paper Chinese lantern for each child.

    a. Fold a piece of color paper in half along the long length (hot dog style).

    b. On the fold side, cut one-inch strips up to a spot about one inch from the edge of the paper (see Figure 29.1).

    c. Unfold the paper and create circles with the uncut edges. Use tape to hold these circles together in the shape of a lantern (see Figure 29.2).

    d. Tape a length of yarn, approximately six inches, to one side of the lantern to hang the lantern.

2. Invite children to decorate paper lantern with chalk, crayons, or colored pens.

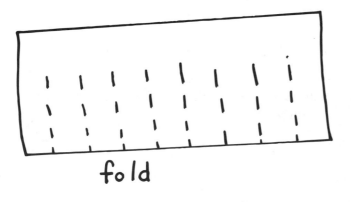

Figure 29.1
Fold-and-cut lines for Chinese lantern

Figure 29.2
Chinese lantern

Bonus Storytime Resources

More Books

Bee-Bim Bop! by Linda Sue Park, illustrated by Ho Baek Lee

Bringing in the New Year by Grace Lin

Fortune Cookies by Albert Bitterman, illustrated by Chris Rascha

Lanterns and Firecrackers: A Chinese New Year Story by Jonny Zucker and Jan
  Barger Cohen

Red Is a Dragon: A Book of Colors by Roseanne Thong, illustrated by Grace Lin

Extra Action Song

Sung to the tune of "Three Blind Mice"

Dragons Dance in the Parade

Dragons dance, dragons dance,
(Dance around, waving hands.)

In the parade, in the parade.
(March in place.)

They dance on their tippy toes.
(Walk on tiptoes.)

They jump up and down a lot.
(Jump.)

They prance around all over town.
(Spin around.)

Dragons dance,
(Dance around, waving hands.)

In the parade.
(March in place.)

Additional Art Experience

Dragon:

1. Print out the dragon drawing (use Pattern 29.1).
2. Precut a large supply of one-inch colorful tissue paper squares.
3. Invite children to decorate the dragon by gluing tissue paper dragon scales onto it.

Pattern 29.1 **Dragon**

Monsters

Opening Song and Rhyme

Book #1 *Five Ugly Monsters* by Tedd Arnold

Stand-Up Activity

Monster, Monster
(Suit actions to words.)

Monster, monster, turn around.
Monster, monster, stomp on the ground.
Monster, monster, claw up high.
Monster, monster, stare with your eyes.
Monster, monster, show a scowl.
Monster, monster, give a howl.
Monster, monster, sit on your bed.
Monster, monster, eat your bread.

Flannel Board

Pieces: One little monster, one medium-sized monster, and one big monster
Sung to the tune of "Mary Had a Little Lamb"

If You See a Monster

If you see a little monster, little monster, little monster,
If you see a little monster, wave your hand hello.

If you see a medium monster, medium monster, medium monster,
If you see a medium monster, bow your head in greeting.

If you see a great big monster, great big monster, great big monster,
If you see a great big monster, run away and hide.

Book #2 *Go Away, Big Green Monster!* by Ed Emberley

Action Song

Sung to the tune of "The Ants Go Marching"

The Monsters around the House

The monsters stomp around the house. Hooray! Hooray!
(Stomp.)
The monsters stomp around the house. Hooray! Hooray!
The monsters stomp around house. They giggle and shout, as they roar about.
And they all make lots of noise, around the house.
Boom, boom, boom, boom!
(Clap for each boom.)

The monsters jump around the house. Hooray! Hooray!
(Jump.)
The monsters jump around the house. Hooray! Hooray!
The monsters jump around house. They giggle and shout, as they roar about.
And they all make lots of noise, around the house.
Boom, boom, boom, boom!
(Clap for each boom.)

The monsters run around the house. Hooray! Hooray!
(Run in place.)
The monsters run around the house. Hooray! Hooray!
The monsters run around house. They giggle and shout, as they roar about.
And they all make lots of noise, around the house.
Boom, boom, boom, boom!
(Clap for each boom.)

The monsters sleep around the house. Hooray! Hooray!
(Put hands together on side of face.)
The monsters sleep around the house. Hooray! Hooray!
The monsters sleep around house. They giggle and shout, as they snore about.
And they all make lots of noise, around the house.
Snore, snore, snore, snore!

Closing Song

Art Experience

Monster mask:

1. Print off and cut out one monster mask for each child (use Pattern 30.1).
2. Tape or glue a craft stick to each mask for a handle.
3. Precut a large supply of sewing notions (ribbon, lace, cloth scraps) into one-inch chunks.
4. Invite children to decorate the masks with glue and sewing notions.

Bonus Storytime Resources

More Books

Dogzilla by Dav Pilkey

Glad Monster, Sad Monster: A Book about Feelings by Ed Emberley and Anne Miranda

Into the Castle by June Crebbin, illustrated by John Bendall-Brunello

Skateboard Monsters by Daniel Kirk

There's Something in My Attic by Mercer Mayer

Extra Action Song #1

Sung to the tune of "I'm a Little Teapot"

I'm a Little Monster

I'm a little monster hear me growl. (*Point to self, then growl.*)

Here are my big ears. (*Point to ears.*)

Here arc my claws. (*Wave hands in the air like claws.*)

When I get all sneaky, I tiptoe up. (*Bend over slightly and walk in place on toes.*)

I jump in the air and give a big ROAR! (*Jump, then roar.*)

Extra Action Song #2

"Monster Boogie" action song from *Buzz Buzz* by Laurie Berkner

Additional Art Experience

Monster doorknob hanger:

1. Precut one colorful cardstock doorknob hanger for each child (use Pattern 30.2).
2. Precut two white circles for each child, approximately two-inch diameter.
3. Invite children to glue one button or dot sticker into the center of each circle to create an eye. Next, glue the circles onto the doorknob hanger for eyes. Create more monster features with crayons or color pens.

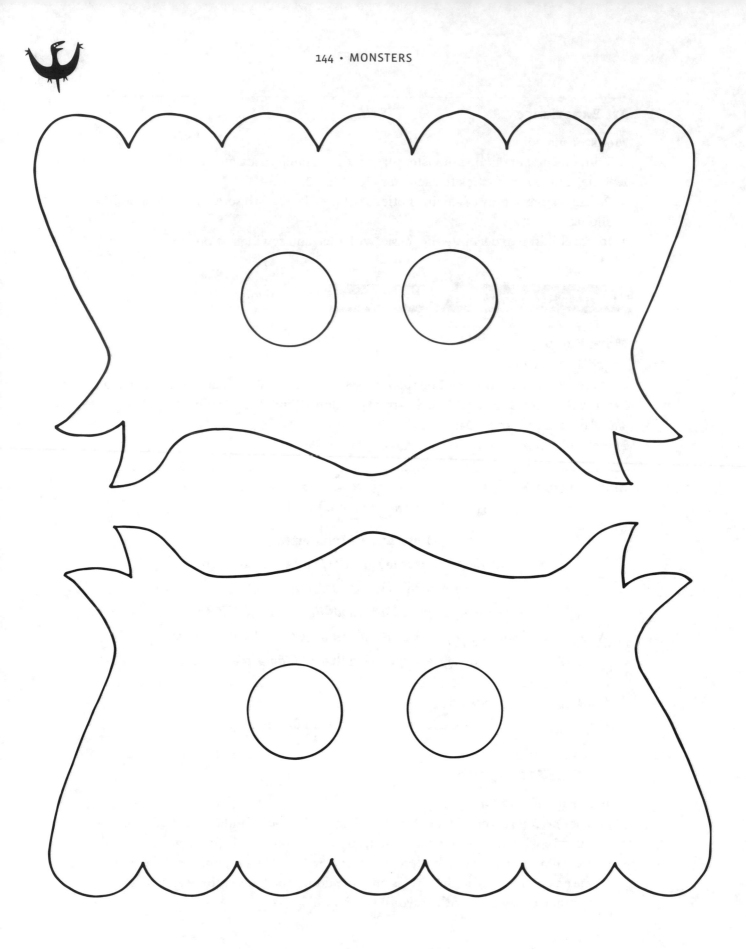

Pattern 30.1 **Monster masks**

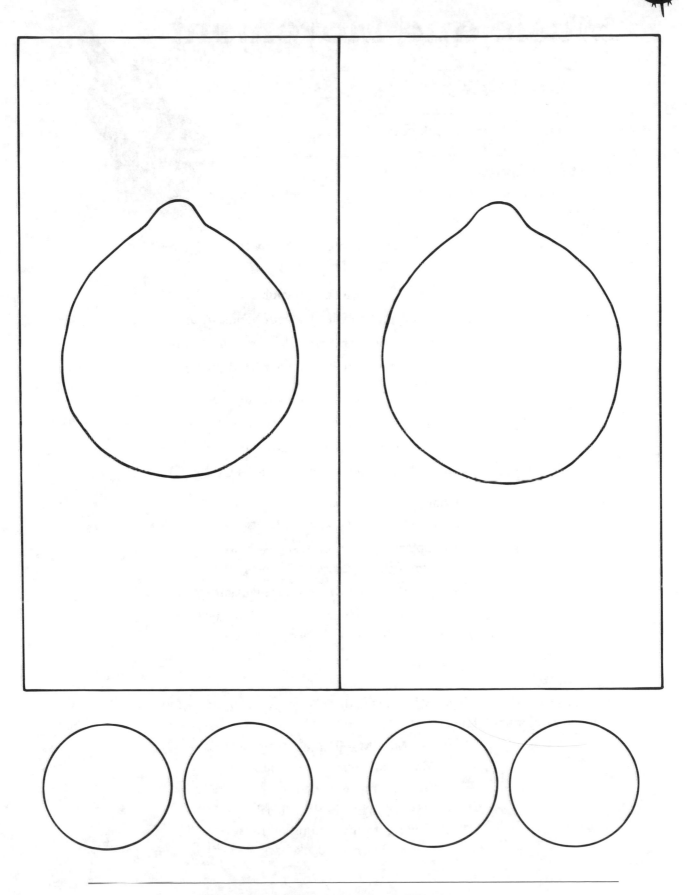

Pattern 30.2 **Monster doorknob hangers**

Music and Movement

Opening Song and Rhyme

Book #1 *Move!* by Steve Jenkins and Robin Page

Stand-Up Activity

Favorite source: Songs for Wiggleworms by Old Town School of Folk Music

If You're Happy and You Know It
(Traditional)

If you're happy and you know it, clap your hands. *(Clap.)*

If you're happy and you know it, clap your hands. *(Clap.)*

If you're happy and you know it, then your face will surely show it,

If you're happy and you know it, clap your hands. *(Clap.)*

If you're happy and you know it, stomp your feet. *(Stomp.)*

If you're happy and you know it, stomp your feet. *(Stomp.)*

If you're happy and you know it, then your face will surely show it,

If you're happy and you know it, stomp your feet. *(Stomp.)*

If you're happy and you know it, shout "Hurray!"
(Raise arms high as you cheer "Hoo-ray.")

If you're happy and you know it, shout "Hurray!"
(Raise arms high as you cheer "Hoo-ray.")

If you're happy and you know it, then your face will surely show it,

If you're happy and you know it, shout "Hurray!"
(Raise arms high as you cheer "Hoo-ray.")

Flannel Board

Pieces: Girl dressed in black (Miss Mary), three to five silver buttons, mother, two quarters, elephant, fence

Miss Mary Mack
(Traditional jump rope rhyme)

Miss Mary Mack, Mack, Mack,
All dressed in black, black, black,
With silver buttons, buttons, buttons,
All down her back, back, back.

She asked her mother, mother, mother,
For 50 cents, cents, cents,
To see the elephants, elephants, elephants,
Jump over the fence, fence, fence.

They jumped so high, high, high,
They reached the sky, sky, sky,
And they didn't come back, back, back,
'Til the 4th of July, ly, ly!

Book #2 *The Little Band* by James Sage, illustrated by Keiko Narahashi

---

Fingerplay

Favorite source: Wee Sing: Children's Songs & Fingerplays by Pamela Conn Beall and Susan Hogen Nipp

Where Is Thumbkin?

(Traditional song)

Where is Thumbkin? Where is Thumbkin?

Here I am! *(Show and wiggle one thumb.)*

Here I am! *(Show and wiggle other thumb.)*

How are you today, Sir? Very well, I thank you! *(Pretend thumbs talk to each other.)*

Run away. *(Hide first thumb behind back.)*

Run away. *(Hide other thumb behind back.)*

Where is Pointer? Where is Pointer?

Here I am! *(Show and wiggle one forefinger.)*

Here I am! *(Show and wiggle other forefinger.)*

How are you today, Sir? Very well, I thank you! *(Pretend fingers talk to each other.)*

Run away. *(Hide first forefinger behind back.)*

Run away. *(Hide other forefinger behind back.)*

Where is Tall Man . . .

Where is Ring Man . . .

Where is Pinky . . .

Closing Song

Art Experience

Paper plate maracas:

1. Fold a paper plate in half. Staple or tape the folded plate closed but place a few dried beans or popcorn inside before sealing completely.
2. Precut a large supply of crepe papers approximately one-foot long, about five to eight for each child.
3. Invite children to decorate the maracas with stickers and then glue on crepe paper streamers (see Figure 31.1).

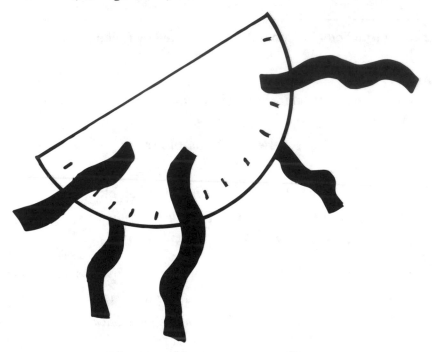

Figure 31.1 **Paper plate maracas**

Bonus Storytime Resources

More Books

Dancing Feet by Lindsey Craig, illustrated by Marc Brown

Emily Loves to Bounce by Stephen Michael King

How Do You Wokka-Wokka? by Elizabeth Bluemle, illustrated by Randy Cecile

If You're Happy and You Know It: Jungle Edition by James Warhola

Tumble Bumble by Felicia Bond

Extra Action Song

"Clap Your Hands" action song from *Toddler Action Songs* by Cedarmont Kids

Extra Fingerplay

Open, Shut Them
(Traditional)

Open, shut them. Open, shut them.
(Open and close both fists.)

Give a little clap. *(Clap.)*

Open, shut them. Open, shut them.
(Open and close both fists.)

Lay them in your lap.
(Place hands in lap.)

Creep them, creep them, right up to your chin.
(Walk fingers up chest.)

Open up your little mouth,
(Open mouth wide.)

But do not let them in.
(Shake head and hide hands behind back.)

Open, shut them. Open, shut them.
(Open and close both fists.)

Give a little clap. *(Clap.)*

Open, shut them. Open, shut them.
(Open and close both fists.)

Lay them in your lap.
(Place hands in lap.)

Additional Art Experience

Papier-mâché rattle:

1. Make one papier-mâché pill bottle for each child.

   a. Tear up a large supply of white paper strips, approximately one inch wide.

   b. Place a few dried beans or popcorn inside an empty, clean pill bottle. Close the lid.

   c. One at a time, dip the paper strips in a bowl of watery glue and then wrap this wet paper around the pill bottle. Continue until the pill bottle is completely covered.

   d. Let dry for three to five days. (If the papier-mâché is not thick enough, add another layer of glue-wet strips of paper and allow to dry.)

2. Invite children to decorate this rattle with color pens.

My Body and Me

Opening Song and Rhyme

Book #1 *Hello Toes! Hello Feet!* by Ann Whitford Paul, illustrated by Nadine Bernard Westcott

Stand-Up Activity

Favorite source: Where Is Thumbkin? by Kimbo

Head, Shoulders, Knees and Toes
(Traditional)

Head, shoulders, knees and toes, knees and toes.
(Point to body part as you say it.)

Head, shoulders, knees and toes, knees and toes.

Eyes and ears and mouth and nose.

Head, shoulders, knees and toes, knees and toes.
(Repeat at a faster pace.)

Flannel Board

Pieces: Bird, dog, beetle, spider

How Many Feet?

I have two feet.
Birds have two.
Dogs have four.
Beetles have six.
Spiders have eight.
That's quite a lot more than me,
Because I only have two feet!

Book #2 *What Can Rabbit Hear?* by Lucy Cousins (lift-flap)

Action Rhyme

Two Little Hands

(Traditional)

(Suit actions to words.)

Two little hands go clap, clap, clap.
Two little feet go tap, tap, tap.
Two little hands go thump, thump, thump.
Two little feet go jump, jump, jump.
One body turns all around.
Then we sit quietly down.

Closing Song

Art Experience

Rice cracker face:

1. Give each child one large rice cracker, a large dollop of cream cheese, a handful of raisins, and a clean plastic knife or craft stick.
2. Invite children to spread some cream cheese onto the rice cracker with the plastic knife or craft stick.
3. Next, arrange the raisins in the design of a face (see Figure 32.1).

Figure 32.1 **Rice cracker face**

Bonus Storytime Resources

More Books

Five for a Little One by Chris Raschka

From Head to Toe by Eric Carle

My Hands Can by Jean Holzenthaler, illustrated by Nancy Tafuri

My Nose, Your Nose by Melanie Walsh

My Two Hands, My Two Feet by Rick Walton, illustrated by Julia Gorton

Extra Fingerplay

Ten Little Fingers

(Traditional)

I have ten little fingers. They all belong to me. *(Show ten fingers.)*

I can make them do things. Would you like to see?

I can close them up tight. *(Close both hands as fists.)*

I can open them up wide. *(Show open hands.)*

I can hold them up high. *(Raise hands up high.)*

I can hold them down low. *(Lower hands to the ground.)*

I can wave them to and fro. *(Wave both hands.)*

And I can fold them just so. *(Fold hands together and place them in lap.)*

Additional Art Experience

Stick puppet people:

1. Precut one construction paper body shape for each child (use Pattern 32.1).
2. Tape or glue a craft stick onto each shape.
3. Invite children to decorate their people with color chalk or color pens.

Pattern 32.1 **Stick puppet people**

Nighttime

Opening Song and Rhyme

Book #1 *Good Night, Poppy and Max: A Bedtime Counting Book* by Lindsey Gardiner

Stand-Up Activity

Going to Bed

I put on my pajamas. *(Pretend to put on clothes.)*

I brush my teeth. *(Pretend to brush teeth.)*

I read some books. *(Use sign language for "book.")*

Then I jump on my bed. *(Jump.)*

I find my teddy bear. *(Use sign language for "bear.")*

I drink some water. *(Use sign language for "water.")*

I pet the cat. *(Use sign language for "cat.")*

Then I fall asleep.
(Place hands together on the side of the head and make snoring sound.)

Flannel Board

Pieces: Five monkeys

Five Little Monkeys Jumping on the Bed
(Traditional)

Five little monkeys jumping on a bed.
One fell off and bumped his head.
Mama called the doctor and the doctor said,
"No more monkeys jumping on the bed."

Four little monkeys jumping on a bed.
One fell off and bumped his head.
Mama called the doctor and the doctor said,
"No more monkeys jumping on the bed."

(Repeat down to zero.)

Book #2 *Sweet Dreams, Maisy* by Lucy Cousins

Fingerplay

Favorite source: Car Songs: Songs to Sing Anywhere by Dennis Buck

Twinkle, Twinkle Little Star

(Nursery rhyme)

Twinkle, twinkle little star, *(Flutter fingers.)*

How I wonder what you are.

Up above the world so high. *(Point high in the air.)*

Like a diamond in the sky. *(Make a diamond shape with fingers.)*

Twinkle, twinkle little star, *(Flutter fingers.)*

How I wonder what you are.

Closing Song

Art Experience

Shooting star:

1. Spiral cut one paper plate for each child.
2. Precut one star for each child (use Pattern 33.1).
3. Invite children to glue the star onto the spiral (see Figure 33.1).
4. Next, decorate the shooting star with color pens or crayons.

Figure 33.1 **Shooting star**

Bonus Storytime Resources

More Books

Napping House by Audrey Wood, illustrated by Don Wood
Papa, Please Get the Moon for Me by Eric Carle
Ten in the Bed by Jane Cabrera
Tuck Me In by Dean Hacohen and Sherry Scharschmidt
Where to Sleep by Kandy Radzinski

Extra Fingerplay

Ready for Bed

This little child is ready for bed. (*Show one finger.*)

He's rubbing his eyes. (*Rub eyes.*)

He's yawning big yawns. (*Pretend to yawn.*)

He looks out his window and waves at the stars. (*Wave.*)

Then of course, he blows a kiss to the moon. (*Blow a kiss.*)

He lays down on his bed.
(*Place the one finger onto the palm of the other hand.*)

And covers himself up.
(*Bend fingers of the other hand to cover the one finger.*)

The child then drifts off asleep with a light little snore.
(*Make snoring sound.*)

Additional Art Experiences

Moon bed:

1. Precut one crescent moon shape for each child (use Pattern 33.2).
2. Precut one cardstock rectangle for each child, approximately four inches by six inches.
3. Precut one rectangular piece of fabric for each child, approximately four inches by six inches.
4. Invite children to decorate the moon with crayons or color pens.
5. Next, glue the moon to the rectangular cardstock. Then glue the fabric over the moon to tuck it into bed.

Stars in the night sky:

1. Give each child one piece of black construction paper and one piece of white chalk.
2. Invite children to draw their own star patterns onto the paper with the chalk.

Pattern 33.1 **Stars**

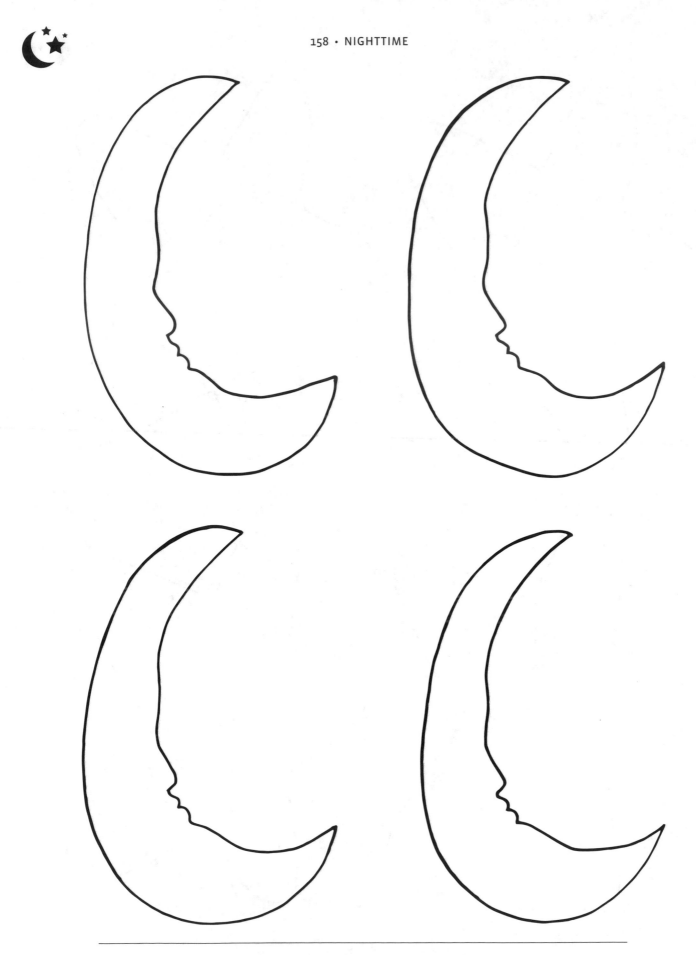

Pattern 33.2 **Crescent moons**

Nocturnal Animals

Opening Song and Rhyme

Book #1 *Owl Babies* by Martin Waddell, illustrated by Patrick Benson

Stand-Up Activity

The Owl
(Traditional)

There's a wide-eyed owl,
(Circle eyes with fingers.)

With a pointed nose,
(Point to nose.)

Two pointed ears,
(Extend forefingers up from head for ears.)

And claws for toes.
(Bend fingers and arms in front of chest for claws.)

When he sits up in the tree,
(Point up high.)

And he looks at me,
(Point at self.)

He flaps his wings and he says, "Whoo! Whoo!"
(Fold arms into armpits and flap wings as you hoot like an owl.)

Flannel Board
Pieces: Five bats (use Pattern 34.1)

Five Little Bats

Five little bats hanging in a cave.
Five little bats upside down during the day.
One little bat, off he goes, looking for food far away.

Four little bats hanging in a cave.
Four little bats upside down during the day.
One little bat, off he goes, looking for food far away.
(Repeat down to zero bats.)

Now the day is coming with light's first ray,
Flying back, here they come, five bats in a cave.

Book #2 *Where Is Tippy Toes?* by Betsy Lewin

Action Chant

During the Night

During the night I know that,

Stars twinkle in the sky. (*Flutter fingers high in the air.*)

Bats fly and swoop through the air. (*Flap arms like wings.*)

Owls flap their wings before saying, "Who-Who."
(*Tuck arms to the side and flap them.*)

Cats jump from place to place. (*Jump.*)

Opossums climb up trees. (*Pretend to climb.*)

Raccoons run across the grass. (*Run in place.*)

Wolves howl at the moon. (*Howl.*)

And I lie in my bed to sleep.

(*Place hands to the side of your head.*)

Closing Song

Art Experience

Feathered owl:
1. Print out the owl drawing (use Pattern 34.2).
2. Cut out one small orange triangle for each child.
3. Hand each child one owl drawing, one orange triangle, two buttons, and some feathers.
4. Invite children to glue the feathers onto the owl. Then add buttons for eyes and a triangle for a beak.

Bonus Storytime Resources

More Books

Baby Bat's Lullaby by Jacquelyn Mitchard, illustrated by Julia Noonan

Good-Night, Owl! by Pat Hutchins

Oliver's Wood by Sue Hendra

Who's in the Forest? by Phillis Gershator, illustrated by Jill McDonald

Wow! Said the Owl by Tim Hopgood

Extra Action Rhyme

Little Bat

Little bat, little bat, fly up high. *(Flap arms for wings.)*

Little bat, little bat, drop on by. *(Drop to the ground.)*

Little bat, little bat, listen for your lunch. *(Put hands to your ears.)*

Little bat, little bat, give a punch. *(Pretend to punch the air.)*

Little bat, little bat, let's do a spin. *(Turn around.)*

Little bat, little bat, let's see a grin. *(Point to your smile.)*

Little bat, little bat, hang by your feet. *(Point to your feet.)*

Little bat, little bat, have a seat. *(Sit on floor.)*

Additional Art Experience

Bat finger puppet:

1. Precut one black construction paper bat for each child (use Pattern 34.1).
2. Cut two small slits on the body of the bat so that a child can place a finger through the holes in the paper.
3. Invite children to decorate the bat with color chalk.

Pattern 34.1 **Bat finger puppets**

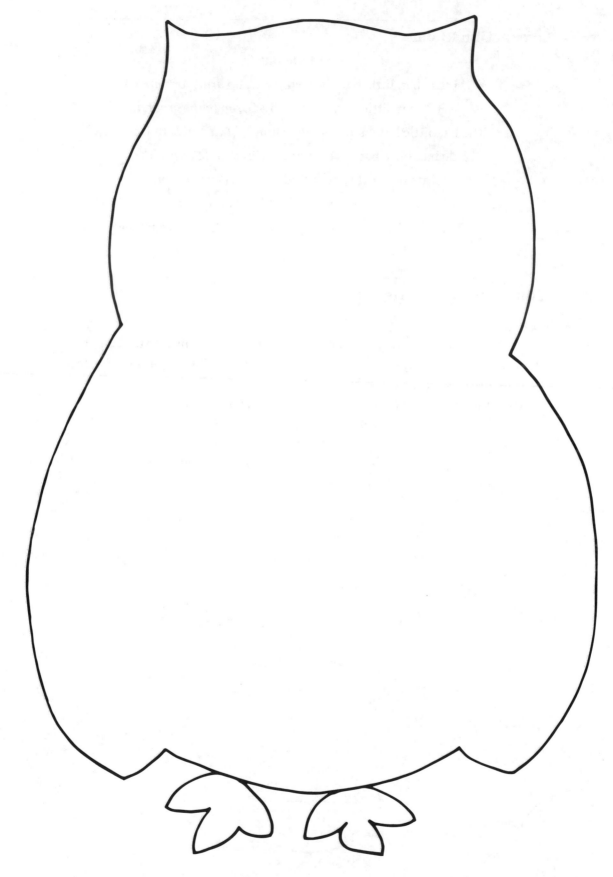

Pattern 34.2 **Feathered owl**

Opposites

Opening Song and Rhyme

Book #1 *Dinosaur Roar!* by Paul and Henrietta Stickland

Stand-Up Activity

Sometimes Tall, Sometimes Small
(Traditional)

Sometimes I am tall. *(Raise hands up high.)*

Sometimes I am small. *(Crouch close to ground.)*

Sometimes I am very, very tall. *(Stand on tiptoes with hands up high.)*

Sometimes I am very, very small. *(Crouch close to the ground.)*

Sometimes tall, *(Stand up with hands up high.)*

Sometimes small, *(Crouch.)*

See how I am now. *(Stand normally.)*

Flannel Board

Graph your favorite shade of blue:

Pieces: Squares of light and dark blue

Directions: Invite children to tape their favorite shade of blue onto a flannel board or wall to make a simple graph. Count how many squares for each color. Which has more? Which is smaller?

Book #2 *Maisy Big, Maisy Small: A Book of Maisy Opposites* by Lucy Cousins

Fingerplay
Sung to the tune of "The Farmer in the Dell"

Rolling Hands
(Roll hands over each other as indicated.)

We're rolling our hands, we're rolling our hands,
Roll them high, roll them low, We're rolling our hands.
We're rolling them slow, we're rolling them slow,
Roll them high, roll them low, We're rolling them slow.
We're rolling them fast, we're rolling them fast,
Roll them high, roll them low, We're rolling them fast.

Closing Song

Art Experience

Big, medium, and small squares:

1. Precut one large paper square for each child (wallpaper scraps are fun to use).
2. Precut two medium paper squares for each child.
3. Precut four small paper squares for each child.
4. Invite children to glue these squares into a pretty design onto another plain piece of regular-sized paper.

Bonus Storytime Resources

More Books

Big Is Big (and Little, Little): A Book of Contrasts by J. Patrick Lewis, illustrated by Bob Barner

A Garden of Opposites by Nancy Davis

Opposnakes: A Lift-the-Flap Book about Opposites by Salina Yoon

Over Under by Marthe Jocelyn and Tom Slaughter

Swing High, Swing Low: A Book of Opposites by Fiona Coward, illustrated by Giovanni Manna

Extra Fingerplay

Some Things

Some things are big. (*Stretch hands far to the sides.*)

Some things are small. (*Cup hands together in front of body.*)

Some things are tall. (*Raise hands up high.*)

Some things are short. (*Hold palms horizontally, close together but not touching.*)

Some things are fast. (*Roll hands quickly over each other.*)

Some things are slow. (*Roll hands slowly over each other.*)

Some things are yes. (*Nod head.*)

Some things are no. (*Shake head.*)

Some things are right. (*Point to the right with both hands.*)

Some things are left. (*Point to the left with both hands.*)

Some things are hiding. (*Cover eyes with hands.*)

Some things are . . . BOO!

Extra Action Song

"Slow, Fast Song" action song from *Little Songs for Little Me* by Nancy Stewart

Additional Art Experience

Empty jar, full jar:

1. Print out the drawing of two jars (use Pattern 35.1).
2. Invite children to paint the jars varying degrees of empty and full.

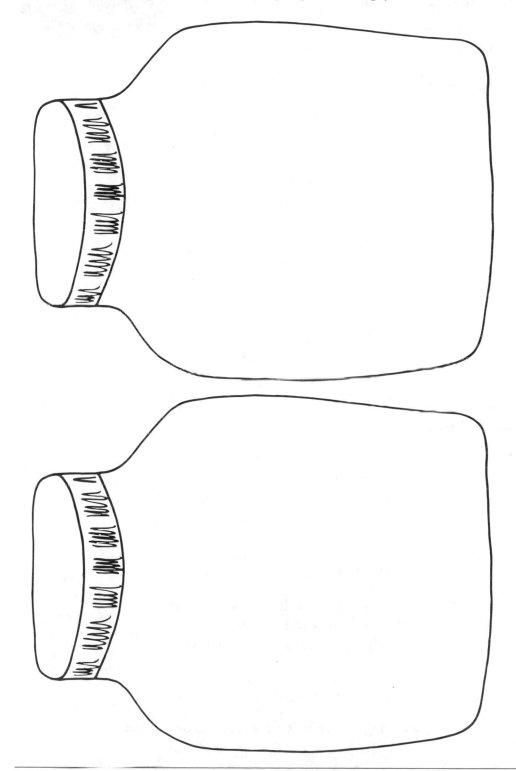

Pattern 35.1 **Empty jar, full jar**

Pet Parade

Opening Song and Rhyme

Book #1 *What Pet to Get?* by Emma Dodd

Stand-Up Activity

I Met a Pet

I never met a pet that I could forget.

A dog says, "Woof, woof!" and wags his tail to let you know he is happy.
(Wiggle body from side to side.)

A cat says, "Meow, meow!" and curls up in your lap with a purr.
(Curl body into a ball.)

A fish says, "Glub, glub!" and swims around his bowl.
(Pretend to swim.)

A hamster says, "Squeak, squeak!" and runs in her exercise wheel.
(Run in place.)

A bird says, "Tweet, tweet!" and flies around your head.
(Flap arms for wings.)

No, I never met a pet that I could forget.

Flannel Board

Pieces: Dog, rabbit, duck, snake, mouse

Playing Drums on the Mat

I have a dog, he plays on the drums.
He keeps me awake when my bedtime comes,

With a rat-tat, rat-a-tat-tat.
(Pat legs—clap, pat legs—clap-clap.)

I have a dog playing drums there on the mat.
I have a rabbit, she plays on the drums.
She keeps me awake when my bedtime comes,

With a rat-tat, rat-a-tat-tat.
(Pat legs—clap, pat legs—clap-clap.)

I have a dog and a rabbit playing drums on the mat.
I have a duck, he plays on the drums.
He keeps me awake when my bedtime comes,

With a rat-tat, rat-a-tat-tat.
(Pat legs—clap, pat legs—clap-clap.)

I have a dog and a rabbit and a duck playing drums on the mat.
I have a snake, she plays on the drums.
She keeps me awake when my bedtime comes,

With a rat-tat, rat-a-tat-tat.
(Pat legs—clap, pat legs—clap-clap.)

I have a dog and a rabbit and a duck and a snake playing drums on the mat.
I have a mouse, he plays on the drums.
He keeps me awake when my bedtime comes,

With a rat-tat, rat-a-tat-tat.
(Pat legs—clap, pat legs—clap-clap.)

I have a dog and a rabbit and a duck and a snake and a mouse
playing drums on the mat.
I tell you right now, I can't get any sleep.
So tonight is the night when I make them all scat!

Book #2 *Dear Zoo: A Pop-Up Book* by Rod Campbell

Action Song
Sung to the tune of "Are You Sleeping?"

I Want a Pet

I want a pet. I want a pet. *(Point to self.)*
That goes bounce-bounce, goes bounce-bounce. *(Jump.)*
I really, really want one. One that goes bounce.
Do you have, a pet for me?

I want a pet. I want a pet. *(Point to self.)*
That runs in a circle, runs in a circle. *(Spin around.)*
I really, really want one. One that runs in a circle.
Do you have, a pet for me?

I want a pet. I want a pet. *(Point to self.)*
That goes up and down, goes up and down. *(Reach up high, then touch toes.)*
I really, really want one. One that goes up-down.
Do you have, a pet for me?

(Continued on page 168)

I want a pet. I want a pet. (*Point to self.*)

That goes sleep-sleep, goes sleep-sleep.
(*Sit down with hands together on the side of the face.*)

I really, really want one. One that goes sleep-sleep.

Do you have, a pet for me?

Closing Song

Art Experience

Fishbowl:

1. Print out the fishbowl drawing on blue paper (use Pattern 36.1).
2. Invite children to glue goldfish crackers onto the fishbowl.

Bonus Storytime Resources

More Books

Counting Pets by Twos by Rebecca Fjelland Davis

Don't Take Your Snake for a Stroll by Karin Ireland, illustrated by David Catrow

An Octopus Followed Me Home by Dan Yaccarino

Peek-a-Pet! by Marie Torres Cimarusti, illustrated by Stephanie Peterson (lift-flap)

Tails Are Not for Pulling by Elizabeth Verdick, illustrated by Marieka Heinlen

Extra Action Song

Sung to the tune of "I'm Bringing Home a Baby Bumblebee"

I'm Bringing Home a Very Special Pet

I'm bringing home a very special pet. (*March in place.*)

Yes, it's true; I have him here on this leash. (*Point to pretend leash in hand.*)

I'm bringing home a very special pet. Ah, he's so cute!
(*Place hands over heart.*)

My very special pet has big fuzzy ears. (*Point to ears.*)

He can hear me with those fuzzy ears.

I'm bringing home a very special pet. Ah, he's so cute!
(*Place hands over heart.*)

My very special pet has a green sniffing nose. (*Point to nose.*)

He can smell most anything around.

I'm bringing home a very special pet. Ah, he's so cute!
(*Place hands over heart.*)

My very special pet is really big. (*Spread arms out wide.*)

He may need his own humongous house.

I'm bringing home a very special pet. Ah, he's so cute!
(*Place hands over heart.*)

My very special pet is a monster. (*Use sign language for "monster."*)

Yes, he's mine. I'm very happy to tell you.

I'm bringing home a very special pet. Ah, my monster's so cute!
(*Place hands over heart.*)

Additional Art Experiences

Mouse face:

1. Precut one mouse head shape (use Pattern 36.2) and one set of mouse ear shapes (use Pattern 36.3) for each child.
2. Invite the children to glue the ears to the face (see Figure 36.1).
3. Next, decorate the mouse face with dot sticker eyes and nose, as well as with crayons.

Figure 36.1 **Mouse faces**

Paper plate snake:

1. Spiral cut one paper plate for each child.
2. Invite children to glue button eyes onto the spiral snake (see Figure 36.2).
3. Next, decorate with color pens.

Figure 36.2 **Paper plate snake**

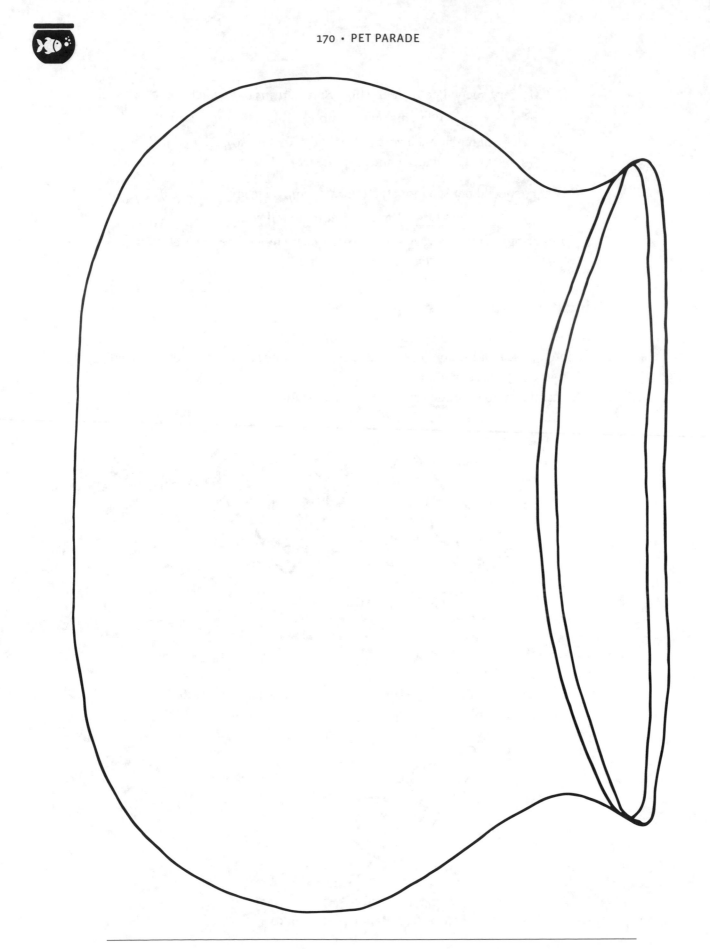

Pattern 36.1 **Fishbowl**

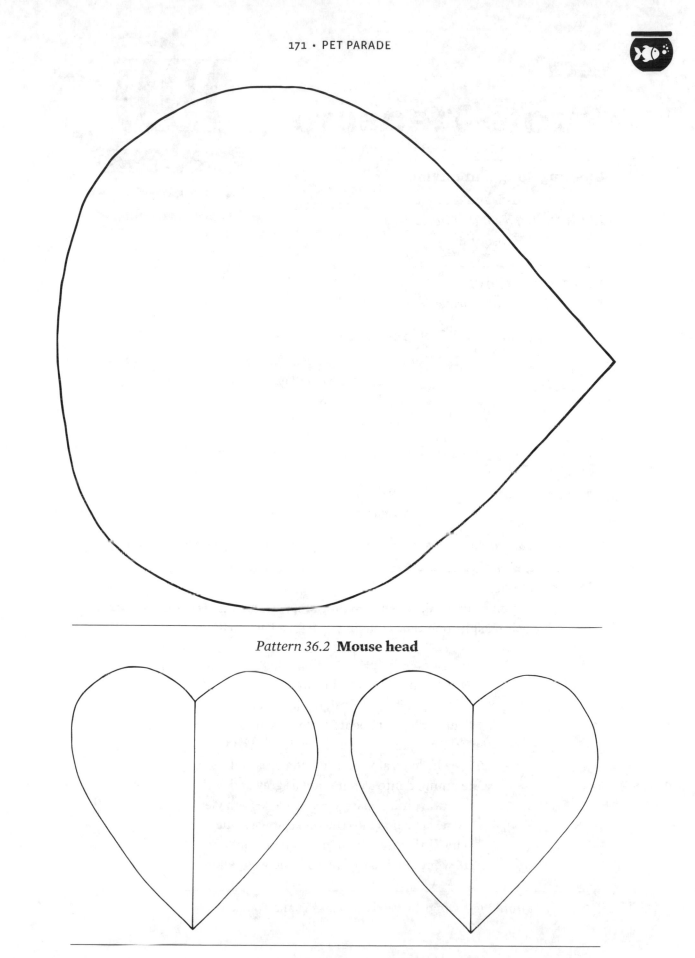

Pattern 36.2 **Mouse head**

Pattern 36.3 **Mouse ears**

Pirate Treasure

Opening Song and Rhyme

Book #1 *Bubble Bath Pirates!* by Jarrett J. Krosoczka

Stand-Up Activity

Sung to the tune of "Farmer in the Dell"

Yo-Ho a Pirate's Gold

A jumping we will go, *(Jump.)*
A jumping we will go,
Yo-ho a pirate's gold,
A jumping we will go.

A swimming we will go, *(Pretend to swim.)*
A swimming we will go,
Yo-ho a pirate's gold,
A swimming we will go.

(Repeat with other action words, such as running, dancing, spinning, etc.)

Flannel Board

Pieces: One green sailing ship, one red sailing ship, one gray and white sailing ship, one blue sailing ship, one yellow sailing ship (use Pattern 8.1, p. 50)

Five Little Pirate Boats

Five little pirate boats, bright and shiny clean.
One tipped over, it was green.
Four little pirate boats, with all sails spread.
One sailed into a storm, it was red.
Three little pirate boats, what a dreadful sight!
One bumped into a shark, it was gray and white.
Two little pirate boats, coming close for a view.
One smashed into the rocks, it was blue.
One little pirate boat, now a lonely fellow.
He went looking for treasure, he was yellow.

Book #2 *Pirate Piggywiggy* by Christyan and Diane Fox

Action Song

Sung to the tune of "Row, Row, Row Your Boat"

Row Your Pirate Ship

Row, row, row your ship, gently across the sea,
(*Pretend to row.*)

Yo-ho, yo-ho, a pirate's life at sea.

Scrub, scrub, scrub the deck, gently across the sea,
(*Move hands back and forth together as if washing the deck.*)

Yo ho, yo ho, a pirate's life at sea.

Furl, furl, furl your sail, gently across the sea,
(*Move hand over hand as if pulling on a rope.*)

Yo ho, yo ho, a pirate's life at sea.

Sway, sway, sway your ship, gently across the sea,
(*Sway body side to side.*)

Yo ho, yo ho, a pirate's life at sea.

Closing Song

Art Experience

Pirate spyglass:

1. Precut a large supply of one-inch squares of colorful tissue paper.
2. Give each child one paper towel tube, some tissue paper squares, and glue.
3. Invite children to decorate their spyglass by gluing the tissue paper squares onto the paper towel tube.

Bonus Storytime Resources

More Books

Do Pirates Take Baths? by Kathy Tucker, illustrated by Nadine Bernard Westcott

I Love My Pirate Papa by Laura Leuck, illustrated by Kyle M. Stone

Maisy's Pirate Treasure Hunt by Lucy Cousins (lift-flap)

Sail Away by Florence McNeil and David McPhail

Sheep on a Ship by Nancy Shaw, illustrated by Margot Apple

Extra Action Chant

One-Eyed Pirate Adventure

I'm a one-eyed pirate,
(Cover one eye with one hand.)

Captain of my ship.
(Stand tall and salute.)

I stride the deck,
(Walk in place.)

With hands on my hips.
(Stand with hands on hips.)

I use my spyglass to watch the seas.
(Make circles with hands and put them together in front of one eye.)

I find gold with my treasure map.
(Put hands together and open up like a book.)

The sails are up,
(Open arms out wide.)

And the wind blows me,
(Blow the wind.)

On an adventure!

Additional Art Experiences

Paper bag treasure map:
1. Cut one large rectangle out of a brown paper bag for each child.
2. Crinkle the brown paper rectangle and then straighten it out flat.
3. Invite children to draw a treasure map onto the brown paper rectangle with color chalk or color pens.

Treasure chest:
1. Print out the treasure chest drawing (use Pattern 37.1).
2. Invite children to use dot stickers or bingo paint bottles to add colorful treasure to the chest.

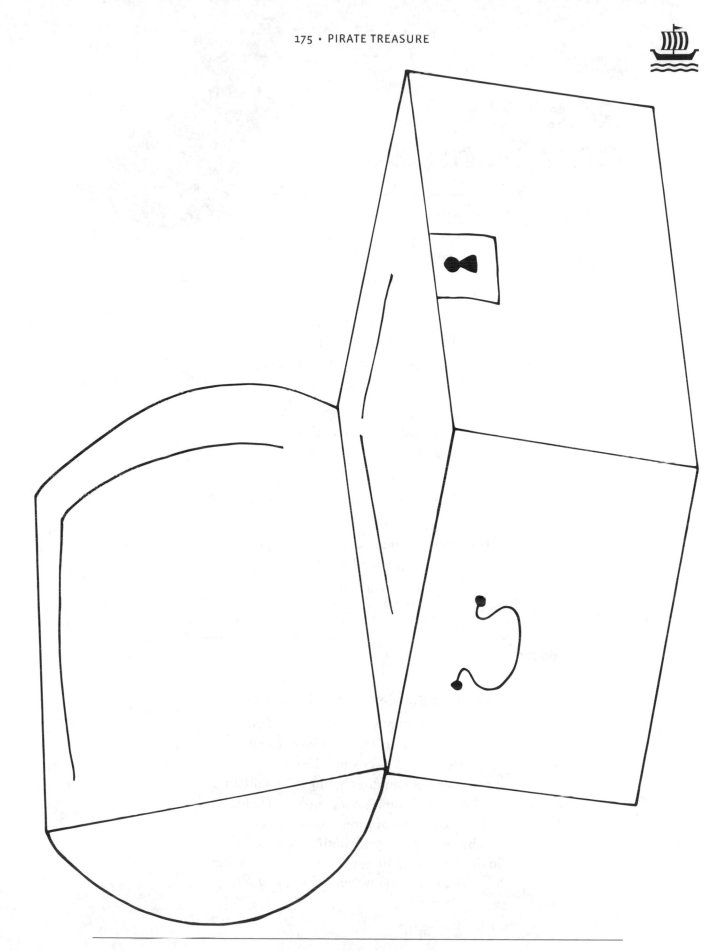

Pattern 37.1 **Treasure chest**

Rabbits and Bunnies

Opening Song and Rhyme

Book #1 *Bunny and Me* by Adele Aron Greenspun and Joanie Schwarz

---

Stand-Up Activity

I Saw a Little Bunny
(Traditional)

I saw a little rabbit go hop, hop, hop.
(Jump.)

I saw his ears go flop, flop, flop.
(Put hands on head for ears and then flop these ears.)

I saw his eyes go blink, blink, blink.
(Blink eyes.)

I saw his nose go twink, twink, twink.
(Wiggle nose.)

This little rabbit ate a carrot on the ground,
(Pretend to eat.)

Then he hopped around.
(Jump.)

Flannel Board
Pieces: Five or more rabbits

Little Bunnies in a Field of Clover

One little bunny hopping onto a field,
Finding lots of yummy clover to eat,
He ate and he ate until he was full.
So he asked for another bunny to join the fun.
Two little bunnies hopping onto a field,
Finding lots of yummy clover to eat,
They ate and they ate until they were full.
So they asked for another bunny to join the fun.
(Repeat as many times as you wish.)

Book #2 *Munch Munch, Peter Rabbit: A Lift-the-Flap Book* by Beatrix Potter
(board book)

Fingerplay

Here's a Bunny

(Traditional)

Here's a bunny with two long ears.
(Show two fingers.)

Here is her hole in the ground.
(Make hole with other arm at waist.)

This bunny likes to come out to sniff around and eat.
(Sniff the air, then pretend to eat.)

But when she gets scared,
She pricks up her ears,
(Show two fingers again.)

And jumps into her hole.
(Put finger ears into the hole at waist.)

Closing Song

Art Experience

Colorful bunny ears:
1. Precut two rabbit-shaped ears for each child (use Pattern 38.1). Optional: These rabbit ears look even better enlarged onto legal-size paper.
2. Precut long strips of paper for a headband, approximately two inches wide.
3. Tape the ears to the long, narrow headband.
4. Invite children to decorate their ears with color pens or crayons.
5. Tape another strip of paper to the headband to fit around a child's head.

Bonus Storytime Resources

More Books

Biscuit and the Bunny by Alyssa Satin Capucilli, illustrated by Pat Schories (board book)

Bunnies on the Go: Getting from Place to Place by Rick Walton, illustrated by Paige Miglio

Bunny, Bunny by Kristen Hall, illustrated by Kathy Wilburn

Little White Rabbit by Kevin Henkes

What Can Rabbit See? by Lucy Cousins (lift-flap)

Extra Action Rhyme

Jumping Bunny

Jumping bunny, jumping bunny, jump so fast.
(Jump.)

Jumping bunny, jumping bunny, jump so slow.

Jumping bunny, jumping bunny, start to run.
(Run in place.)

Running bunny, running bunny, run so fast.

Running bunny, running bunny, run so slow.

Running bunny, running bunny, start to spin.
(Turn around.)

Spinning bunny, spinning bunny, spin so fast.

Spinning bunny, spinning bunny, spin so slow.

Spinning bunny, spinning bunny, start to slide.
(Move feet side to side.)

Sliding bunny, sliding bunny, slide so fast.

Sliding bunny, sliding bunny, slide so slow.

Sliding bunny, sliding bunny, start to jump.
(Jump.)

Jumping bunny, jumping bunny, jump so fast.

Jumping bunny, jumping bunny, jump so slow.

Jumping bunny, jumping bunny, come to a stop.
(Use sign language for "stop.")

Additional Art Experience

Rabbit paper bag puppet:

1. Precut two puppet-sized rabbit ears for each child (use Pattern 38.2).
2. Supply each child with a paper lunch bag, two rabbit ears, two large googly eyes or buttons, a pom-pom nose, and some yarn pieces for whiskers.
3. Invite children to glue the rabbit face onto the bottom of the paper bag to create a simple puppet (see Figure 38.1).

Figure 38.1 **Rabbit paper bag puppet**

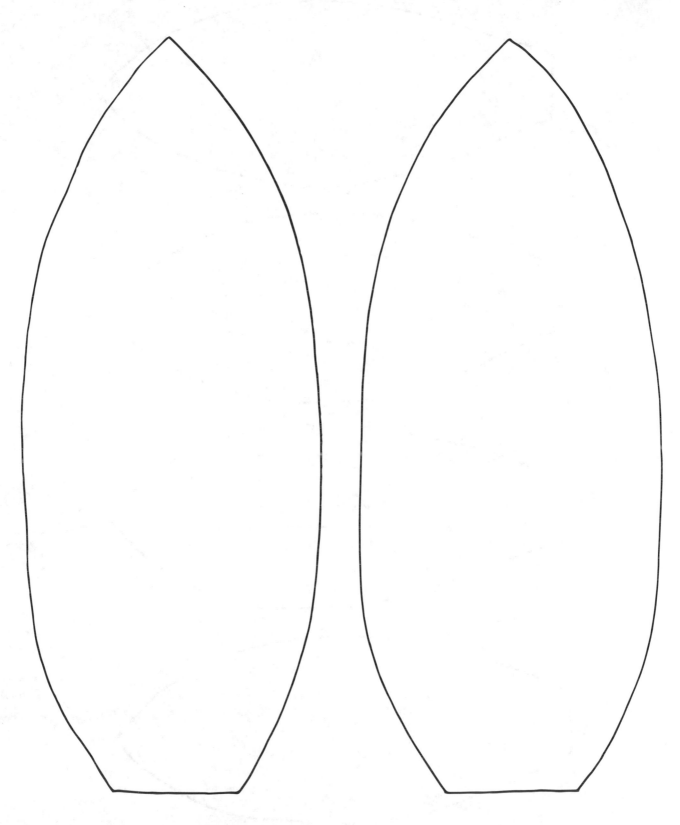

Pattern 38.1 **Bunny ears for headband**

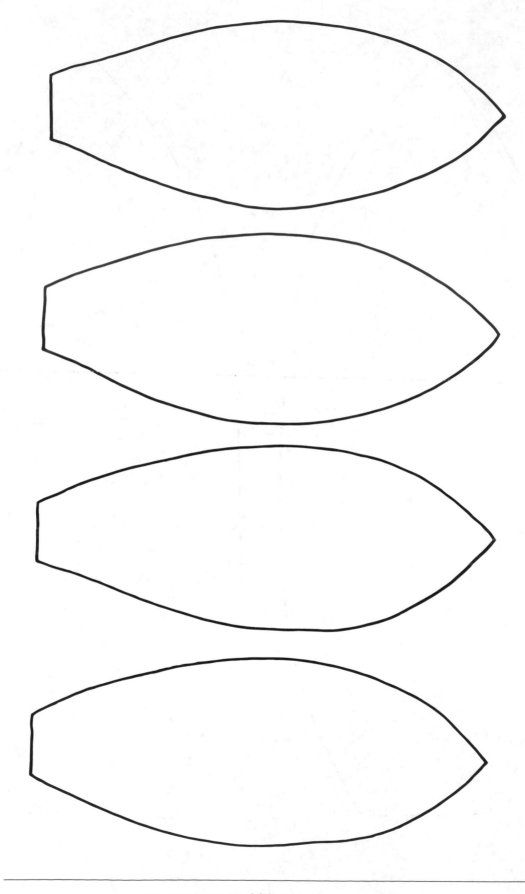

Pattern 38.2 **Rabbit ears for puppet**

Royalty

Opening Song and Rhyme

Book #1 *King Bidgood's in the Bathtub* by Audrey Wood, illustrated by Don Wood

Stand-Up Activity

Favorite source: More Tickles & Tunes by Kathy Reid-Naiman

Grand Old Duke of York

(Traditional)

The grand old Duke of York, he had ten thousand men.
(March in place.)

He marched them up a hill,
(Raise arms up high.)

And he marched them down again.
(Lower hands, touching ground.)

And when you're up, you're up;
(Raise arms up high.)

And when you're down, you're down.
(Lower hands, touching ground.)

And when you're only halfway up,
(Place hands at hip level.)

You're neither up,
(Raise arms up high.)

Nor down.
(Lower hands, touching ground.)

Flannel Board

Pieces: Pie with blackbirds on top, king, queen, maid, blackbird

Sing a Song of Sixpence

(Nursery rhyme)

Sing a song of sixpence, a pocket full of rye,
Four-and-twenty blackbirds baked in a pie.
When the pie was opened the birds began to sing.
Wasn't that a dainty dish to set before a king?

(Continued on page 182)

The king was in his counting house, counting out his money;
The queen was in the parlor, eating bread and honey.
The maid was in the garden, hanging out the clothes.
When down came a blackbird and snapped at her nose.

Book #2 *The Missing Tarts* by B. G. Hennessy, illustrated by Tracey Campbell Pearson

Fingerplay

Lords and Ladies in a Row

Five ladies in waiting, standing in a row, (*Show fingers of one hand.*)

They bow their heads to honor the queen. (*Bend fingers slightly.*)

Five noble lords, standing in a row, (*Show fingers of the other hand.*)

They bow their heads to honor the king. (*Bend fingers slightly.*)

They stand in two straight lines and politely applaud. (*Clap.*)

Then they come together, (*Put hands together.*)

And dance at the ball. (*Flutter fingers.*)

Closing Song

Art Experience

Paper plate crown:

1. Precut one paper plate crown for each child.

    a. Cut a hole in the center of each paper plate.

    b. From the hole cut several lines going out to within one inch of the edge of the plate (see Figure 39.1).

    c. Fold these triangles up to make a crown (see Figure 39.2).

2. Invite children to decorate their crowns by gluing on buttons.

Figure 39.1
Paper plate crown cut lines

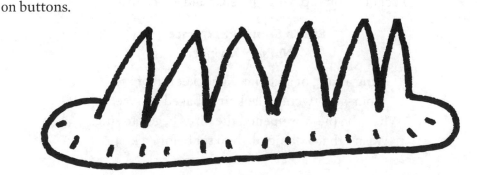

Figure 39.2 **Paper plate crown**

Bonus Storytime Resources

More Books

Do Princesses Wear Hiking Boots? by Carmela LaVigna Coyle, illustrated by Mike Gordon

Falling for Rapunzel by Leah Wilcox, illustrated by Lydia Monks

Giddy-Up! Let's Ride! by Flora McDonnell

Princess Party by Joy Allen

17 Kings and 42 Elephants by Margaret Mahy, illustrated by Patricia MacCarthy

Extra Action Chant

Not Much Different

A prince has a crown,
(Circle hands on top of head.)

And he bows to say, "Hello."
(Bow.)

A princess has a crown,
(Circle hands on top of head.)

And she curtseys to say, "How do you do?"
(Curtsey.)

They can run,
(Run.)

They can dance,
(Dance.)

They can jump,
(Jump.)

They can sit.
(Sit.)

They are not much different from you,
(Point to other person.)

Or me.
(Point to self.)

Additional Art Experience

Royal shield:

1. Precut or print out a shield shape on colorful cardstock paper (use Pattern 39.1).
2. Invite children to decorate their shields with stickers, color pens, and crayons.

Pattern 39.1 **Royal shield**

Silly Fun

Opening Song and Rhyme

Book #1 *Silly Sally* by Audrey Wood

Stand-Up Activity
Sung to the tune of "Row, Row, Row Your Boat"

Silliness Is Fun

Walk, walk, walk with me, walking a silly path. *(Walk in place.)*

Silliness is fun, don't you agree? Walking is so much fun.

Leap, leap, leap with me, leaping a silly path. *(Jump.)*

Silliness is fun, don't you agree? Leaping is so much fun.

(Repeat with more action words, such as flying, spinning, running, sleeping, etc.)

Flannel Board
Pieces: Goose, moose, llama wearing red pajamas, whale with a polka-dot tail, fly wearing a tie, bear, comb, plus more rhyming animals and words
Favorite source: Singable Songs for the Very Young by Raffi

Down by the Bay
(Traditional song)

Down by the bay, where the watermelons grow,
Back to my home, I dare not go,
For if I do, my mother will say,
"Did you ever see a goose,
Kissing a moose,
Down by the bay?"

Down by the bay, where the watermelons grow,
Back to my home, I dare not go,
For if I do, my mother will say,
"Did you ever see a llama,
Wearing red pajamas,
Down by the bay?"

(Repeat with other rhyming animals and words, such as whale/polka-dot tail, fly/ wearing a tie, bear/combing his hair, etc.)

Book #2 *The Seals on the Bus* by Lenny Hort, illustrated by G. Brian Karas

Fingerplay

Not So Crazy Fingers

I have crazy ears, *(Point to ears.)*

And a crazy nose, *(Rub nose.)*

Crazy shoulders, *(Wiggle shoulders.)*

And crazy toes, *(Wiggle toes.)*

Crazy hair, *(Pat hair.)*

And a crazy chin, *(Point to chin.)*

But my fingers sit quietly like so. *(Fold hands together into lap.)*

Closing Song

Art Experience

Paper plate mask:

1. Cut a supply of paper plates in half.
2. In each half plate, cut two eye holes.
3. Tape or glue a craft stick onto the half plate for a handle (see Figure 40.1).
4. Precut a colorful supply of tissue paper squares, approximately one inch square.
5. Invite children to decorate their masks with glue, feathers, and tissue paper squares.

Figure 40.1 **Paper plate mask**

Bonus Storytime Resources

More Books

Down by the Bay (Raffi Songs to Read) by Raffi, illustrated by Nadine Bernard Westcott
Eight Silly Monkeys by Steve Haskamp
The Noisy Counting Book by Susan Schade and Jon Buller
Silly Suzy Goose by Petr Horáček
What! Cried Granny: An Almost Bedtime Book by Kate Lum, illustrated by Adrian Johnson

Extra Action Song #1

Favorite source: Rhythm of the Rocks: A Multicultural Journey by Marylee & Nancy

Rum Sum, Sum
(Moroccan folk song)

A rum sum, sum, a rum sum, sum,
(Clap thighs.)
Guli, guli, guli, guli, guli,
(Roll hands over each other.)
Rum sum, sum.
(Clap thighs.)
A rafi, a rafi,
(Shake hands high in the air.)
Guli, guli, guli, guli, guli,
(Roll hands over each other.)
Rum sum, sum.
(Clap thighs.)

Extra Action Song #2

"Shake My Sillies Out" action song from *More Singable Songs* by Raffi

Additional Art Experience

Balloon prints:

1. For each child, inflate a small balloon to a size that will easily fit in the palm of a child's hand (this should be done before storytime starts).
2. In a pie tin or shallow bowl, place a thin layer of two different colored tempera paints (do not worry if they mix together).
3. Invite children to dip the balloon into the paints and then press onto a large piece of paper.

Spiders

Opening Song and Rhyme

Book #1 *Very Busy Spider* by Eric Carle

Stand-Up Activity

Sung to the tune of "The Farmer in the Dell"

The Spider on His Web

The spider walks her web.
(Walk in place.)

The spider walks her web.

Up and down and all around, the spider walks her web.
(Reach up and down, then spin around.)

The spider spins her web.
(Roll hands over each other.)

The spider spins her web.

Up and down and all around, the spider spins her web.
(Reach up and down, then spin around.)

(Repeat with more action words, such as run, jump, weave, etc.)

Flannel Board

Pieces: Five elephants

One Little Elephant Went Out to Play upon a Spider's Web One Day
(Nursery rhyme)

One little elephant went out to play upon a spider's web one day.
He had such enormous fun; he called for another to join the fun.
Two little elephants went out to play upon a spider's web one day.
They had such enormous fun; they called for another to join the fun.

(Continue counting up to five elephants.)

Five little elephants went out to play upon a spider's web one day.
The web went creak, the web went crack,
And all of the elephants went running back!

Book #2 *Spider on the Floor* (Raffi Songs to Read) by Raffi and Bill Russell, illustrated by True Kelley

Fingerplay

Itsy Bitsy Spider
(Nursery rhyme)

The itsy bitsy spider climbed up the water spout.
(Climb opposite thumbs and index fingers upward.)

Down came the rain,
(Flutter fingers down.)

And washed the spider out.
(Sweep arms in front of body.)

Out came the sun and dried up all the rain,
(Form circle over head with arms.)

So the itsy bitsy spider climbed up the spout again.
(Climb opposite thumbs and index fingers upward.)

Closing Song

Art Experience

Spider leg headband:
1. Precut a supply of long colorful strips of paper, approximately one inch by eleven inches.
2. Precut some larger strips of black paper, approximately two inches wide.
3. Tape two lengths of the long black paper together to fit a child's head.
4. Give each child one black headband and eight colorful strips of paper.
5. Invite children to glue the eight smaller strips onto the headband to create spider legs (see Figure 41.1).
6. Glue googly eyes or dot stickers onto the black headband for spider eyes.

Figure 41.1 **Spider leg headband**

Bonus Storytime Resources

More Books

Aaaarrgghh! Spider! by Lydia Monks
Itsy Bitsy Spider by Lorianne Siomades
Little Miss Muffet by Tracey Campbell Pearson (board book)
Miss Spider's New Car by David Kirk
Roly Poly Spider by Jill Sardegna, illustrated by Tedd Arnold

Extra Fingerplay

Icky Sticky Spiderweb

Icky sticky spiderweb, spiderweb, spiderweb, *(Clap thighs.)*

Icky sticky spiderweb, stretches from here to there. *(Point left, then right.)*

Icky sticky spiderweb, spiderweb, spiderweb, *(Clap thighs.)*

Icky sticky spiderweb, is used to catch bugs. *(Use sign language for "bug.")*

Icky sticky spiderweb, spiderweb, spiderweb, *(Clap thighs.)*

Icky sticky spiderweb, is home to a spider. *(Use sign language for "spider.")*

Icky sticky spiderweb, spiderweb, spiderweb, *(Clap thighs.)*

Icky sticky spiderweb, is interesting to watch. *(Circle eyes with fingers.)*

Additional Art Experience

Paper plate spiderweb:

1. Precut six to ten small slits around the outside edge of a paper plate.
2. Give each child one paper plate with slits and one really long length of yarn, approximately five feet long.
3. Invite children to wrap the yarn around the paper plate and into the slits to make a web design (see Figure 41.2).

Figure 41.2 **Paper plate spiderweb**

Springtime

Opening Song and Rhyme

Book #1 *My Spring Robin* by Anne Rockwell, illustrated by Harlow Rockwell and Lizzy Rockwell

Stand-Up Activity

Sung to the tune of "Mary Had a Little Lamb"

We Love Spring

We love rain in the spring, in the spring, in the spring.
(Flutter fingers down.)
We love rain in the spring; it is a jolly time.

We love birds in the spring, in the spring, in the spring.
(Flap arms to the side for wings.)
We love birds in the spring; it is a jolly time.

We love grass in the spring, in the spring, in the spring.
(Touch the ground.)
We love grass in the spring; it is a jolly time.

We love tulips in the spring, in the spring, in the spring.
(Cup hands for the head of a tulip flower.)
We love tulips in the spring; it is a jolly time.

Flannel Board

Pieces: Five ducks
Favorite source: Rise and Shine by Raffi

Five Little Ducks Went Out One Day

(Traditional)

Five little ducks went out one day, over the hills and far away.
Mother Duck said, "Quack, Quack, Quack, Quack,"
But only four little ducks came back.
Four little ducks went out one day, over the hills and far away.
Mother Duck said, "Quack, Quack, Quack, Quack,"
But only three little ducks came back.
(Repeat counting down to "But no little ducks came back.")
Sad mother duck went out one day, over the hills and far away.
Mother Duck said, "Quack, Quack, Quack, Quack,"
And five little ducks came back.

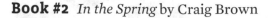

Book #2 *In the Spring* by Craig Brown

Fingerplay

Ten Spring Flowers

Flowers tall,
(Raise hands up high.)

Flowers small,
(Move hands down low.)

Count the flowers as they sway in the springtime breeze.
(Move hands side to side.)

1, 2, 3, 4, 5, 6, 7, 8, 9, 10!
(Point to each finger as you count.)

Closing Song

Art Experience

Paper tube windsock:
1. Precut one paper towel tube for each child, approximately five or six inches long.
2. Tape or staple a six-inch length of yarn to one end of the tube.
3. Precut a supply of colorful crepe paper, approximately 18 inches long.
4. Invite children to create a windsock by gluing the crepe paper onto the paper tube (see Figure 42.1).

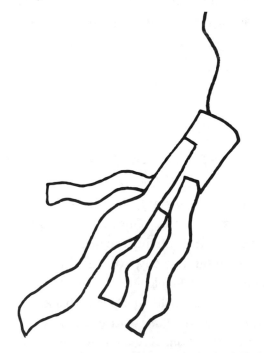

Figure 42.1 **Paper tube windsock**

Bonus Storytime Resources

More Books

Hurray for Spring! by Patricia Hubbell, illustrated by Taia Morley

Mouse's First Spring, by Lauren Thompson, illustrated by Buket Erdogan

Splish, Splash, Spring by Jan Carr, illustrated by Dorothy Donohue

Spring Things by Bob Raczka, illustrated by Judy Stead

Wake Up, It's Spring! by Lisa Campbell Ernst

Extra Action Song

Sung to the tune of "Are You Sleeping?"

Springtime Flowers

In the springtime, in the springtime,
(Use sign language for "spring.")

Come the flowers, come the flowers,
(Use sign language for "flower.")

Everywhere, here and there. Everywhere, all around,
(Spin around.)

We find the flowers, growing on the ground.
(Touch ground.)

Additional Art Experience

Muffin cup flower:

1. Give each child one large sheet of paper, one colorful muffin cup for cooking, one length of green yarn approximately six inches long, and a small pinch of birdseed.
2. Invite children to create a flower by gluing the flower head muffin cup and yarn stem onto the larger paper (see Figure 42.2). Then add some birdseed.

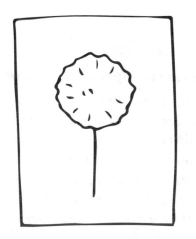

Figure 42.2 **Muffin cup flower**

Summer in the Sun

Opening Song and Rhyme

Book #1 *Summer Wonders* by Bob Raczka, illustrated
by Judy Stead

Stand-Up Activity

Favorite source: Sing Along with Bob #1 by Bob McGrath

Mister Sun

(Traditional)

Oh, mister sun, sun, mister golden sun,
(Form circle over head with arms.)

Please shine down on me.
(Flutter fingers down.)

Oh, mister sun, sun, mister golden sun,
(Form circle over head with arms.)

Hiding behind the tree. *(Place hands over eyes.)*

These little children are asking you, to please come out so we can play with you.
(Use sign language for "play.")

Oh, mister sun, sun, mister golden sun,
(Form circle over head with arms.)

Please shine down on, *(Flutter fingers down.)*

Won't you shine down on, please shine down on me.
(Point to self.)

Flannel Board

Pieces: Five ice cream scoops, one ice cream cone

Scoops on My Ice Cream Cone

Five scoops on my ice cream cone.
Five scoops looking oh so yummy.
The sun was high on this hot summer day, and I ate a scoop right away.
Four scoops on my ice cream cone.
Four scoops looking oh so yummy.
The sun was high on this hot summer day, and I ate a scoop right away.
(Count down to zero scoops.)

Zero scoops on my ice cream cone.
So then I ate up all the cone. Yum!

Book #2 *Wemberly's Ice Cream Star* by Kevin Henkes

Action Song
Sung to the tune of "The Farmer in the Dell"

It's Time to Go Outside

It's time to go outside, it's time to go and run,
(*Run in place.*)

In summertime it's so much fun to run and run and run.

It's time to go outside, it's time to go and swim,
(*Pretend to swim.*)

In summertime it's so much fun to swim and swim and swim.

It's time to go outside, it's time to go and jump,
(*Jump.*)

In summertime it's so much fun to jump and jump and jump.

It's time to go outside, it's time to go and climb,
(*Pretend to climb.*)

In summertime it's so much fun to climb and climb and climb.

(*Repeat with more action words, such as spin, fly, sit, dance, etc.*)

Closing Song

Art Experience

Sun visor:
1. Precut one cardstock sun visor shape for each child (use Pattern 43.1).
2. Punch a small hole at each end of the sun visor.
3. Precut one length of thin elastic string for each child, approximately six inches.
4. Invite children to decorate the sun visor with color pens and stickers.
5. Tie the elastic string to both ends of the sun visor to complete this summer hat.

Bonus Storytime Resources

More Books
Beach Day by Karen Roosa, illustrated by Maggie Smith
Claude Has a Picnic by Dick Gackenbach
Maisy Goes to the Playground: A Maisy Lift-the-Flap Classic by Lucy Cousins
Mouse's First Summer by Lauren Thompson, illustrated by Buket Erdogan
A Summer Day by Doug Florian

Extra Action Song

Sung to the tune of "Three Blind Mice"

Playing in the Sprinklers

Splish, splash, jump,
(Wave one hand, wave the other hand, then jump.)

Splish, splash, jump,
(Wave one hand, wave the other hand, then jump.)

Playing in the sprinklers. Playing in the sprinklers.
(Spin around.)

The water feels oh so good. On this hot summer day.
(Use sign language for "water.")

The sun is up.
(Form circle over head with arms.)

My friends are around.
(Use sign language for "friend.")

Splish, splash, jump.
(Wave one hand, wave the other hand, then jump.)

Splish, splash, jump.
(Wave one hand, wave the other hand, then jump.)

Additional Art Experience

Triangle sun:

1. Precut one large yellow circle for each child (use Pattern 43.2).
2. Precut a large supply of yellow, red, and orange triangles of different sizes.
3. Invite children to glue their sun circle onto a plain white or blue regular paper and then decorate this sun with the triangles.

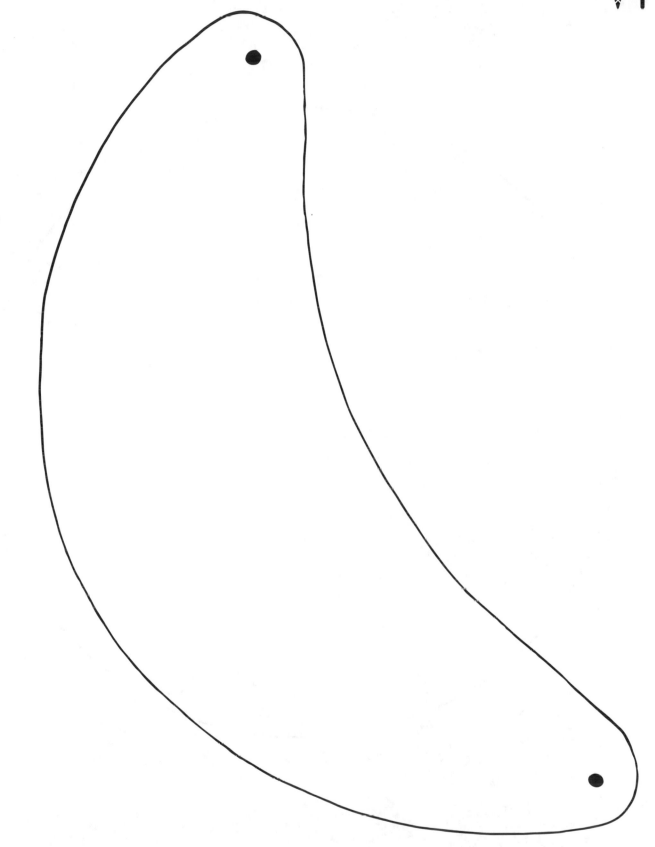

Pattern 43.1 **Sun visor**

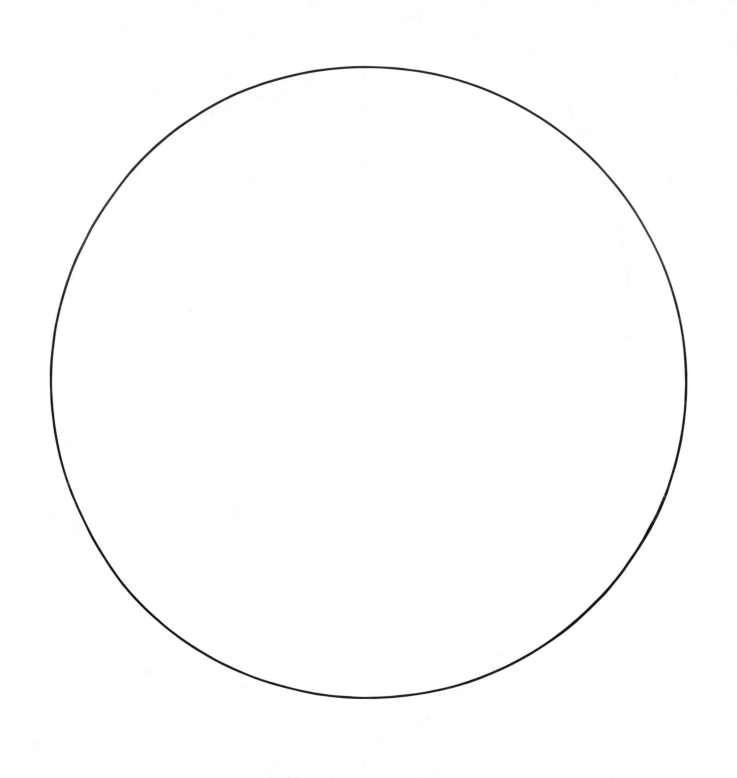

Pattern 43.2 **Sun circle**

Thanksgiving Turkeys

Opening Song and Rhyme

Book #1 *Biscuit Is Thankful* by Alyssa Satin Capucilli, illustrated by Pat Schories (board book)

Stand-Up Activity
Sung to the tune of "I'm a Little Teapot"

I'm a Thankful Turkey

I'm a little turkey short and fat.
(Make large circle with arms in front of body.)

I tend to show up around Thanksgiving Day.
(Shake forefinger.)

When you want to give thanks to your family,
(Use sign language for "thank you.")

Just shake my feathers,
(Put hands under armpits and flap arms like wings.)

And say, "I love you."
(Use sign language for "I love you.")

Flannel Board
Pieces: Ten turkeys (use Pattern 44.1)

Turkey Cheese Fondue

One, two, make some fondue.
Three, four, make some more.
Five, six, together they mix.
Seven, eight, where's the plate?
Nine, ten, let's make it again.
Ten turkeys eating cheese fondue.

Book #2 *Five Silly Turkeys* by Salina Yoon (board book)

Action Song

Sung to the tune of "Hokey Pokey"

Gobble-Gobble Pokey
(Suit actions to words.)

Put your right wing in, put your right wing out,
Put your right wing in and shake it all about.
Go gobble-gobble-gobble and turn yourself around;
that's how we shake our feathers.

Put your left wing in, put your left wing out,
Put your left wing in and shake it all about.
Go gobble-gobble-gobble and turn yourself around;
that's how we shake our feathers.

Put your tail feathers in, put your tail feathers out,
Put your tail feathers in and shake them all about.
Go gobble-gobble-gobble and turn yourself around;
that's how we shake our feathers.

Put your head in, put your head out,
Put your head in and shake it all about.
Go gobble-gobble-gobble and turn yourself around;
that's how we shake our feathers.

Closing Song

Art Experience

Feathered turkey:
1. Print out the turkey shape (use Pattern 44.1).
2. Invite children to decorate the turkey by gluing on colored feathers.

Bonus Storytime Resources

More Books

One Little, Two Little, Three Little Pilgrims by B. G. Hennessy, illustrated by Lynne Cravath

1, 2, 3 Thanksgiving by W. Nikola-Lisa, illustrated by Robin Kramer

Thanksgiving in the Barn: A Pop-Up Book by Nadine Bernard Westcott

This First Thanksgiving Day: A Counting Story by Laura Krauss Melmed, illustrated by Mark Buehner

The Turkey Ball by David Steinberg, illustrated by Liz Conrad

Extra Action Chant

Ten Strutting Turkeys
(Action chant)

Ten fat turkeys,
(Hold up all ten fingers.)

Strutting around looking for food.
(Walk in place.)

They jump over fences.
(Jump.)

They run over fields.
(Run in place.)

They flap their wings,
(Flap arms.)

And say, "Gobble, gobble."

But when Thanksgiving Day comes around they hide.
(Show fingers, then put them behind your back.)

Because they don't want to become your dinner.
(Rub tummy.)

Extra Fingerplay

"Mr. Turkey and Mr. Duck" fingerplay song from *Little Songs for Little Me* by Nancy Stewart

Additional Art Experience

Coffee filter turkey:

1. Precut one turkey head for each child (use Pattern 11.2).
2. Give each child one turkey head and one white coffee filter.
3. Invite children to decorate the turkey head and coffee filter with color pens.
4. To complete the turkey, glue the turkey head to the coffee filter tail feathers.

Pattern 44.1 **Feathered turkey**

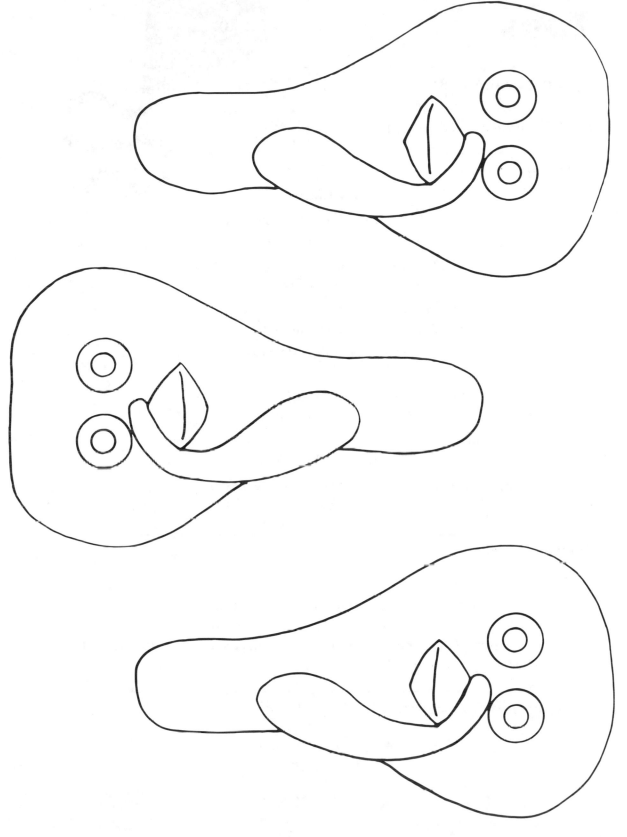

Pattern 44.2 **Turkey heads**

Toys

Opening Song and Rhyme

Book #1 *Peekaboo Bedtime* by Rachel Isadora

Stand-Up Activity

Toy Chant

Fire truck, fire truck, roll on the ground.
(Touch the ground.)

Magic pony, magic pony, come get crowned.
(Circle hands on head.)

Paper airplane, paper airplane, take off and fly.
(Make airplane arms out to the sides.)

Baby doll, baby doll, start to cry.
(Rub eyes.)

Bulldozer, bulldozer, move dirty earth's crust.
(Push hands away from body.)

Fairy wand, fairy wand, sprinkle me with pixie dust.
(Flutter fingers.)

Special blanket, special blanket, wrap me up so I feel good.
(Hug self.)

Flannel Board

Color teddy bear pattern:

Pieces: Ten teddy bears of three different colors (use Pattern 5.1, p. 38)

Directions: Start a color pattern with the teddy bear pieces. Let the children help finish the pattern. For example: Blue bear, blue bear, green bear, yellow bear, blue bear, blue bear, green bear, yellow bear.

Book #2 *I Know a Rhino* by Charles Fuge

Action Chant

Stuffed Animals

One, two, three, four, five, stuffed animals in a row. *(Show five fingers.)*

One is a bear. *(Use sign language for "bear.")*

One is a dog. *(Use sign language for "dog.")*

One is a pink bunny rabbit that likes to jump. *(Jump.)*

One is an owl. *(Use sign language for "owl.")*

And one is a giraffe with a really long neck.
(Move hands from neck to up high in the air.)

All lined up on my bed, they keep me company as I go to sleep.
(Put hands together on the side of the face.)

Closing Song

Art Experience

Paper bag kite:
1. For each child, tie a length of string or yarn, approximately 30 inches, to two sides of a brown paper bag. The holes in the paper bag may need to be reinforced with cellophane tape so they do not tear.
2. Precut a large supply of crepe paper streamers, approximately one foot long.
3. Invite children to decorate the paper bag by gluing on crepe paper streamers and coloring with color pens.
4. Tie another long length of kite string to the first string to make this a kite that flies (see Figure 45.1).

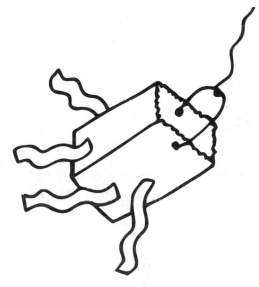

Figure 45.1 **Paper bag kite**

Bonus Storytime Resources

More Books

Baby Danced the Polka by Karen Beaumont, illustrated by Jennifer Plecas (lift-flap)

The Ball Bounced by Nancy Tafuri

Block City by Robert Louis Stevenson, illustrated by Daniel Kirk

Saucepan Game by Jan Ormerod

Wrapping Paper Romp by Patricia Hubbell, illustrated by Jennifer Plecas (board book)

Extra Action Song

Sung to the tune of "Wheels on the Bus"

Dancing Dolly

My dolly can dance all around, all around, all around.
(Spin around.)
My dolly can dance all around, here at storytime.

My dolly can dance on her toes, on her toes, on her toes.
(Walk on tiptoes.)
My dolly can dance on her toes, here at storytime.

My dolly can dance side to side, side to side, side to side.
(Move feet and sway left and then right.)
My dolly can dance side to side, here at storytime.

My dolly can dance up and down, up and down, up and down.
(Move arms up high and then down low.)
My dolly can dance up and down, here at storytime.

My dolly can dance sitting on the ground, on the ground, on the ground.
(Sit on floor.)
My dolly can dance sitting on the ground, here at storytime.

Additional Art Experience

Tangram design:

1. Precut one colorful paper tangram set for each child (use Pattern 45.1).
2. Invite children to glue these shapes onto another piece of white paper in a pretty design.

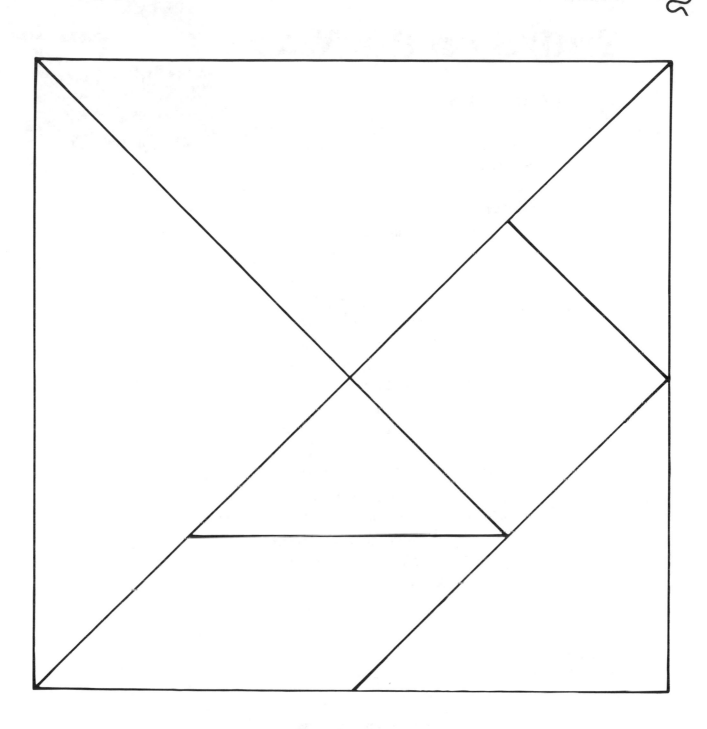

Pattern 45.1 **Tangram pieces**

Trains on the Track

Opening Song and Rhyme

Book #1 *I Love Trains!* by Philemon Sturges, illustrated by Shari Halpern

Stand-Up Activity

Choo Choo Train
(Traditional)

This is a choo-choo train,
(Bend arms at elbows.)

Puffing down the track.
(Rotate forearms in rhythm.)

Now it's going forward,
(Walk forward, continuing arm motion.)

Now it's going back.
(Walk backward, continuing arm motion.)

Now the bell is ringing.
(Pretend to pull a bell cord with a closed fist.)

Now the whistle blows.
(Hold fist near mouth and make "Toot, Toot" sound.)

What a lot of noise it makes.
(Cover ears with hands.)

Everywhere it goes.
(Stretch out arms.)

Flannel Board

Pieces: Train engine, coal car, box car, mail car, caboose
Sung to the tune of "Three Blind Mice"

First Comes the Engine

Choo-choo train, choo-choo train,
Coming down the track, coming down the track.
First comes the engine,
Followed by the coal car,
The box car,
The tanker,
The caboose is last, the caboose is last.

Book #2 *Freight Train* by Donald Crews

Fingerplay

Train Cars in a Row

Ten train cars all in a row.
(Show ten fingers.)

Ten train cars line up on the track, just so.

They travel east.
(Move hands to the right.)

They travel west.
(Move hands to the left.)

They travel north.
(Move hands up.)

And they travel south.
(Move hands down.)

They travel all around,
(Move hands in a circle.)

Up and down.
(Move hands up in the air and then down.)

Always in a row, when they come through town.

Closing Song

Art Experience

Train cars:
1. Precut two colorful paper or cardstock rectangles for each child, approximately three inches by five inches.
2. Give each child two rectangles, a regular size piece of paper, and some wheelie or rotelle pasta.
3. Invite children to glue the rectangles and wheelie pasta pieces onto the regular size paper to create two train cars.

Bonus Storytime Resources

More Books

Clickety Clack by Rob and Amy Spence, illustrated by Margaret Spengler

Dinosaur Train by John Steven Gurney

Terrific Trains by Tony Mitton and Ant Parker

This Train by Paul Collicutt

A Train Goes Clickety-Clack by Jonathan London, illustrated by Denis Roche

Extra Action Chant

Choo-Choo Train Zooming down the Track

Choo-choo train, choo-choo train, go so slow.
(Bend arms at elbows and rotate in a slow circle.)

Choo-choo train, choo-choo train, go so fast.
(Speed up arms a little.)

Choo-choo train, choo-choo train, zooming down the track.
(Speed up arms a little more and run in place.)

Choo-choo train, choo-choo train, slowing down.
(Slow down arms and stop running.)

Choo-choo train, choo-choo train, stopping at a station.
(Stand still.)

Additional Art Experience

Train engine:

1. Precut one black construction paper train engine shape for each child (use Pattern 46.1).
2. Invite children to decorate this train engine with color chalk.

Pattern 46.1 **Train engine**

Under the Sea

Opening Song and Rhyme

Book #1 *Hooray for Fish* by Lucy Cousins

Stand-Up Activity
Sung to the tune of "The Farmer in the Dell"

The Ocean Is a Wonder

The fish are swimming today, the fish are swimming today.
(Pretend to swim.)

The ocean is a wonderful place; the fish are swimming today.

The crabs are snapping today; the crabs are snapping today.
(Snap at the air with crab hands.)

The ocean is a wonderful place; the crabs are snapping today.

The dolphins are jumping today; the dolphins are jumping today.
(Jump.)

The ocean is a wonderful place; the dolphins are jumping today.

The eels are slithering today; the eels are slithering today.
(Put hands and arms together and move them around in a slithering fashion.)

The ocean is a wonderful place; the eels are slithering today.

The sharks are chomping today; the sharks are chomping today.
(Bring arms together in front of body as if they are a large mouth eating something.)

The ocean is a wonderful place; the sharks are chomping today.

The skates are gliding today; the skates are gliding today.
(Walk around with airplane arms out to the sides.)

The ocean is a wonderful place; the skates are gliding today.

The starfish are sitting today; the starfish are sitting today.
(Sit on floor.)

The ocean is a wonderful place; the starfish are sitting today.

Flannel Board

Pieces: Five starfish (use Pattern 47.1)

Five Lovely Starfish

Five lovely starfish sitting on the beach,
Along came a wave and now there are four.
Four lovely starfish sitting on the beach,
Along came a wave and now there are three.
(Count down to zero.)

Book #2 *Fish Wish* by Bob Barner

Action Song

Sung to the tune of "Are You Sleeping?"

Great Big Shark

Great big shark, great big shark,
(Move arms out wide to the sides.)

Swimming through the water, swimming through the water.
(Pretend to swim.)

Looking for lunch, looking for lunch.
(Circle eyes with hands.)

Chomp, chomp, chomp! Chomp, chomp, chomp!
(Bring arms together in front of body as if they are a large mouth eating something.)

Closing Song

Art Experience

Fish scales:

1. Print out the fish shape (use Pattern 47.2).
2. Precut a large supply of colorful tissue paper squares, approximately one inch square.
3. Invite children to add fish scales by gluing the tissue paper squares onto the fish.

Bonus Storytime Resources

More Books

Baby Beluga (Raffi Songs to Read) by Raffi, illustrated by Ashley Wolff

Fish, Fish, Fish by George Adams, illustrated by Brigitte Willgoss

I'm the Biggest Thing in the Ocean by Kevin Sherry

Ten Little Fish by Audrey Wood and Bruce Wood

Way Down Deep in the Deep Blue Sea by Jan Peck, illustrated by Valeria Petrone

Extra Action Song #1

Sung to the tune of "I'm a Little Teapot"

I'm a Whale

I'm a great big whale. *(Point to self.)*

And I can swim. *(Pretend to swim.)*

There is my tail. *(Point behind you.)*

And here's my dorsal fin. *(Place one hand on hip.)*

When I want to show off with my friend,

I jump into the air, *(Jump.)*

And wiggle my rear end. *(Wiggle bottom.)*

Extra Action Song #2

"Goldfish" action song from *Victor Vito* by Laurie Berkner

Additional Art Experiences

Jellyfish:

1. Cut a paper plate in half.
2. Precut a supply of crepe paper or tissue paper streamers, approximately one foot long.
3. Give each child one half of a paper plate and some colorful streamers.
4. Invite children to glue the streamers onto the straight edge of the half plate to create tentacles for the jellyfish (see Figure 47.1).

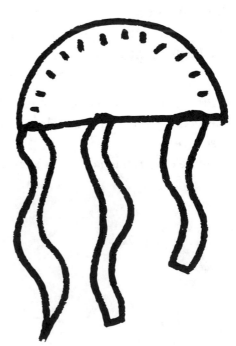

Figure 47.1 **Jellyfish**

Starfish:

1. Print out the starfish shape (use Pattern 47.1).
2. Invite children to decorate the starfish with star stickers and crayons.

Pattern 47.1 **Starfish**

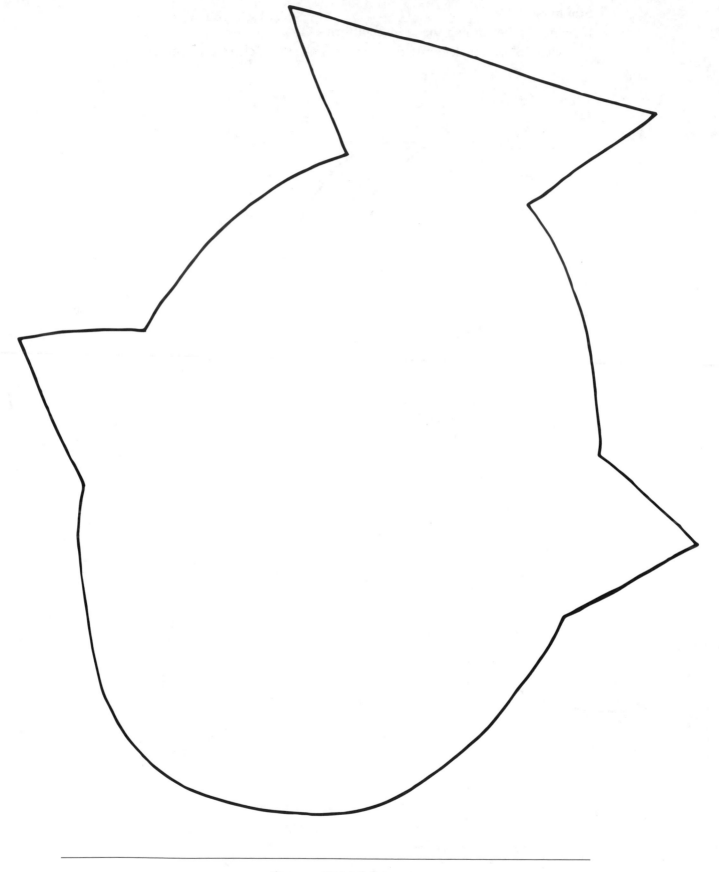

Pattern 47.2 **Fish**

Valentine Hugs and Kisses

Opening Song and Rhyme

Book #1 *Snappy Little Hugs* by Dugald Steer, illustrated by Derek Matthews (pop-up)

Stand-Up Activity

Sung to the tune of "Jingle Bells"

Valentine's Day Is Here to Stay

Hug a friend, hug a friend, hug a friend today. (*Hug self.*)

Valentine's Day is here to stay. Let's celebrate all day!

Blow a kiss, blow a kiss, blow a kiss today. (*Blow kisses.*)

Valentine's Day is here to stay. Let's celebrate all day!

Jump around, jump around, jump around today. (*Jump.*)

Valentine's Day is here to stay. Let's celebrate all day!

Dance and clap, dance and clap, dance and clap today.
(*Dance around and clap hands.*)

Valentine's Day is here to stay. Let's celebrate all day!

Flannel Board

Pieces: Eight Valentine's Day cards

Eight Valentine Cards

Eight little valentine cards I bought at the store.

I gave one to my mother.

I gave one to my grandma.

Now I have six cards for me to sort.

One is for my sister.

And one is for my cat.

One is for my Uncle Paul who likes to play ball.

That leaves three more cards for me to give.

I can't forget my brother.

And I can't forget my father.

My teacher also needs one because she is as busy as a beaver.

Now my valentines are gone. There are no more for me to give.

I wonder how many I will get from all my family and friends.

Book #2 *Where Is Baby's Valentine?* by Karen Katz (lift-flap board book)

Action Rhyme

Valentine, Valentine

(Suit actions to words.)

Valentine, valentine, turn around.
Valentine, valentine, touch the ground.
Valentine, valentine, blow a kiss.
Valentine, valentine, swim like a fish.
Valentine, valentine, give a hug.
Valentine, valentine, jump like a bug.
Valentine, valentine, find your feet.
Valentine, valentine, take your seat.

Closing Song

Art Experience

Valentine heart:
1. Precut one large colorful heart for each child (use Pattern 48.1).
2. Invite children to decorate this heart by gluing on small foam hearts or candy conversation hearts.

Bonus Storytime Resources

More Books

Be Mine, Be Mine, Sweet Valentine by Sarah Weeks, illustrated by Fumi Kosaka
How About a Kiss for Me? by Todd Tarpley, illustrated by Liza Woodruff
Kiss Kiss! by Margaret Wild and Bridget Strevens-Marzo
Lilly's Chocolate Heart by Kevin Henkes
My Heart Is Like a Zoo by Michael Hall

Extra Action Chant

Put Your Valentine on Your Nose

Put your valentine on your nose, on your nose.
(Touch nose.)

Put your valentine on your nose, on your nose.

It's a heart for love and friendship,
(Use sign language for "friend.")

A hug for everyone.
(Hug self.)

Put your valentine on your nose, on your nose.
(Touch nose.)

Put your valentine on your toes, on your toes.
(Touch toes.)

Put your valentine on your toes, on your toes.

It's a heart for love and friendship,
(Use sign language for "friend.")

A hug for everyone.
(Hug self.)

Put your valentine on your toes, on your toes.
(Touch toes.)

Put your valentine on your head, on your head.
(Touch head.)

Put your valentine on your head, on your head.

It's a heart for love and friendship,
(Use sign language for "friend.")

A hug for everyone.
(Hug self.)

Put your valentine on your head, on your head.
(Touch head.)

(Repeat with more body parts, such as arm, shoulder, tummy, etc.)

Additional Art Experience

Valentine's Day greeting card:
1. Print off the Valentine's Day greeting card (use Pattern 48.2).
2. Invite children to decorate this greeting card with thumbprints for a personal valentine touch.

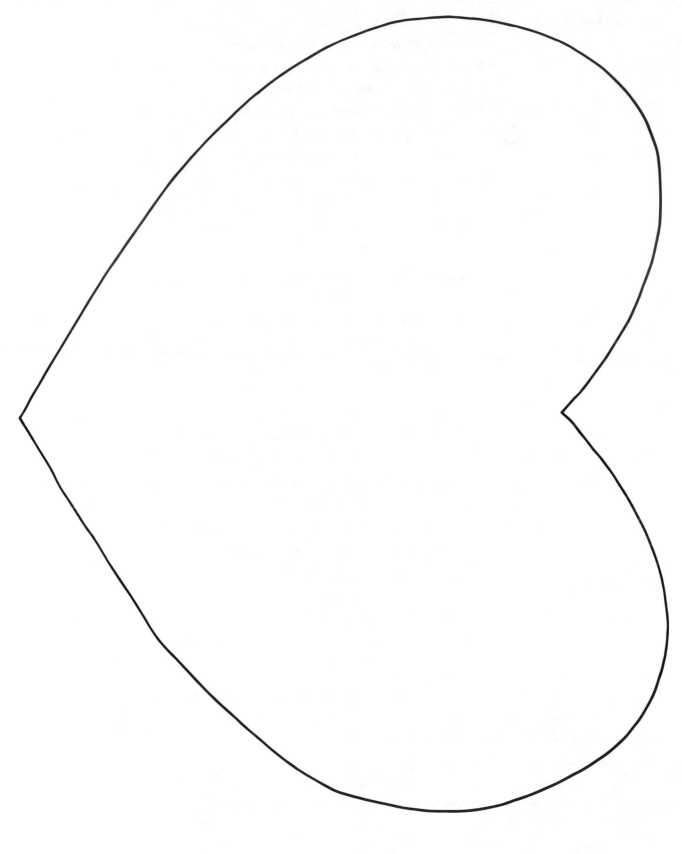

Pattern 48.1 **Valentine heart**

Pattern 48.2 **Valentine's Day greeting card**

Weather

Opening Song and Rhyme

Book #1 *Kite Flying* by Grace Lin

Stand-Up Activity
Sung to the tune of "Farmer in the Dell"

Weather Goes Drifting

A cloud goes drifting by, a cloud goes drifting by.
(Cup hands together up high and move from left to right.)

What will the weather bring us today? A cloud goes drifting by.

The rain comes falling down, the rain comes falling down.
(Flutter fingers.)

What will the weather bring us today? The rain comes falling down.

The wind starts to blow, the wind starts to blow.
(Sway back and forth.)

What will the weather bring us today? The wind starts to blow.

The sun shines bright and hot, the sun shines bright and hot.
(Form circle over head with arms.)

What will the weather bring us today? The sun shines bright and hot.

Flannel Board
Pieces: Five kites

Five Beautiful Kites

Five beautiful kites flying high in the sky.

Along came a big gust of wind,

And whooooosh, *(Loudly blow air out of mouth.)*

One of the kites flies away.

Four beautiful kites flying high in the sky.

Along came a big gust of wind,

And whooooosh, *(Loudly blow air out of mouth.)*

One of the kites flies away.

(Continue counting down to zero kites.)

Book #2 *Kipper's Rainy Day* by Mick Inkpen (lift-flap)

Action Song

Sung to the tune of "Sing a Song of Sixpence"

Puddle Jump

Pitter patter raindrops falling on the ground. *(Flutter fingers down.)*

Pitter patter raindrops falling on my head. *(Point to head.)*

Up goes my umbrella, *(Pretend to open an umbrella.)*

As I begin to stomp. *(Stomp.)*

I love to go puddle jumping on any rainy day. *(Jump.)*

Closing Song

Art Experience

Fluffy clouds:

1. Print out the cloud drawing on blue paper (use Pattern 49.2).
2. Invite children to glue cotton balls onto the paper to make fluffy clouds.

Bonus Storytime Resources

More Books

The Big Storm: A Very Soggy Counting Book by Nancy Tafuri

It Looked Like Spilt Milk by Charles G. Shaw

Like a Windy Day by Frank Asch and Devin Asch

Little Cloud by Eric Carle

Raindrop, Plop! by Wendy Cheyette Lewison, illustrated by Pam Paparone

Extra Action Song

Sung to the tune of "Did You Ever See a Lassie?"

Did You See the Wind Blow?

Did you ever see the wind blow, the wind blow, the wind blow?
(Sway from side to side.)

Did you ever see the wind blow, blow all-all around?
(Spin around with arms out.)

It blows this way up high,
(Move arms up high to the right.)

And that way down low.
(Move arms down low to the left.)

Did you ever see the wind blow, blow this way and that?
(Sway from side to side.)

Additional Art Experience

Umbrella in the rain:

1. Print out the umbrella drawing on colorful paper (use Pattern 49.1).
2. Invite children to add raindrops around the umbrella by using a Q-tip dipped in blue paint.

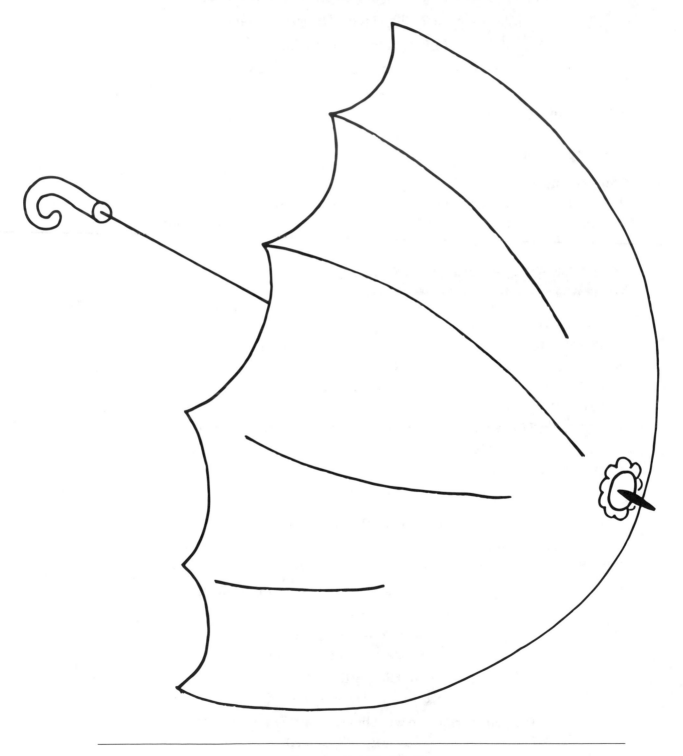

Pattern 49.1 **Umbrella**

Pattern 49.2 **Fluffy cloud**

Wheels on the Road

Opening Song and Rhyme

Book #1 *My Car* by Byron Barton

Stand-Up Activity

I See a Traffic Light

I see a traffic light,
(Circle eyes with fingers.)

Standing tall and straight.
(Stand tall with arms down to the sides.)

When the light turns to red,
(Use sign language for "red.")

All the cars go stop.
(Put hand out for stop.)

When the light turns yellow,
(Use sign language for "yellow.")

All the cars go slow.
(Use sign language for "slow.")

When the light turns green,
(Use sign language for "green.")

All the cars go, go, go!
(Roll hands over each other.)

Flannel Board

Pieces: Yellow bus, motorcycle, blue truck, red car, pink scooter white van, and other vehicles

Sung to the tune of "Mary Had a Little Lamb"

I Want To Ride

I want to ride on your yellow bus, your yellow bus, your yellow bus,
I want to ride on your yellow bus. I want to ride today.
I want to ride on your motorcycle, your motorcycle, your motorcycle,
I want to ride on your motorcycle. I want to ride today.

(Repeat with more vehicles, such as blue truck, red car, pink scooter, white van, etc.)

Book #2 *Truck Duck* by Michael Rex

Action Song
Favorite source: Rise and Shine by Raffi

Wheels on the Bus
(Traditional)

The wheels on the bus go round and round, round and round, round and round.
(Roll hands over each other.)

The wheels on the bus go round and round, all over town.

The wipers on the bus go swish, swish, swish, swish, swish, swish,
swish, swish, swish.
(Move arms back and forth for windshield wipers.)

The wipers on the bus go swish, swish, swish, all over town.

The lights on the bus go blink, blink, blink, blink, blink, blink, blink, blink, blink.
(Open and shut hands.)

The lights on the bus go blink, blink, blink, all over town.

The doors on the bus go open and shut, open and shut, open and shut.
(Move arms to open and shut positions.)

The doors on the bus go open and shut, all over town.

The driver on the bus says move on back, move on back, move on back.
(Point thumb behind you.)

The driver on the bus says move on back, all over town.

The people on the bus go up and down, up and down, up and down.
(Move arms up and down.)

The people on the bus go up and down, all over town.

Closing Song

Art Experience

Graham cracker traffic light:
1. Give each child one graham cracker, a dollop of white frosting or cream cheese, a plastic knife or craft stick to spread the frosting, one red M&M candy, one yellow M&M candy, and one green M&M candy.
2. Invite children to spread the frosting onto the graham cracker and then arrange the candy to resemble a traffic light (see Figure 50.1).

Figure 50.1 **Graham cracker traffic light**

Bonus Storytime Resources

More Books

The Bridge Is Up by Babs Bell, illustrated by Rob Hefferan

Maisy Drives the Bus by Lucy Cousins

Toot Toot Beep Beep by Emma Garcia

Truck Jam by Paul Stickland (pop-up)

Wheels on the Race Car by Alexander Zane, illustrated by James Warhola

Extra Fingerplay

I'm a Little Piece of Tin

(Traditional)

I'm a little piece of tin. *(Point to self.)*

Nobody knows what shape I'm in. *(Shake head.)*

Got four wheels, *(Show four fingers.)*

And a runnin' board, *(Wave arm in front of body.)*

I'm a four-door, I'm a Ford!

Honk, honk, *(Push nose twice.)*

Rattle, rattle, *(Roll hands over each other.)*

Crash, *(Slap legs with both hands.)*

Beep, beep. *(Clap twice.)*

Honk, honk, *(Push nose twice.)*

Rattle, rattle, *(Roll hands over each other.)*

Crash, *(Slap legs with both hands.)*

Beep, beep, *(Clap twice.)*

Honk, honk! *(Push nose twice.)*

Additional Art Experiences

Paper plate steering wheel:

1. Precut three holes in a paper plate to form a steering wheel.
2. Precut a construction paper circle to be the horn of the steering wheel.
3. Invite children to glue on the horn and then decorate the steering wheel with crayons (see Figure 50.2).

Figure 50.2 **Paper plate steering wheel**

Tire track painting:

1. Hand each child one regular piece of white paper and one small toy car.
2. Invite children to dip the wheels of the toy car into a thin layer of paint and then drive the car over the paper.

Wild Animals

Opening Song and Rhyme

Book #1 *The Loudest Roar* by Thomas Taylor

Stand-Up Activity

Going on a Hike

I was going for a hike one day. During my walk, I saw lots of animals.
(Walk in place.)

I saw a bear eating some berries.
(Use sign language for "bear.")

I saw an eagle flying over the lake.
(Flap arms as wings straight out to the sides.)

I saw a mouse scurry across the path.
(Run in place.)

I saw a beaver building a dam.
(Use sign language for "beaver.")

But as soon as I saw the skunk,
(Use sign language for "skunk.")

I walked away!
(Walk in place holding nose.)

Flannel Board

Pieces: Five monkeys

Five Little Monkeys Swinging from the Tree
(Traditional)

Five little monkeys swinging in a tree.
Teasing Mr. Alligator, "Can't catch me. Can't catch me."
Along came Mr. Alligator quiet as can be,
And snapped one monkey out of that tree.

Four little monkeys swinging in a tree.
Teasing Mr. Alligator, "Can't catch me. Can't catch me."
Along came Mr. Alligator quiet as can be,
And snapped one monkey out of that tree.

(Continue counting down to zero monkeys.)

Book #2 *Ziggy the Zebra* by Libby Ellis, illustrated by Salina Yoon (pop-up)

Action Chant

Great to Be Wild and Free
(Suit actions to words.)

I'm running with the zebras. I'm running with the zebras.
Isn't it great to be wild and free? I'm running with the zebras.
I'm slithering with the snakes. I'm slithering with the snakes.
Isn't it great to be wild and free? I'm slithering with the snakes.
I'm howling with the wolves. I'm howling with the wolves.
Isn't it great to be wild and free? I'm howling with the wolves.
I'm chomping with the crocs. I'm chomping with the crocs.
Isn't it great to be wild and free? I'm chomping with the crocs.

(Repeat with more animal action words, such as flying with the eagles, waddling like a porcupine, scurrying like a lizard, etc.)

Closing Song

Art Experience

Stripes on a zebra:
1. Print out the zebra shape (use Pattern 51.1).
2. Precut a large supply of thin black construction paper stripes, approximately ¼ inch by 3 inches.
3. Invite children to glue the black stripes onto the zebra shape to make a one-of-a-kind zebra.

Bonus Storytime Resources

More Books

Jazzy in the Jungle by Lucy Cousins
Over in the Grasslands by Anna Wilson and Alison Bartlett
Panda Bear, Panda Bear, What Do You See? by Bill Martin Jr. and Eric Carle
Simms Taback's City Animals by Simms Taback
Snappy Little Jungle by Dugald Steer, illustrated by Derek Matthews (pop-up)

Extra Action Rhyme

Sung to the tune of "Three Blind Mice"

I'm a Tiger

I'm a tiger. I'm a tiger.
(Use sign language for "tiger.")

Hear me roar. Hear me roar.
(Roar.)

I love to sleep up high in a tree.
(Put hands together on the side of the face.)

And jump at all the other animals.
(Jump.)

In all the jungle I'm number one.
(Show one finger.)

I'm a tiger,
(Use sign language for "tiger.")

Hear me roar!
(Roar.)

Additional Art Experiences

Elephant finger puppet:

1. Precut one finger puppet for each child (use Pattern 51.2). Don't forget to cut out the nose hole.
2. Invite children to decorate their elephant with color pens or crayons.

Lion mane:

1. Print out the lion face drawing (use Pattern 51.3).
2. Invite children to decorate the lion's mane with paint.

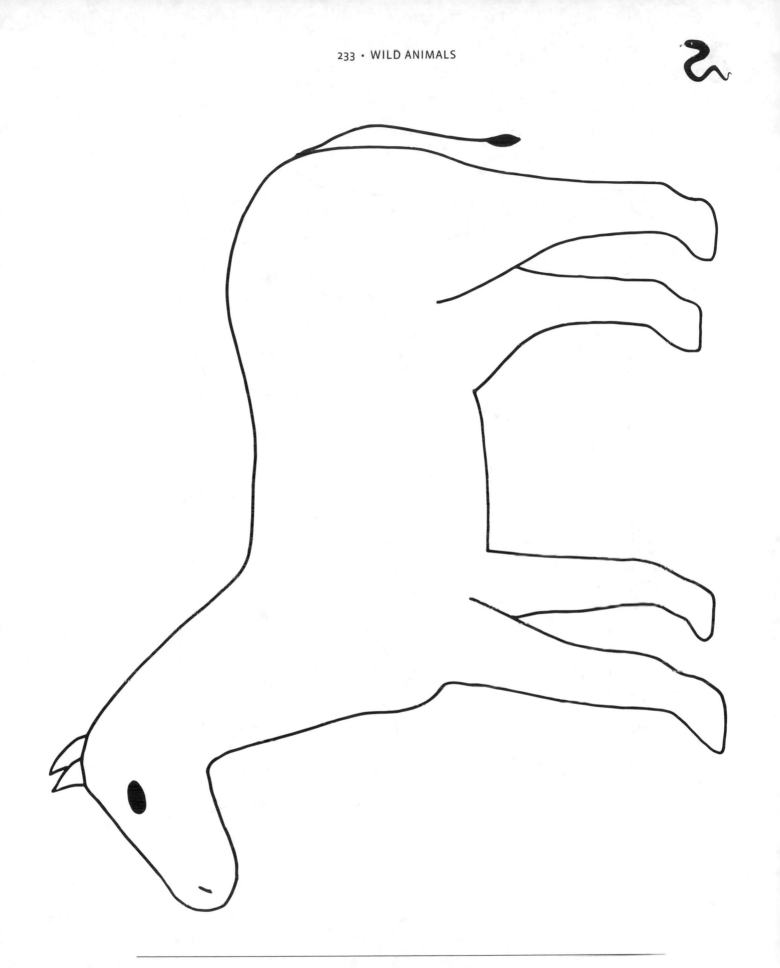

Pattern 51.1 **Zebra shape**

Pattern 51.2 **Elephant finger puppets**

Pattern 51.3 **Lion mane**

Winter Snow

Opening Song and Rhyme

Book #1 *Cleo in the Snow* by Caroline Mockford

Stand-Up Activity
Sung to the tune of "Here We Go 'Round the Mulberry Bush"

This Is the Way We Play in the Snow
(Suit actions to words.)

This is the way we stomp through the snow,
stomp through the snow,
stomp through the snow.
This is the way we stomp through the snow,
when we go out to play.

This is the way we hop through the snow,
hop through the snow,
hop through the snow.
This is the way we hop through the snow,
when we go out to play.

This is the way we spin through the snow,
spin through the snow,
spin through the snow.
This is the way we spin through the snow,
when we go out to play.

This is the way we crawl through the snow,
crawl through the snow,
crawl through the snow.
This is the way we crawl through the snow,
when we go out to play.

This is the way we sit in the snow,
sit in the snow,
sit in the snow.
This is the way we sit in the snow,
when we go out to play.

Flannel Board

Pieces: Five snowmen (use Pattern 52.1)

Five Little Snowmen

Five little snowmen standing in a row.
Five little snowmen all made with love.

The first one said, "I'm off to find a freezer so I won't melt when the sun comes out."
The second one said, "I'm going sledding with those kids over there."
The third one said, "I'm going to learn how to ski today."
The fourth one said, "I'm off to the nearest ice skating rink to practice my jumps and twirls."
The fifth one said, "I know there is a hockey stick calling for me."

Now there are zero snowmen standing in a row.

Book #2 *Max and Ruby's Snowy Day* by Rosemary Wells (board book)

Action Song

Sung to the tune of "Are You Sleeping?"

Make Some Snowballs

Snow is falling, snow is falling,
(Flutter fingers down.)

All around, all around.
(Spin around.)

Come let's make some snowballs. Come let's make some snowballs.
(Pretend to make a snowball with hands.)

Throw them here. Throw them there.
(Pretend to throw.)

Closing Song

Art Experience

Snow scene:
1. Give each child a sheet of dark blue construction paper, one Q-tip, and some white paint.
2. Invite children to paint with the Q-tip to make a unique snow scene.

Bonus Storytime Resources

More Books

Downhill Fun: A Counting Book about Winter by Michael Dahl, illustrated by Todd Ouren

Mouse's First Snow by Lauren Thompson, illustrated by Buket Erdogan

Snow by Manya Stojic

Snow! Snow! Snow! by Lee Harper

Snowballs by Lois Ehlert

Extra Action Chant

Dance Little Snowflake

Dance little snowflake. Dance little snowflake.
(Dance.)

Dance around the town.
(Spin around.)

Dance upon your tiptoes.
(Walk on tiptoes.)

Dance from side to side.
(Sway side to side.)

Twirling up and down, twirling up and down,
(Move arms high up and down low.)

While you dance around the town.
(Spin around.)

Additional Art Experience

Snowman stick puppet:

1. Precut one snowman for each child (use Pattern 52.1).
2. Glue or tape a craft stick to each snowman.
3. Invite children to glue cotton balls onto their snowman stick puppet.

Pattern 52.1 **Snowman stick puppets**

about the author

Carol Garnett Hopkins is a children's librarian at a stand-alone municipal library in western Washington. She is a Jill-of-all-trades around the library, but her specialties include toddler storytimes, programming for children, ordering children's books and movies, plus matching Accelerated Reader books with young readers. In her spare time, she plays video games, reads manga, and digs in her garden. She lives in Puyallup (pronounced Pew-all-up) with her husband and son, as well as two cats and a large garden, which is in desperate need of more attention.

index

A

Aaaarrgghh! Spider! (Monks), 190
Acorns Everywhere (Sherry), 25
action chant/song/rhyme
    Apple Munching theme, 18
    Autumn theme, 25, 26
    Aviation theme, 29, 30
    Bath Time Bubbles theme, 33, 34
    Bears theme, 37
    Berry Delicious theme, 40–41
    Birds of a Feather theme, 46
    Boats in the Water theme, 49
    Bugs and Other Creepy Crawlies theme, 54
    Cats and Kittens theme, 59
    Chickens theme, 62
    Clothing and Hats theme, 65–66
    Colors and Patterns theme, 68–69
    Community Workers theme, 73, 74
    Construction Site theme, 77, 78
    Cool Pool of Water theme, 81, 82
    Counting theme, 86
    Dinosaurs theme, 87, 88
    Dogs and Puppies theme, 93
    Farm Animals theme, 95, 96
    Fire Trucks and Firefighters theme, 100, 101
    Flowers and Gardens theme, 106
    Food, Yummy Food theme, 108, 109

action chant/song/rhyme (*cont'd*)
    Frogs and Toads theme, 114, 115
    Garbage and Recycling theme, 119
    Gingerbread and Other Cookies theme, 124, 125
    Green for St. Patrick's Day theme, 129–130
    Halloween theme, 133
    Lunar New Year theme, 137–138, 139
    Monsters theme, 142, 143
    Music and Movement theme, 148
    My Body and Me theme, 151
    Nocturnal Animals theme, 160, 161
    Opposites theme, 164
    Pet Parade theme, 167–169
    Pirate Treasure theme, 173, 174
    Rabbits and Bunnies theme, 178
    Royalty theme, 183
    Under the Sea theme, 213, 214
    Silly Fun theme, 187
    Springtime theme, 193
    Summer in the Sun theme, 195, 196
    Thanksgiving Turkeys theme, 200, 201
    Toys theme, 205, 206
    Trains on the Track theme, 210
    Valentine Hugs and Kisses theme, 218, 219
    Weather theme, 223
    Wild Animals theme, 231, 232
    Winter Snow theme, 236, 237

Adams, George, 214
Air Show (Suen), 29
Alborough, Jez, 65
All for Pie, Pie for All (Martin), 41
All My Little Ducklings (Wellington), 46
Allen, Joy, 183
Along Came Toto (Axworthy), 92
aluminum foil, 4
American Sign Language (ASL) dictionary, 13
Appelt, Kathi, 33
Apple, Margot, 173
Apple Farmer Annie (Wellington), 19
Apple Munching theme, 18–23
Apple Pie Tree (Hall), 18
Apples! Apples! (Yoon), 18
Arnold, Tedd, 141, 190
Arnosky, Jim, 25
art, craft vs., 1–2
art and craft activities
    learning opportunities through, xi
    as open-ended art experiences, xii
    reasons for, xii–xiv
    See also toddler art fundamentals
art experience
    Apple Munching theme, 19
    Autumn theme, 25, 26
    Aviation theme, 29, 30
    Bath Time Bubbles theme, 33, 34
    Bears theme, 37, 38
    Berry Delicious theme, 41
    Birds of a Feather theme, 45, 46
    Boats in the Water theme, 49, 50
    Bugs and Other Creepy Crawlies theme,
        54, 55
    Cats and Kittens theme, 58, 59
    Chickens theme, 62, 63
    Clothing and Hats theme, 66, 67
    Colors and Patterns theme, 68, 70
    Community Workers theme, 73, 74
    Construction Site theme, 77, 78
    Cool Pool of Water theme, 81, 82
    Counting theme, 85, 86
    Dinosaurs theme, 88, 89
    Dogs and Puppies theme, 92, 93
    Farm Animals theme, 95, 96
    Fire Trucks and Firefighters theme, 100–
        101, 102
    Flowers and Gardens theme, 105, 106
    Food, Yummy Food theme, 108, 109
    Frogs and Toads theme, 115
    Garbage and Recycling theme, 119, 120
    Gingerbread and Other Cookies theme, 125
    Green for St. Patrick's Day theme, 129

art experience *(cont'd)*
    Halloween theme, 133, 134
    Lunar New Year theme, 138, 139
    mediums, use of different, 2–3
    Monsters theme, 143
    Music and Movement theme, 148, 149
    My Body and Me theme, 151, 152
    Nighttime theme, 155, 156
    Nocturnal Animals theme, 160, 161
    Opposites theme, 164, 165
    Pet Parade theme, 168, 169
    Pirate Treasure theme, 173, 174
    Rabbits and Bunnies theme, 177, 178
    Royalty theme, 182, 183
    Under the Sea theme, 213, 214–215
    Silly Fun theme, 186, 187
    Spiders theme, 189, 190
    Springtime theme, 192, 193
    in storytime routine, 14
    Summer in the Sun theme, 195, 196
    Thanksgiving Turkeys theme, 200, 201
    Toys theme, 205, 206
    Trains on the Track theme, 209, 210
    Valentine Hugs and Kisses theme, 218, 219
    Weather theme, 223, 224
    Wheels on the Road theme, 227–228, 229
    Wild Animals theme, 231, 232
    Winter Snow theme, 236, 237
art supplies
    cost-saving measures, 3–4
    list of, 4–9
"Artsy Helper Sheets," xiv
artsy storytime program
    routine of, 11
    routine steps, 12–14
    storytime themes, 14
    tips for working with toddlers at storytime,
        14–15
Artsy Toddler Storytimes (Hopkins)
    art and craft activities, reasons for, xii–xiv
    goal of, xi
    how to use, xii
Asch, Devin, 223
Asch, Frank, 223
Autumn theme, 24–27
Aviation theme, 28–31
Axworthy, Ann, 92

B

Baby Bat's Lullaby (Mitchard), 160
Baby Beluga (Raffi Songs to Read) (Raffi), 214
Baby Danced the Polka (Beaumont), 206
Bad Frogs (Hurd), 115

Baker, Keith, 61, 129
baking cups, 4
Ball Bounced, The (Tafuri), 206
Bark, George (Feiffer), 91
Barner, Bob
   Big Is Big (and Little, Little): A Book of Contrasts, 164
   Bugs, Bugs, Bugs!, 53
   Dinosaur Bones, 88
   Fish Wish, 213
Barnyard Banter (Fleming), 94
Bartlett, Alison, 231
Barton, Byron
   Boats, 49
   Dinosaurs, Dinosaurs, 88
   Jump Frog Jump, 115
   Machines at Work, 77
   My Car, 226
Bath Time (Spinelli), 33
Be Mine, Be Mine, Sweet Valentine (Weeks), 218
Beach Day (Roosa), 195
Beall, Pamela Conn, 147
Bear Wants More (Wilson), 41
Bears on Chairs (Parenteau), 37
Beaumont, Karen, 124, 206
Bee-Bim Bop! (Park), 139
Bell, Babs, 228
Benson, Patrick, 159
Berkner, Laurie
   "Airplane" song, 30
   "I Know a Chicken" song, 13, 62
   "Monster Boogie" song, 143
   Victor Vito, 214
   "We Are the Dinosaurs" song, 88
Best of the Laurie Berkner Band (Berkner), 13
Big Earth, Little Me (Wiley), 119
Big Fat Hen (Baker), 61
Big Is Big (and Little, Little): A Book of Contrasts (Lewis), 164
Big Machines! Big Buildings! (Lewis), 77
Big Red Tub (Jarman), 32
Big Smelly Bear (Teckentrup), 33
Big Storm: A Very Soggy Counting Book, The (Tafuri), 223
bingo bottle paints, 4
Birds (Henkes), 44
Birds of a Feather theme, 44–47
Biscuit and the Bunny (Capucilli), 177
Biscuit Is Thankful (Capucilli), 199
Biscuit Visits the Pumpkin Patch (Capucilli), 134
Bitterman, Albert, 139
Blackberry Banquet (Pierce), 41

Blackstone, Stella, 28
Block City (Stevenson), 206
Bluemle, Elizabeth, 148
Boats (Barton), 49
Boats (Rockwell), 48
Boats for Bedtime (Litowinsky), 49
Boats in the Water theme, 48–51
Bond, Felicia, 148
book #1, in storytime routine, 12
book #2, in storytime routine, 13
Brandenberg, Alexa, 74
Bridge Is Up, The (Bell), 228
Bringing in the New Year (Lin), 139
Brooks, Karen Stormer, 62
Brown, Craig, 192
Brown, Marc, 148
Brown, Ruth, 113
Brown Bear, Brown Bear What Do You See? (Martin & Carle), 36
Bubble Bath Pirates! (Krosoczka), 172
Bubbles, Bubbles (Appelt), 33
Buck, Dennis, 13, 155
Bugs, Bugs, Bugs! (Barner), 53
Bugs and Other Creepy Crawlies theme, 52–56
Bugs at Work (Carter), 74
Buller, Jon, 187
Bunnies on the Go: Getting from Place to Place (Walton), 177
Bunny, Bunny (Hall), 177
Bunny and Me (Greenspun & Schwarz), 176
Bunting, Eve, 62
Busy Little Squirrel (Tafuri), 25
Butterfly, Butterfly: A Book of Colors (Horáček), 54
Butterworth, Nick, 105
buttons, 4
Buzz Buzz (Berkner), 143

C

Cabrera, Jane
   Cat's Colors, 70
   Dog's Day, 92
   Kitty's Cuddles, 58
   Ten in the Bed, 156
Campbell, Rod, 167
Can You Moo? (Wojtowycz), 95
Capucilli, Alyssa Satin, 134, 177, 199
Car Songs: Songs to Sing Anywhere (Buck), 13, 155
cardstock, 4
Carle, Eric
   Brown Bear, Brown Bear What Do You See?, 36

Carle, Eric (*cont'd*)
    From Head to Toe, 152
    Little Cloud, 223
    1, 2, 3 to the Zoo: A Counting Book, 85
    Panda Bear, Panda Bear, What Do You See?, 231
    Papa, Please Get the Moon for Me, 156
    Very Busy Spider, 188
    Very Quiet Cricket, 52
Carr, Jan, 193
Carrot Seed, The (Krauss), 106
Carter, David A., 74
Cartwright, Reg, 77
Casanova, Mary, 49
Catalanotto, Peter, 74
Catrow, David, 168
Cats and Kittens theme, 57–60
Cat's Colors (Cabrera), 70
Cats Sleep Anywhere (Farjeon), 57
Cecile, Randy, 148
Cedarmount Kids, 148
chalk, 4–5
chant
    See action chant/song/rhyme
Charlie Chick (Denchfield & Parker), 61
Chick: A Pop-Up Book (Vere), 62
Chickens theme, 61–64
Chodos-Irvine, Margaret, 66
Church, Caroline Jayne, 19
Cimarusti, Marie Torres, 168
"Clap Your Hands" (song), 148
Claude Has a Picnic (Gackenbach), 195
Clemesha, David, 119
Cleo in the Snow (Mockford), 236
Clickety Clack (Spence), 210
closing, in storytime routine, 13–14
cloth, 5
Clothesline (Alborough), 65
Clothing and Hats theme, 65–67
coffee filters, 5
Cohen, Jan Barger, 139
Collicutt, Paul, 29
color pens, 5
coloring, with different mediums, 3
coloring sheets, 10
Colors and Patterns theme, 68–71
Come Here, Cleo! (Mockford), 58
Community Workers theme, 72–75
Compost! Growing Gardens from Your Garbage (Glaser), 119
Conrad, Liz, 200
Construction Countdown (Olson), 77
construction paper, 5

Construction Site theme, 76–79
Cookie Count: A Tasty Pop-Up (Sabuda), 124
Cookie's Week (Ward & DePaola), 57
Cordell, Matthew, 115
cost, of art supplies, 3–4
cotton balls, 5
cotton fiberfill, 5
Count! (Fleming), 85
Counting Kisses (Katz), 85
Counting Pets by Twos (Davis), 168
Counting theme, 84–86
Cousins, Lucy
    Hooray for Fish, 212
    Jazzy in the Jungle, 231
    Maisy at the Farm, 62
    Maisy Big, Maisy Small: A Book of Maisy Opposites, 163
    Maisy Drives the Bus, 228
    Maisy Goes to the Playground: A Maisy Lift-the-Flap Classic, 195
    Maisy Makes Gingerbread, 124
    Maisy Takes a Bath, 32
    Maisy's Fire Engine, 100
    Maisy's Halloween, 134
    Maisy's Pirate Treasure Hunt, 173
    Maisy's Pool, 80
    Maisy's Rainbow, 70
    Sweet Dreams, Maisy, 154
    What Can Rabbit Hear?, 150
    What Can Rabbit See?, 177
Cow Loves Cookies, The (Wilson), 123
Coward, Fiona, 164
Coyle, Carmela LaVigna, 183
craft, art vs., 1–2
craft foam shapes, 5
craft sticks/popsicle sticks, 5
Craig, Lindsey, 148
Cravath, Lynne, 200
crayons, 5–6
Crebbin, June, 143
crepe paper streamers, 6
Crews, Donald
    Flying, 28
    Freight Train, 209
    Harbor, 49
    Ten Black Dots, 84
Crowley, Joy, 33

D
dabber dot markers, 4
Dahl, Michael, 77, 237
Dancing Feet (Craig), 148
Davis, Nancy, 164

Davis, Rebecca Fjelland, 168
Day, Nancy Raines, 58
Dear Zoo: A Pop-Up Book (Campbell), 167
Degan, Bruce, 40
Denchfield, Nick, 61
DePaola, Tomie, 57
"Did You Ever See a Lassie?" (song), 14
Dinosaur Bones (Barner), 88
Dinosaur Roar! (Stickland), 163
Dinosaur Stomp! A Monster Pop-Up Book
　　(Stickland), 87
Dinosaur Train (Gurney), 88, 210
Dinosaurs, Dinosaurs (Barton), 88
Dinosaurs theme, 87–90
Dinosaurumpus (Mitton), 88
DiPucchio, Kelly S., 46
directions, xiii
Do Pirates Take Baths? (Tucker), 173
Do Princesses Wear Hiking Boots? (Coyle), 183
Dodd, Emma
　　Dog's Colorful Day: A Messy Story about
　　　Colors and Counting, 70
　　I Don't Want a Cool Cat!, 58
　　What Pet to Get?, 166
Dogs (Gravett), 91
Dogs and Puppies theme, 91–93
Dog's Colorful Day: A Messy Story about Colors
　　and Counting (Dodd), 70
Dog's Day (Cabrera), 92
Dogzilla (Pilkey), 143
donations, of art supplies, 3, 4
Donohue, Dorothy, 193
Don't Take Your Snake for a Stroll (Ireland), 168
Down by the Bay (Raffi Songs to Read) (Raffi),
　　187
Down by the Cool of the Pool (Mitton), 80
Downey, Lisa, 41
Downhill Fun: A Counting Book about Winter
　　(Dahl), 237
Downing, Johnette, 14
"Drive the Fire Truck" (song), 101
Dronzek, Laura, 44

E

Earth Book, The (Parr), 119
Eco People on the Go! (Gerardi), 118
Ehlert, Lois
　　Feathers for Lunch, 44
　　Growing Vegetable Soup, 106
　　Leaf Man, 25
　　Pie in the Sky, 41
　　Rrralph, 92
　　Snowballs, 237

Eight Silly Monkeys (Haskamp), 187
Ella Sarah Gets Dressed (Chodos-Irvine), 66
Ellis, Libby, 231
Elmer's glue, 8
Emberley, Ed, 141, 143
Emily Loves to Bounce (King), 148
Endle, Kate, 119
Erdogan, Buket
　　Mouse's First Fall, 25
　　Mouse's First Snow, 237
　　Mouse's First Spring, 193
Ericsson, Jennifer A., 70
Ernst, Lisa Campbell, 193
Every Autumn Comes the Bear (Arnosky), 25
eye and hand coordination, xiii

F

Falling for Rapunzel (Wilcox), 183
Farjeon, Eleanor, 57
Farm Animals theme, 94–98
Faulkner, Keith, 115
feathers, 6
Feathers for Lunch (Ehlert), 44
Feiffer, Jules, 91
felt, 6
fingerplay
　　Apple Munching theme, 19
　　Birds of a Feather theme, 45
　　Boats in the Water theme, 50
　　Cats and Kittens theme, 58
　　Chickens theme, 61–62
　　Colors and Patterns theme, 70
　　Counting theme, 84–85, 86
　　Dogs and Puppies theme, 92
　　Flowers and Gardens theme, 105
　　Food, Yummy Food theme, 108
　　Garbage and Recycling theme, 120
　　Green for St. Patrick's Day theme, 129
　　Halloween theme, 134
　　Music and Movement theme, 146–147, 149
　　My Body and Me theme, 152
　　Nighttime theme, 155, 156
　　Opposites theme, 163, 164
　　Rabbits and Bunnies theme, 177
　　Royalty theme, 182
　　Silly Fun theme, 186
　　Spiders theme, 189, 190
　　Springtime theme, 192
　　Thanksgiving Turkeys theme, 201
　　Trains on the Track theme, 209
　　Wheels on the Road theme, 228–229
Fire Fighter Piggywiggy (Fox), 99
Fire Truck (Sís), 101

Fire Trucks and Firefighters theme, 99–103

Firefighters! Speeding! Spraying! Saving! (Hubbell), 101

Fish, Fish, Fish (Adams), 214

Fish Wish (Barner), 213

Fitz-Gibbon, Sally, 66

Five for a Little One (Raschka), 152

"Five Little Monkeys" (song by Dennis Buck), 13

Five Little Pumpkins (Yaccarino), 134

Five Silly Turkeys (Yoon), 199

Five Trucks (Floca), 29

Five Ugly Monsters (Arnold), 141

flannel board

    Apple Munching theme, 18

    Autumn theme, 24

    Aviation theme, 28

    Bath Time Bubbles theme, 32

    Bears theme, 36

    Berry Delicious theme, 40

    Birds of a Feather theme, 44

    Boats in the Water theme, 48

    Bugs and Other Creepy Crawlies theme, 52–53

    Cats and Kittens theme, 57

    Chickens theme, 61

    Clothing and Hats theme, 65

    Colors and Patterns theme, 68

    Community Workers theme, 72

    Construction Site theme, 76

    Cool Pool of Water theme, 80

    Counting theme, 84

    Dinosaurs theme, 87

    Dogs and Puppies theme, 91

    Farm Animals theme, 94

    Fire Trucks and Firefighters theme, 100

    Flowers and Gardens theme, 104–105

    Food, Yummy Food theme, 107–108

    Frogs and Toads theme, 113–114

    Garbage and Recycling theme, 118

    Gingerbread and Other Cookies theme, 124

    Green for St. Patrick's Day theme, 128

    Halloween theme, 132–133

    Lunar New Year theme, 137

    Monsters theme, 141

    Music and Movement theme, 146–147

    My Body and Me theme, 150

    Nighttime theme, 154

    Nocturnal Animals theme, 159

    Opposites theme, 163

    Pet Parade theme, 166–167

    Pirate Treasure theme, 172

flannel board *(cont'd)*

    Rabbits and Bunnies theme, 176

    Royalty theme, 181–182

    Silly Fun theme, 185

    Spiders theme, 188

    Springtime theme, 191

    in storytime routine, 12

    Summer in the Sun theme, 194

    Thanksgiving Turkeys theme, 199

    Toys theme, 204

    Trains on the Track theme, 208

    Under the Sea theme, 213

    Valentine Hugs and Kisses theme, 217

    Weather theme, 222

    Wheels on the Road theme, 226

    Wild Animals theme, 230

    Winter Snow theme, 236

Flashing Fire Engines (Mitton & Parker), 101

Flather, Lisa, 36

Fleming, Candace, 46

Fleming, Denise

    Barnyard Banter, 94

    Count!, 85

    Lunch, 107

    In the Small, Small Pond, 81

    In the Tall, Tall Grass, 54

"Flitter, Flutter" (song by Johnette Downing), 14

Floca, Brian, 29

Florian, Douglas, 106, 195

Flowers and Gardens theme, 104–106

Flying (Crews), 28

food, 9

Food, Yummy Food theme, 107–112

Fortune Cookies (Bitterman), 139

Four Brave Sailors (Ginsburg), 49

Fox, Christyan and Diane

    Fire Fighter Piggywiggy, 99

    Goodnight Piggywiggy, 74

    Pirate Piggywiggy, 172

Fox, Mem

    Magic Hat, The, 65

    Where Is the Green Sheep?, 128

Frazier, Craig, 129

Freight Train (Crews), 209

Froggy Gets Dressed (London), 115

Frogs and Toads theme, 113–117

From Head to Toe (Carle), 152

Fuge, Charles, 204

G

Gackenbach, Dick, 195

Garbage and Recycling theme, 118–122

Garcia, Emma, 77, 228
Garden of Opposites, A (Davis), 164
Gardiner, Lindsey
   Good Night, Poppy and Max: A Bedtime Counting Book, 154
   Here Come Poppy and Max, 92
   When Poppy and Max Grow Up, 72
Garofoli, Viviana, 101
Gerardi, Jan, 118
Gershator, Phillis, 160
Giddy-Up! Let's Ride! (McDonnell), 183
Gilchrist, Jan Spivey, 81
Gingerbread and Other Cookies theme, 123–127
Ginsburg, Mira, 49
Glad Monster, Sad Monster: A Book about Feelings (Emberley & Miranda), 143
Glaser, Linda, 119
glue
   art supplies to have on hand, 8
   with different mediums, 3
   toddlers' experimentation with, xiii, xiv
glue sticks, 6
Go Away, Big Green Monster! (Emberley), 141
Godwin, Laura, 101
Goembel, Ponder, 108
"Goin' on a Bear Hunt" (song), 13
"Goldfish" (song), 214
Gómez, Rebecca, 129
Good Night, Poppy and Max: A Bedtime Counting Book (Gardiner), 154
Good-Night, Owl! (Hutchins), 160
Goodnight Piggywiggy (Fox), 74
googly eyes, 6
Gordon, David, 77
Gordon, Mike, 183
Gorton, Julia, 152
Got, Yves, 134
Gravett, Emily, 19, 91
Green, Anne Canevari, 54
Green for St. Patrick's Day theme, 128–131
Green Means Go (Ring), 129
Greenberg, Melanie Hope, 49
Greenfield, Eloise, 81
Greenspun, Adele Aron, 176
Grover, Max, 28
Growing Vegetable Soup (Ehlert), 106
Grumpy Bird (Tankard), 46
Gurney, John Steven, 88, 210

H

Hacohen, Dean, 156
Hall, Kristen, 177
Hall, Marcellus, 123
Hall, Michael, 218
Hall, Zoe, 18, 106
Halloween Countdown (Prelutsky), 133
Halloween Night (Hatch), 134
Halloween theme, 132–136
Halls, Kelly Milner, 62
Halpern, Shari
   Apple Pie Tree, 18
   I Love Bugs!, 54
   I Love Planes!, 29
   I Love Trains!, 208
   I Love Trucks!, 77
   Surprise Garden, The, 106
Harbor (Crews), 49
Harper, Lee, 237
Harris, Trudy, 54
Harshmann, Marc, 25
Haskamp, Steve, 187
Hatch, Elizabeth, 134
Hats, Hats, Hats (Morris), 66
Have You Seen Birds? (Oppenheim & Reid), 46
Hector, Julian, 101
Hefferan, Rob, 228
Heinlen, Marieka, 168
Hello Toes! Hello Feet! (Paul), 150
Hendra, Sue, 160
Henkes, Kevin
   Birds, 44
   Lilly's Chocolate Heart, 218
   Little White Rabbit, 177
   My Garden, 106
   Wemberley's Ice Cream Star, 195
Hennessy, B. G., 182, 200
Here Come Poppy and Max (Gardiner), 92
Heyman, Ken, 66
"*Hi, Pizza Man!*" (Walter), 108
Hill, Eric, 92
Hillenbrand, Will
   "I'm a Little Teapot" song, 108
   Moon Might Be Milk, The, 124
   Smash! Mash! Crash! There Goes the Trash!, 119
   This Little Piggy & Other Rhymes to Sing & Play, 124
Hines, Anna Grossnickle, 84
Holm, Sharon Lane, 68
Holzenthaler, Jean, 152
Hooray for Fish (Cousins), 212
Hop Jump (Walsh), 114
Hopgood, Tim, 160
Horacek, Judy, 128
Horáček, Petr, 54, 187

Hort, Lenny, 186
How About a Kiss for Me? (Tarpley), 218
How Do Dinosaurs Say Goodnight? (Yolen & Teague), 87
How Do I Put It On? (Watanabe), 66
How Do You Wokka-Wokka? (Bluemle), 148
Hoyt, Ard, 49
Hubbell, Patricia, 101, 193, 206
Hurd, Thacher, 115
Hurray for Spring! (Hubbell), 193
Hurry! Hurry! (Bunting), 62
Hush Little Polar Bear (Mack), 37
Hutchins, Pat, 19, 160

I

I Am Me! (Brandenberg), 74
I Bought a Baby Chicken (Halls), 62
I Don't Want a Cool Cat! (Dodd), 58
I Heard a Little Baa (MacLeod & Phillips), 95
"I Know a Chicken" (song), 13, 62
I Know a Rhino (Fuge), 204
"I Like My Hat" (song), 66
I Love Animals (McDonnell), 95
I Love Bugs! (Sturges), 54
I Love Cats (Saltzberg), 58
I Love My Pirate Papa (Leuck), 173
I Love Planes! (Sturges), 29
I Love Trains! (Sturges), 208
I Love Trucks! (Sturges), 77
I Stink (McMullan), 118
I Went Walking (Williams), 94
I Wish I Were a Pilot (Blackstone), 28
If You Give a Moose a Muffin (Numeroff), 108
If You Give a Mouse a Cookie (Numeroff), 124
If You're Happy and You Know It: Jungle Edition (Warhola), 148
"I'm a Little Teapot" (song), 108, 124
I'm Dirty (McMullan), 76
I'm Mighty (McMullan & McMullan), 48
I'm the Biggest Thing in the Ocean (Sherry), 214
impulse control, xiii
In the Small, Small Pond (Fleming), 81
In the Spring (Brown), 192
In the Tall, Tall Grass (Fleming), 54
ink stamp pads, 6
Inkpen, Mick, 105, 222
Into the Castle (Crebbin), 143
Ireland, Karin, 168
Isadora, Rachel, 204
It Looked Like Spilt Milk (Shaw), 223
It's St. Patrick's Day! (Gómez), 129
Itsy Bitsy Spider (Siomades), 190

J

Jabar, Cynthia, 33
Jamberry (Degan), 40
Jarman, Julie, 32
Jasper's Beanstalk (Butterworth & Inkpen), 105
Jazzy in the Jungle (Cousins), 231
Jenkins, Steve, 146
Jocelyn, Marthe, 164
Johnson, Adrian, 187
Johnson, Cathy Ann, 108
Jonas, Ann, 81
Jump Frog Jump! (Kalan), 115

K

Kalan, Robert, 115
Karas, G. Brian, 186
Katz, Karen
    Counting Kisses, 85
    My First Chinese New Year, 137
    Where Is Baby's Valentine?, 218
Kelley, True, 189
Kids in Action (Greg & Steve), 13
King, Stephen Michael, 148
King Bidgood's in the Bathtub (Wood), 181
Kipper's Rainy Day (Inkpen), 222
Kirk, Daniel, 143, 206
Kirk, David, 190
Kiss Kiss! (Wild & Strevens-Marzo), 218
Kite Flying (Lin), 222
Kitten Red Yellow Blue (Catalanotto), 74
Kitten's Year, A (Day), 58
Kittinger, Jo S., 74
Kitty's Cuddles (Cabrera), 58
Knutson, Kimberley, 24
Kosaka, Fumi, 33, 218
Kramer, Robin, 200
Krauss, Ruth, 106
Krosoczka, Jarrett J., 172

L

Lambert, Jonathan, 115
Lanterns and Firecrackers: A Chinese New Year Story (Zucker & Cohen), 139
Lawrence, John, 62
Leaf Man (Ehlert), 25
Leap Back Home to Me (Thompson), 115
learning opportunities, xi
Lee, Ho Baek, 139
Lee, Kate, 70
Leuck, Laura, 173
Lewin, Betsy, 160
Lewis, J. Patrick, 164

Lewis, Kevin, 77
Lewison, Wendy Cheyette, 223
Like a Windy Day (Asch & Asch), 223
Lilly's Chocolate Heart (Henkes), 218
Lin, Grace, 139, 222
"Listen to the Water" (song), 82
Litowinsky, Olga, 49
Little Apple Goat (Church), 19
Little Band, The (Sage), 147
Little Cloud (Carle), 223
Little Green (Baker), 129
Little Miss Muffet (Pearson), 190
Little Mouse, the Red Ripe Strawberry, and the Big Hungry Bear (Wood & Wood), 40
Little Songs for Little Me (Stewart), 164, 201
Little White Duck (Whippo), 81
Little White Rabbit (Henkes), 177
London, Jonathan, 115, 210
Loudest Roar, The (Taylor), 230
Lovely Day for Amelia Goose (Rong), 81
Lucas, Margeaux, 74
Lukasewich, Lori, 101
Lum, Kate, 187
Lunar New Year theme, 137–140
Lunch (Fleming), 107

M

MacCarthy, Patricia, 183
Machines at Work (Barton), 77
Mack, Jeff, 37, 62
MacLeod, Elizabeth, 95
Magic Hat, The (Fox), 65
Mahy, Margaret, 183
Maisy at the Farm (Cousins), 62
Maisy Big, Maisy Small: A Book of Maisy Opposites (Cousins), 163
Maisy Drives the Bus (Cousins), 228
Maisy Goes to the Playground: A Maisy Lift-the-Flap Classic (Cousins), 195
Maisy Makes Gingerbread (Cousins), 124
Maisy Takes a Bath (Cousins), 32
Maisy's Fire Engine (Cousins), 100
Maisy's Halloween (Cousins), 134
Maisy's Pirate Treasure Hunt (Cousins), 173
Maisy's Pool (Cousins), 80
Maisy's Rainbow (Cousins), 70
Maitland, Barbara, 36
Mama's Little Bears (Tafuri), 37
Manna, Giovanni, 164
Mariniello, Cecco, 29
Markes, Julie, 72
Martin, Bill, Jr., 36, 231
Martin, David, 41

Marylee & Nancy, 187
math activity, 12
Matthews, Derek
    Snappy Little Colors, 70
    Snappy Little Dinosaurs, 88
    Snappy Little Dogs, 217
    Snappy Little Farmyard, 95
    Snappy Little Halloween, 132
    Snappy Little Jungle, 231
Max and Ruby's Snowy Day (Wells), 236
Mayer, Mercer, 143
McDonald, Jill, 160
McDonnell, Flora, 95, 183
McGrath, Bob, 194
McMullan, Kate and Jim, 48, 76, 118
McNeil, Florence, 173
McPhail, David, 173
mediums, 2–3
Melmed, Laura Krauss, 200
Miglio, Paige, 177
"Milkshake" (song), 108
Miller, Virginia, 19
Miranda, Anne, 143
Miss Spider's New Car (Kirk), 190
Missing Tarts, The (Hennessy), 182
Mitchard, Jacquelyn, 160
Mitton, Tony
    Dinosaurumpus, 88
    Down by the Cool of the Pool, 80
    Flashing Fire Engines, 101
    Terrific Trains, 210
Mockford, Caroline, 58, 236
Monks, Lydia, 183, 190
"Monster Boogie" (song), 143
Monsters theme, 141–145
Moon Might Be Milk, The (Shulman), 124
More Tickles and Tunes (Reid-Naiman), 82, 181
Morley, Taia, 193
Morris, Ann, 66
Mortimer, Anne, 57, 58
Mouse Count (Walsh), 85
Mouse Paint (Walsh), 68
Mouse's First Fall (Thompson), 25
Mouse's First Snow (Thompson), 237
Mouse's First Spring (Thompson), 193
Mouse's First Summer (Thompson), 195
Move! (Jenkins & Page), 146
movement activity, 12, 13
Mr. Cookie Baker (Wellington), 124
"Mr. Turkey and Mr. Duck" (song), 201
Mrs. McNosh and the Great Big Squash (Weeks), 104
Mrs. McNosh Hangs Up Her Wash (Weeks), 66

Mrs. Wishy-Washy (Crowley), 33
Munch Munch, Peter Rabbit: A Lift-the-Flap Book (Potter), 177
muscle control, 2, 10
Music and Movement theme, 146–149
My Bear and Me (Maitland), 36
My Body and Me theme, 150–153
My Car (Barton), 226
My First Chinese New Year (Katz), 137
My Garden (Henkes), 106
My Hands Can (Holzenthaler), 152
My Heart Is Like a Zoo (Hall), 218
My Little Polar Bear (Rueda), 37
My Nose, Your Nose (Walsh), 152
My Pop Pop and Me (Smalls), 108
My Spring Robin (Rockwell), 191
My Two Hands, My Two Feet (Walton), 152

N

Napping House (Wood), 156
Narahashi, Keiko, 147
Night before St. Patrick's Day, The (Wing), 129
Night Fire (Lukasewich), 101
Nighttime theme, 154–158
Nikola-Lisa, W., 200
Nipp, Susan Hogen, 147
Nocturnal Animals theme, 159–162
Noisy Counting Book, The (Schade & Buller), 187
Noonan, Julia, 160
Numeroff, Laura Joeffe, 108, 124

O

Octopus Followed Me Home, An (Yaccarino), 168
Odanaka, Barbara, 119
O'Graden, Irene, 33
Ohtomo, Yasuo, 66
Old Town School of Music, 101, 108
Oliver's Wood (Hendra), 160
Olson, K. C., 77
1, 2, Buckle My Shoe (Hines), 84
1, 2, 3 Thanksgiving (Nikola-Lisa), 200
1, 2, 3 to the Zoo: A Counting Book (Carle), 85
One Bear, One Dog (Stickland), 37
One Big Building: A Counting Book about Construction (Dahl), 77
One Dog Canoe (Casanova), 49
One Little, Two Little, Three Little Pilgrims (Hennessy), 200
One Little Blueberry (Salzano), 41
opening, of storytime, 12
Oppenheim, Joanne, 46

Opposites theme, 163–165
Opposnakes: A Lift-the-Flap Book about Opposites (Yoon), 164
Orange Pear Apple Bear (Gravett), 19
Ormerod, Jan, 206
Ouren, Todd, 77, 237
Over in the Grasslands (Wilson & Bartlett), 231
Over Under (Jocelyn & Slaughter), 164
Owl Babies (Waddell), 159

P

Page, Robin, 146
paint (tempera paint), 6
paintbrushes, 6
painting, 3
Paley, Joan, 81
Panda Bear, Panda Bear, What Do You See? (Martin & Carle), 231
Papa, Please Get the Moon for Me (Carle), 156
Paparone, Pam, 223
paper, 7
paper lunch sacks, 7
paper plates, 7
paper towel tubes, 7
Parenteau, Shirley, 37
parents
    safety for artsy storytime, 9
    working with toddlers at storytime, 15
Park, Linda Sue, 139
Parker, Ant
    Charlie Chick, 61
    Flashing Fire Engines, 101
    Terrific Trains, 210
Parker-Rees, Guy, 80, 88
Parkins, David, 72
Parr, Todd, 119
pasta, 9
Pattern Bugs (Harris), 54
patterns
    Apple Munching theme, 20–23
    Autumn theme, 26–27
    Aviation theme, 31
    Bath Time Bubbles theme, 35
    Bears theme, 38–39
    Berry Delicious theme, 42–43
    Birds of a Feather theme, 47
    Boats in the Water theme, 51
    Bugs and Other Creepy Crawlies theme, 56
    Cats and Kittens theme, 60
    Chickens theme, 63–64
    Clothing and Hats theme, 67
    Colors and Patterns theme, 71

patterns *(cont'd)*
    Community Workers theme, 75
    Construction Site theme, 79
    Cool Pool of Water theme, 83
    Dinosaurs theme, 89–90
    Farm Animals theme, 97–98
    Fire Trucks and Firefighters theme, 102–103
    Food, Yummy Food theme, 110–112
    Frogs and Toads theme, 116–117
    Garbage and Recycling theme, 121–122
    Gingerbread and Other Cookies theme, 126–127
    Green for St. Patrick's Day theme, 131
    Halloween theme, 135–136
    Lunar New Year theme, 140
    Monsters theme, 144–145
    My Body and Me theme, 153
    Nighttime theme, 157–158
    Nocturnal Animals theme, 161–162
    Opposites theme, 165
    Pet Parade theme, 170–171
    Pirate Treasure theme, 175
    Rabbits and Bunnies theme, 179–180
    Royalty theme, 184
    Under the Sea theme, 215–216
    Summer in the Sun theme, 197–198
    Thanksgiving Turkeys theme, 202–203
    Toys theme, 207
    Trains on the Track theme, 211
    Valentine Hugs and Kisses theme, 220–221
    Weather theme, 224–225
    Wild Animals theme, 233–235
    Winter Snow theme, 237
Paul, Ann Whitford, 150
Pearson, Tracey Campbell, 182, 190
Peck, Jan, 214
Pedersen, Janet, 33
Peekaboo Bedtime (Isadora), 204
Peek-a-Pet! (Cimarusti), 168
Pet Parade theme, 166–171
Peterson, Carole, 66
Peterson, Stephanie, 168
Petrone, Valeria, 214
Phillips, Louise, 95
Pickering, Jimmy, 134
Pie in the Sky (Ehlert), 41
pie tins, 7
Piece of Chalk, A (Ericsson), 70
Pierce, Terry, 41
Pilkey, Dav, 143
pill bottles, 7

Pirate Piggywiggy (Fox), 172
Pirate Treasure theme, 172–175
Planes (Rockwell), 29
plastic tablecloths, 7
Playtime: 49 Favorite Action and Sing-Along Songs (CEMA Special Markets), 14
Plecas, Jennifer, 206
Potter, Beatrix, 177
Prelutsky, Jack, 133
Princess Party (Allen), 183
puppets, 13

Q
Q-tips, 7

R
Rabbits and Bunnies theme, 176–180
Raczka, Bob, 193, 194
Radzinski, Kandy, 156
Raffi
    Baby Beluga (Raffi Songs to Read), 214
    Down by the Bay (Raffi Songs to Read), 187
    Spider on the Floor (Raffi Songs to Read), 189
Raindrop, Plop! (Lewison), 223
Raschka, Chris, 139, 152
Red Are the Apples (Harshmann & Ryan), 25
Red Is a Dragon: A Book of Colors (Thong), 139
Reid, Barbara, 46
Reid-Naiman, Kathy, 82, 181
Remkiewicz, Frank, 115
Repchuck, Caroline, 70
resources
    See storytime resources
Rex, Michael, 227
Reynolds, Adrian, 32
rhyme
    See action chant/song/rhyme
Rhythm of the Rocks: A Multicultural Journey (Marylee & Nancy), 187
Ring, Susan, 129
Roche, Denis, 210
Rockwell, Anne, 29, 48, 191
Rockwell, Harlow, 191
Rockwell, Lizzy, 191
Roly Poly Spider (Sardegna), 190
Rong, Yu, 81
Roosa, Karen, 195
Rosen, Michael, 54
routines, storytime, 11–14
Royalty theme, 181–184
Rrralph (Ehlert), 92

Ruby's Tea for Two (Wells), 108
Rueda, Claudia, 37
Russell, Bill, 189
Ryan, Cheryl, 25

S
Sabuda, Robert, 124
safety, 9–10
Sage, James, 147
Sail Away (McNeil & McPhail), 173
Saltzberg, Barney, 58
Salzano, Tammi, 41
Sardegna, Jill, 190
Saucepan Game (Ormerod), 206
Schade, Susan, 187
Scharschmidt, Sherry, 156
Schories, Pat, 134, 199
Schwarz, Joanie, 176
scissors, 2
Scotch tape, 7
Scrubbly-Bubbly Car Wash (O'Graden), 33
Seals on the Bus, The (Hort), 186
Second Line, The (Downing), 14
Seven Hungry Babies (Fleming), 46
17 Kings and 42 Elephants (Mahy), 183
sewing notions, 8
"Shake My Sillies Out" (song), 187
Shapiro, Michelle, 70
shaving cream, 8
shaving cream finger painting, 33
Shaw, Charles G., 223
Shaw, Nancy, 173
Shea, Pegi Deito, 137
Sheep on a Ship (Shaw), 173
Sherry, Kevin, 25, 214
Shhhh! Everybody's Sleeping (Markes), 72
Shulman, Lisa, 124
sign language, 13
Silly Fun theme, 185–187
Silly Sally (Wood), 185
Silly Suzy Goose (Horáček), 187
Simms Taback's City Animals (Taback), 231
Sing Along with Bob #1 (McGrath), 194
Siomades, Lorianne, 190
Sís, Peter, 101
Ska-Tat! (Knutson), 24
Skateboard Monsters (Kirk), 143
Slaughter, Tom, 164
"Slow, Fast Song" (song), 164
small motor control, xii–xiii, 10
Smalls, Irene, 108
Smash! Mash! Crash! There Goes the Trash!
    (Odanaka), 119

Smith, Maggie, 195
Snappy Little Colors (Lee & Repchuck), 70
Snappy Little Dinosaurs (Steer), 88
Snappy Little Dogs (Steer), 217
Snappy Little Farmyard (Steer), 95
Snappy Little Halloween (Matthews), 132
Snappy Little Jungle (Steer), 231
Snow (Stojic), 237
Snow! Snow! Snow! (Harper), 237
Snowballs (Ehlert), 237
songs, 13–14
    See also action chant/song/rhyme
Songs for Wiggleworms (Old Town School of
    Music), 101, 108
Spence, Amy, 210
Spence, Rob, 210
Spengler, Margaret, 210
Spider on the Floor (Raffi Songs to Read)
    (Raffi, Russell, & Kelley), 189
Spiders theme, 188–190
Spinelli, Eileen, 33
Splash! (Jonas), 81
Splish, Splash, Spring (Carr), 193
Spots, Feathers, and Curly Tails (Tafuri), 95
Spring Things (Raczka), 193
Springtime theme, 191–193
St. Patrick's Day Countdown (Yoon), 128
stand-up activity
    Apple Munching theme, 18
    Autumn theme, 24
    Aviation theme, 28
    Bath Time Bubbles theme, 32
    Bears theme, 36
    Berry Delicious theme, 40
    Birds of a Feather theme, 44
    Boats in the Water theme, 48
    Bugs and Other Creepy Crawlies theme,
        52
    Cats and Kittens theme, 57
    Chickens theme, 61
    Clothing and Hats theme, 65
    Colors and Patterns theme, 68
    Community Workers theme, 72
    Construction Site theme, 76
    Cool Pool of Water theme, 80
    Counting theme, 84
    Dinosaurs theme, 87
    Dogs and Puppies theme, 91
    Farm Animals theme, 94
    Fire Trucks and Firefighters theme, 99
    Flowers and Gardens theme, 104
    Food, Yummy Food theme, 107
    Frogs and Toads theme, 113

stand-up activity (*cont'd*)
Garbage and Recycling theme, 118
Gingerbread and Other Cookies theme, 123
Green for St. Patrick's Day theme, 128
Halloween theme, 132
Lunar New Year theme, 137
Monsters theme, 141
Music and Movement theme, 146
My Body and Me theme, 150
Nighttime theme, 154
Nocturnal Animals theme, 159
Opposites theme, 163
Pet Parade theme, 166
Pirate Treasure theme, 172
Rabbits and Bunnies theme, 176
Royalty theme, 181
Under the Sea theme, 212
Silly Fun theme, 185
Spiders theme, 188
Springtime theme, 191
in storytime routine, 12
Summer in the Sun theme, 194
Thanksgiving Turkeys theme, 199
Toys theme, 204
Trains on the Track theme, 208
Valentine Hugs and Kisses theme, 217
Weather theme, 222
Wheels on the Road theme, 226
Wild Animals theme, 230
Winter Snow theme, 236
Stanley Mows the Lawn (Frazier), 129
Stead, Judy, 193, 194
Steer, Dugald
Snappy Little Dinosaurs, 88
Snappy Little Dogs, 217
Snappy Little Farmyard, 95
Snappy Little Jungle, 231
Steinberg, David, 200
Stevenson, Louis, 206
Stewart, Nancy, 164, 201
stickers, 3, 8
Stickland, Henrietta, 163
Stickland, Paul
Dinosaur Roar!, 163
Dinosaur Stomp! A Monster Pop-Up Book, 87
One Bear, One Dog, 37
Ten Terrible Dinosaurs, 85
Truck Jam, 228
Stinky Cake (Peterson), 66
Stojic, Manya, 237
Stone, Kyle M., 173

storytime resources
Apple Munching theme, 19
Autumn theme, 25
Aviation theme, 29
Bath Time Bubbles theme, 33
Bears theme, 37
Berry Delicious theme, 41
Birds of a Feather theme, 46
Boats in the Water theme, 49
Cats and Kittens theme, 58
Chickens theme, 62
Clothing and Hats theme, 66
Colors and Patterns theme, 69
Community Workers theme, 74
Construction Site theme, 77
Cool Pool of Water theme, 81
Counting theme, 85
Dinosaurs theme, 88
Dogs and Puppies theme, 92
Farm Animals theme, 95
Fire Trucks and Firefighters theme, 101
Flowers and Gardens theme, 106
Frogs and Toads theme, 115
Garbage and Recycling theme, 119
Gingerbread and Other Cookies theme, 124
Green for St. Patrick's Day theme, 129
Halloween theme, 134
Lunar New Year theme, 139
Monsters theme, 143
Music and Movement theme, 148
My Body and Me theme, 152
Nighttime theme, 156
Nocturnal Animals theme, 160
Opposites theme, 164
Pet Parade theme, 168
Pirate Treasure theme, 173
Rabbits and Bunnies theme, 177
Royalty theme, 183
Silly Fun theme, 187
Spiders theme, 190
Springtime theme, 193
Summer in the Sun theme, 195
Thanksgiving Turkeys theme, 200
Toys theme, 206
Trains on the Track theme, 210
Under the Sea theme, 214
Valentine Hugs and Kisses theme, 218
Weather theme, 223
Wheels on the Road theme, 228
Wild Animals theme, 231
Winter Snow theme, 237

storytime themes
    Apple Munching, 18–23
    Autumn, 24–27
    Aviation, 28–31
    Bath Time Bubbles, 32–35
    Bears, 36–39
    Berry Delicious, 40–43
    Birds of a Feather, 44–47
    Boats in the Water, 48–51
    Bugs and Other Creepy Crawlies, 52–56
    Cats and Kittens, 57–60
    Chickens, 61–64
    Clothing and Hats, 65–67
    Colors and Patterns, 68–71
    Community Workers, 72–75
    Construction Site, 76–79
    Cool Pool of Water, 80–83
    Counting, 84–86
    Dinosaurs, 87–90
    Dogs and Puppies, 91–93
    Farm Animals, 94–98
    Fire Trucks and Firefighters, 99–103
    Flowers and Gardens, 104–106
    Food, Yummy Food, 107–112
    Frogs and Toads, 113–117
    Garbage and Recycling, 118–122
    Gingerbread and Other Cookies, 123–127
    Green for St. Patrick's Day, 128–131
    Halloween, 132–136
    Lunar New Year, 137–140
    Monsters, 141–145
    Music and Movement, 146–149
    My Body and Me, 150–153
    Nighttime, 154–158
    Nocturnal Animals, 159–162
    Opposites, 163–165
    for organizational purposes only, 14
    Pet Parade, 166–171
    Pirate Treasure, 172–175
    Rabbits and Bunnies, 176–180
    Royalty, 181–184
    Silly Fun, 185–187
    Spiders, 188–190
    Springtime, 191–193
    Summer in the Sun, 194–198
    Thanksgiving Turkeys, 199–203
    Toys, 204–207
    Trains on the Track, 208–211
    Under the Sea, 212–216
    Valentine Hugs and Kisses, 217–221
    Weather, 222–225
    Wheels on the Road, 226–229

storytime themes (cont'd)
    Wild Animals, 230–235
    Winter Snow, 236–239
storytimes
    learning opportunities through, xi
    plans, use of, xii
    routine steps, 11–14
    tips for working with toddlers at, 14–15
Strevens-Marzo, Bridget, 218
Sturges, Philemon
    I Love Bugs!, 54
    I Love Planes!, 29
    I Love Trains!, 208
    I Love Trucks!, 77
Suen, Anastasia, 29
Summer Day, A (Florian), 195
Summer in the Sun theme, 194–198
Summer Wonders (Raczka), 194
Surprise Garden, The (Hall), 106
Sweet Dreams, Maisy (Cousins), 154
Swing High, Swing Low: A Book of Opposites (Coward), 164

T

Taback, Simms, 231
Tafuri, Nancy
    Ball Bounced, The, 206
    Big Storm: A Very Soggy Counting Book, The, 223
    Busy Little Squirrel, 25
    Four Brave Sailors, 49
    Mama's Little Bears, 37
    My Hands Can, 152
    Spots, Feathers, and Curly Tails, 95
Tails Are Not for Pulling (Verdick), 168
Tankard, Jeremy, 46
tape, 7
Tarpley, Todd, 218
Taylor, Thomas, 230
Teague, Mark, 87
Teckentrup, Britta, 33
Ten Black Dots (Crews), 84
Ten in the Bed (Cabrera), 156
Ten Little Fish (Wood), 214
Ten Mice for Tet (Shea & Weill), 137
Ten Red Apples (Hutchins), 19
Ten Red Apples: A Bartholomew Bear Counting Book (Miller), 19
Ten Terrible Dinosaurs (Stickland), 85
Terrific Trains (Mitton & Parker), 210
Thanksgiving in the Barn: A Pop-Up Book (Westcott), 200
Thanksgiving Turkeys theme, 199–203

themes
    See storytime themes
There's Something in My Attic (Mayer), 143
This First Thanksgiving Day: A Counting Story (Melmed), 200
This Is the Firefighter (Godwin), 101
This Little Chick (Lawrence), 62
This Little Piggy & Other Rhymes to Sing & Play (Yolen & Hillenbrand), 108, 124
This Plane (Collicutt), 29
Thompson, Lauren
    Leap Back Home to Me, 115
    Mouse's First Fall, 25
    Mouse's First Snow, 237
    Mouse's First Spring, 193
    Mouse's First Summer, 195
Thong, Roseanne, 139
Tiny Little Fly (Rosen), 54
Tip Tip Dig Dig (Garcia), 77
tissue paper, 8
Toad (Brown), 113
Toddler Action Songs (Cedarmount Kids), 148
toddler art fundamentals
    art supplies to have on hand, 3–9
    coloring sheets, 10
    craft vs. art, 1–2
    food as a medium, 9
    mediums, use of different, 2–3
    safety, 9–10
    See also art and craft activities
toddlers, working with, 14–15
Toot Toot Beep Beep (Garcia), 228
Toys theme, 204–207
Train Goes Clickety-Clack, A (London), 210
Trains on the Track theme, 208–211
Trashy Town (Zimmerman & Clemesha), 119
Truck Duck (Rex), 227
Truck Jam (Stickland), 228
Tuck Me In (Hacohen & Scharschmidt), 156
Tucker, Kathy, 173
Tumble Bumble (Bond), 148
Turkey Ball, The (Steinberg), 200
Tusa, Tricia, 65
Two Shoes, Blue Shoes, New Shoes (Fitz-Gibbon), 66

U

Under the Sea theme, 212–216

V

Valentine Hugs and Kisses theme, 217–221
Vegetable Garden (Florian), 106
Verdick, Elizabeth, 168

Vere, Ed, 62
Very Busy Spider (Carle), 188
Very Quiet Cricket (Carle), 52
Victor Vito (Berkner), 214
Vivas, Julie, 94

W

Waddell, Martin, 159
Wake Up, It's Spring! (Ernst), 193
Waldron, Kevin, 54
Walker, David, 37
Walsh, Ellen Stoll, 68, 85, 114
Walsh, Melanie, 152
Walter, Virginia, 108
Walton, Rick, 152, 177
Ward, Cindy, 57
Warhola, James, 148, 228
Watanabe, Shigeo, 66
Water, Water (Greenfield), 81
Way Down Deep in the Deep Blue Sea (Peck), 214
"We Are the Dinosaurs" (song), 88
Weather theme, 222–225
webpage, for *Artsy Toddler Storytimes*, xiv
Wee Sing: Children's Songs & Fingerplays (Beall & Nipp), 147
Weeks, Sarah
    Be Mine, Be Mine, Sweet Valentine, 218
    Mrs. McNosh and the Great Big Squash, 104
    Mrs. McNosh Hangs Up Her Wash, 66
Weill, Cynthia, 137
Wellington, Monica
    All My Little Ducklings, 46
    Apple Farmer Annie, 19
    Mr. Cookie Baker, 124
Wells, Rosemary, 108, 236
Wemberley's Ice Cream Star (Henkes), 195
Westcott, Nadine Bernard
    Do Pirates Take Baths?, 173
    Down by the Bay (Raffi Songs to Read), 187
    Hello Toes! Hello Feet!, 150
    Mrs. McNosh Hangs Up Her Wash, 66
    Thanksgiving in the Barn: A Pop-Up Book, 200
Whaddaya Think of That? (Berkner), 30, 62, 88
What Can Rabbit Hear? (Cousins), 150
What Can Rabbit See? (Cousins), 177
What! Cried Granny: An Almost Bedtime Book (Lum), 187
What Pet to Get? (Dodd), 166
What's the Magic Word? (DiPucchio), 46

Wheels on the Race Car (Zane), 228
Wheels on the Road theme, 226–229
Whelan, Kat, 41
When I Grow Up (Kittinger), 74
When Poppy and Max Grow Up (Gardiner), 72
Where Is Baby's Valentine? (Katz), 218
Where Is the Green Sheep? (Fox & Horacek), 128
Where Is Tippy Toes? (Lewin), 160
Where to Sleep (Radzinski), 156
Where's Sam? A Lift-the-Flap Book (Got), 134
Where's Spot? (Hill), 92
Whippo, Walt, 81
white glue, 8
Who Ate All the Cookie Dough? (Beaumont), 124
Who's in the Forest? (Gershator), 160
Wide-Mouthed Frog: A Pop-Up Book, The (Faulkner), 115
Wilburn, Kathy, 177
Wilcox, Leah, 183
Wild, Margaret, 218
Wild Animals theme, 230–235
Wiley, Thom, 119
Willgoss, Brigitte, 214
Williams, Sue, 94
Wilson, Anna, 231
Wilson, Karma, 41, 123
Winborn, Marsha, 46
Wing, Natasha, 129
Winter Snow theme, 236–239
Wojtowycz, David, 95
Wolff, Ashley, 214
Wood, Audrey
　　King Bidgood's in the Bathtub, 181
　　Little Mouse, the Red Ripe Strawberry, and the Big Hungry Bear, 40
　　Napping House, 156
　　Silly Sally, 185
　　Ten Little Fish, 214
Wood, Bruce, 214

Wood, Don
　　King Bidgood's in the Bathtub, 181
　　Little Mouse, the Red Ripe Strawberry, and the Big Hungry Bear, 40
　　Napping House, 156
Woodruff, Liza, 218
Wow! Said the Owl (Hopgood), 160
Wrapping Paper Romp (Hubbell), 206
Wummer, Amy, 129

Y
Yaccarino, Dan
　　Five Little Pumpkins, 134
　　Halloween Countdown, 133
　　Octopus Followed Me Home, An, 168
　　Trashy Town, 119
yarn, 8–9
Yelchin, Eugene, 46, 124
Yolen, Jane
　　How Do Dinosaurs Say Goodnight? 87
　　"I'm a Little Teapot" song, 108
　　This Little Piggy & Other Rhymes to Sing & Play, 124
Yoon, Salina
　　Apples! Apples! 18
　　Five Silly Turkeys, 199
　　Opposnakes: A Lift-the-Flap Book about Opposites, 164
　　St. Patrick's Day Countdown, 128
　　Ziggy the Zebra, 231

Z
Zahares, Wade, 25
Zaman, Farida, 66
Zane, Alexander, 228
Ziggy the Zebra (Ellis), 231
Zimmerman, Andrea, 119
Zoe's Hats: A Book of Colors and Patterns (Holm), 68
Zucker, Jonny, 139